D0212885

DYNAMICS OF THE MIXED ECONOMY

Why does one failed intervention always seem to lead to another?

Since the collapse of the centrally planned economies, some form of mixed economy has become the dominant paradigm guiding social and economic policy throughout the world. Yet there has been relatively little analysis of the inherently destabilizing tensions and contradictions within the mixed economy itself, nor of the underlying logic of interventionism that engenders them. *Dynamics of the Mixed Economy* applies the insights of modern Austrian political economy to these issues. By studying the near- and long-term repercussions of intervention under conditions of dispersed knowledge and radical ignorance, in both market and government, it reaches some troubling conclusions about the likely prospects for actual mixed economies.

It compares and contrasts standard approaches to the growth of the state (including public choice) with that of modern Austrian political economy; examines in detail the nature and operation of the interventionist process in the context of nationalization, regulation and the welfare state; analyzes conditions that produce instability under laissez-faire capitalism; argues that the interventionist process is a "spontaneous order"; and offers several "pattern predictions" regarding the character and behaviour of existing economies.

Sanford Ikeda is Associate Professor of Economics at The State University of New York, Purchase. He received his Ph.D. from New York University under Mario J. Rizzo and Israel M. Kirzner. His articles on market-process theory, interventionism, and bureaucracy have appeared in several books and journals.

FOUNDATIONS OF THE MARKET ECONOMY
Edited by Mario J. Rizzo,
New York University
and
Lawrence H. White,
University of Georgia

A central theme of this series is the importance of understanding and assessing the market economy from a perspective broader than the static economics of perfect competition and Pareto optimality. Such a perspective sees markets as causal processes generated by the preferences, expectations and beliefs of economic agents. The creative acts of entrepreneurship that uncover new information about preferences, prices and technology are central to these processes with respect to their ability to promote the discovery and use of knowledge in society.

The market economy consists of a set of institutions that facilitate voluntary cooperation and exchange among individuals. These institutions include the legal and ethical framework as well as more narrowly "economic" patterns of social interaction. Thus the law, legal institutions and cultural or ethical norms, as well as ordinary business practices and monetary phenomena, fall within the analytical domain of the economist.

Other titles in the series
THE MEANING OF MARKET PROCESS
Essays in the development of modern Austrian economics
Israel M. Kirzner

PRICES AND KNOWLEDGE
A market-process perspective
Esteban F. Thomsen

KEYNES' GENERAL THEORY OF INTEREST
A reconsideration
Fiona C. Maclachlan

LAISSEZ-FAIRE BANKING
Kevin Dowd

EXPECTATIONS AND THE MEANING OF INSTITUTIONS
Essays in economics by Ludwig Lachmann
Edited by *Don Lavoie*

PERFECT COMPETITION AND THE TRANSFORMATION OF ECONOMICS
Frank M. Machovec

ENTREPRENEURSHIP AND THE MARKET PROCESS
An enquiry into the growth of knowledge
David Harper

ECONOMICS OF TIME AND IGNORANCE
Gerald O'Driscoll and Mario J. Rizzo

GRACE LIBRARY CARLOW COLLEGE
PITTSBURGH PA 15213

DYNAMICS OF THE MIXED ECONOMY

Toward a theory of interventionism

Sanford Ikeda

HD
87
I38
1997

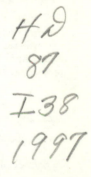

London and New York

CATALOGUED

GRACE LIBRARY CARLOW COLLEGE
PITTSBURGH PA 15213

First published 1997
by Routledge
11 New Fetter Lane, London EC4P 4EE

Simultaneously published in the USA and Canada
by Routledge
29 West 35th Street, New York, NY 10001

© 1997 Sanford Ikeda

Phototypeset in Garamond by Intype London Ltd
Printed and bound in Great Britain by Mackays of Chatham PLC,
Chatham, Kent

All rights reserved. No part of this book may be reprinted or reproduced
or utilized in any form or by any electronic, mechanical, or other
means, now known or hereafter invented, including photocopying and
recording, or in any information storage or retrieval system, without
permission in writing from the publishers.

British Library Cataloguing in Publication Data
A catalogue record for this book is available from the British Library

Library of Congress Cataloguing in Publication Data
Ikeda, Sanford, 1957–
Dynamics of the mixed economy: toward a theory of interventionism
Sanford Ikeda.
p. cm. – (Foundations of the market economy series) Includes
bibliographical references and index.
1. Economic policy. 2. Social policy. 3. Mixed economy.
4. Austria–Economic policy–1945 – I. Title. II. Series HD87. I38 1996
338.9–dc20
96–18544
CIP

This book has been sponsored in part by the Austrian Economics
Program at New York University.

ISBN 0–415–08933–6

How far your eyes may pierce I cannot tell.
Striving to better, oft we mar what's well.
(*King Lear*, Act I, scene IV)

Gift of William McShea 16-22-47

To Jenny and Christopher

CONTENTS

Preface   xi

1 THE CHALLENGE OF THE MIXED ECONOMY   1
   Statement of purpose   2
   The economic theory of regulation and public choice   4
   Theories of government growth and their limitations   14
   Summary and concluding remarks   28

2 THE MEANING OF INTERVENTIONISM   31
   Capitalism, collectivism, and the mixed economy   32
   The economic case for interventionism:
     regulation and redistribution   38
   The critique of interventionism   41
   Limitations of Mises's critique   46
   Ideology, political incentives, and the "knowledge problem"   49
   Concluding remarks   53

3 THE USE OF KNOWLEDGE IN GOVERNMENT
   AND CATALLAXY   55
   Government and catallaxy: theory and practice   55
   The market process   58
   Collectivist central planning   65
   The governmental process   72
   Concluding remarks   89

4 TOWARD A THEORY OF INTERVENTIONISM I:
   THE FRAMEWORK   91
   Lessons for interventionism from the calculation debate   92
   The nature and significance of the knowledge problem
     in mixed economies   94
   The expansionary phase of the interventionist process   99

CONTENTS

The contractionary phase of the interventionist process   137
The interventionist process as a spontaneous order   143
Relaxing the assumption of benevolent public interest   145
Concluding remarks   151

5 TOWARD A THEORY OF INTERVENTIONISM
  II: ROADS TO COLLECTIVISM   152
  Regulatory dynamics   153
  Transfer dynamics   164
  Regulatory and transfer dynamics: a comparison   192

6 THE INSTABILITY OF THE MINIMAL STATE   196
  Description of the minimal state   197
  Analysis   199
  Public goods, monopoly, and bureaucracy   209
  Concluding remarks   211

7 IMPLICATIONS AND PATTERN PREDICTIONS   213
  Propositions   213
  Implications   215
  Interpretations   222
  Examples   226
  Concluding remarks   232

8 WHITHER THE MIXED ECONOMY?   233
  Limitations and questions for further research   234
  The prospects for the mixed economy   236

  Appendices   240
  Notes   248
  References   279
  Index   289

PREFACE

Economists are fond of pointing out the unexpected and frequently unwanted effects of a given public policy. It is our stock in trade. It is less common for us to identify the principles underlying the process by which one policy intervention leads to another, or by which partial decontrol sets into motion forces that push toward either more or less intervention. Indeed, whether politico-economic systems that attempt to unite elements of capitalism and collectivism follow discernible principles of transformation is a question that economists outside the Marxian tradition tend not to ask. If found, those principles could provide deeper insights into the behavior of the mixed economy over time.

While the approach taken in this book views the mixed economy as a complex, spontaneous process that is driven, to a large extent, by its own internal dynamic, it is non-Marxian. Rather, it borrows largely, though not exclusively, from the Austrian market-process tradition in economics to develop an analytical framework that can help to reveal the logic of that dynamic. In particular, it draws heavily from Ludwig von Mises's pioneering critique of interventionism, Friedrich Hayek's insights into the nature of spontaneous orders and the problems of dispersed knowledge, and Israel Kirzner's concept of entrepreneurial discovery as well as his penetrating critique of neoclassical equilibrium analysis. Taken together these provide the basic ingredients of a method of addressing the phenomena of state expansion and contraction that, as I hope to show, exceeds in significant ways the explanatory power of other, better-known approaches to political economy.

The notion of writing a treatise on what Mises called "the hampered market" has been with me almost from the time that I first became interested in economic questions. And so when I was

xi

asked to comment in early 1990 on a paper purporting to analyze "regulation as a process" I was glad finally to have an occasion to organize and put down on paper my thoughts on some problems that I had noticed both in the Misesian critique of interventionism, which nevertheless I had always found appealing, and in the tendency of much contemporary Austrian political economy to overlook what I regarded as the essential and unique contribution of that critique. (See, in particular, my comment in Ebeling (1991: 291–301).) About a year later Professor Mario Rizzo invited me to present a paper to the Austrian Economics Colloquium at New York University, for which occasion I wrote a short essay entitled "Some thoughts on the Misesian critique of interventionism." On the strength of the very positive reception given there to that essay, Professor Rizzo urged me to flesh out my ideas in a longer version, which, after its completion a few months later, eventually became the basis of this book. My original aim was simply to re-examine the Misesian critique of interventionism in light of recent theoretical developments in Austrian economics. I wanted to investigate the logic of interventionism – i.e., the forces that produce genuine politico-economic change in the mixed economy. Early on I began to sense the possibility that such a study, when combined with the Austrian analysis of collectivist economic planning, could reveal certain general but possibly observable patterns that to my knowledge had not previously been articulated.

In addition to the original short essay that began this project, I have had the privilege and invaluable opportunity of presenting drafts of several chapters of the manuscript to the Austrian Economics Colloquium at New York University, and would like to express my gratitude to the participants of that forum for their tough, penetrating, but always fair and constructive criticisms. In particular, I would like to recognize the Austrian faculty of New York University, Israel M. Kirzner, Mario J. Rizzo, Peter J. Boettke, as well as Faculty Research Fellows of the NYU Austrian Program, William N. Butos (Trinity College), Young Back Choi (St Johns University), Roger Koppl (Farleigh Dickinson University), and Joseph Salerno (Pace University), each of whom at various times has given me encouragement from which I frequently drew to persevere through to the completion of the project. Pete Boettke was especially generous in commenting at one time or another on almost every chapter of the manuscript and in his enthusiastic support throughout the entire undertaking, for which I feel enormously indebted. In addition, I would like to thank the graduate-student participants of the Colloquium for their comments, including Sean Keenan, Yisok Kim, George Pavlov, Gilberto Salgado, Charles Steele, Steve Sullivan, and Glen Whitman; and three anonymous referees for their criticisms. My thanks also go to Charles Baird (California State University at Hayward), Roy Cordato (Campbell University), Jeffrey Friedman (Yale University), Walter Grinder, David Harper (The Treasury, New Zealand), David Prychitko (The State University of New York, Oswego), and Lawrence H. White (University of Georgia), for their useful feedback on specific chapters. Ed Lopez and the participants of the Colloquium at the Center for Market Processes, George Mason University, made helpful observations on Chapter 4 for which I am very grateful. Steven Sullivan and Glen Whitman provided research assistance competently and with alacrity. And Jennifer Wada and Sandy Anthony made numerous corrections and editorial suggestions that greatly improved the style and readability of the entire manuscript.

To Alan Jarvis of Routledge, that most patient and supportive of editors, I owe a large debt of gratitude. My deepest thanks, however, go to series co-editor, Mario Rizzo. Here I can say with the utmost confidence that without his efforts on my behalf this book would not have been written. I take particular pleasure in recording the intelligent insights, friendly and useful advice, and kind encouragement that he offered at every stage of its preparation.

While I thus have many to thank for what I have learned, my greatest intellectual debts, in the writing of this volume and in my career as an economist, are (in equal measure) to Ludwig von Mises, Friedrich Hayek, and Israel Kirzner. Responsibility for the shortcomings of this work is, of course, undividedly my own.

I gratefully acknowledge the Earhart Foundation for a grant in the spring of 1992 that freed me from teaching duties to work on the first three chapters; and the Institute for Humane Studies for their summer support in 1993 to continue work on the manuscript, as well as for two travel grants. Purchase College of the State University of New York, also provided travel assistance. In addition to the forums already mentioned, several of the chapters of the manuscript in one form or another were presented at the

Eastern Economic Association, Atlantic Economic Association, and Southern Economic Association.

To my mother and father, who gave me life and their love, I am especially thankful for having given me when I was young the freedom to find my own way, which has often been for them a source of distress but I hope not always of disappointment. Finally, to my own family. Serious writing began on the manuscript for this book about nine months before our son was born. The two have literally grown up together. Despite the intimate role it has played in my family's experiences these last few years, or rather because of it, I am very happy to be bidding the work farewell. For if raising an exuberant little boy can often test the domestic tranquility of first-time parents, taking on another major project such as this one, also a first for us, could have been an enormous trial. Were it not for the steady love, energy, and support of my wife none of these undertakings, which have lately become so important in my life, would have fared so well. This book, then, is dedicated to Jenny and Christopher – the most important of all.

Sanford Ikeda
Brooklyn, New York
January 1996

1

THE CHALLENGE OF THE MIXED ECONOMY

In 1920 Ludwig von Mises, Austrian economist and social theorist, predicted the inevitable failure of collectivist central planning.[1] Since then the inevitable has come to pass. Yet the collapse of "really existing communism" represents both a vindication of and a challenge to "Austrian political economy," of which Mises was perhaps the leading modern exponent. That is, while recent events seem to have borne out Mises's prognosis, they present at the same time the challenge of explaining (1) why systems that have practiced some of the most extreme forms of governmental social management in history have (or had) survived for so long,[2] and (2) what lies ahead for more market-oriented mixed economies such as the United States. They also raise the question of whether current Austrian political economy is capable of making broad predictions about the behavior of mixed economies that are similar in nature to those Mises made about collectivism.

What is perhaps unknown, especially among those who have only recently come to appreciate Mises's vision and analysis of the inherent flaws of collectivism,[3] is that he also addressed the fundamental questions and concerns confronting mixed economies today. Mises published *Kritik des Interventionismus* (Critique of Interventionism) in 1929, nine years after his initial assault on the intellectual basis of socialism and in the same year that marked the beginning of the world-wide economic crisis that followed nearly a decade of government monetary manipulation. In this later work, Mises declared the mixed economy "contradictory and illogical," and dared the advocates of government intervention, in a manner reminiscent of his debate with the advocates of collectivism, to present a set of logically consistent and workable principles sufficient to establish the intellectual foundations of the mixed

1

economy. In contrast to the earlier controversy, however, this invitation has gone essentially unanswered and his critique has been largely neglected outside of Austrian circles.[4] And while his reasoned case against central planning has finally received some measure of the attention and appreciation it deserves, his critique of interventionism, the doctrine of the mixed economy, is still lost in the wilderness. This book is an effort, at what appears to be a timely moment in history, to reintroduce a revised version of Mises's analysis of the mixed economy into the current conversation on public policy. Its point of departure is Mises's critique of interventionism, the development of which spans a number of writings over several decades, beginning in 1912 with a short appraisal of price controls in *The Theory of Money and Credit* (1971: 254–9) and culminating in a lengthy discourse in his *Human Action* (1966: 716–861) in 1949.[5]

STATEMENT OF PURPOSE

The purpose of the present study is to update, extend, and, to some degree, re-interpret and revise the Misesian critique. It will update this critique by bringing to it the contributions of other scholars in the Austrian tradition, such as Friedrich Hayek's studies of knowledge and coordination and Israel Kirzner's investigations into the nature of entrepreneurship and the market process, which, whether Mises fully recognized them or not, have by now become an integral part of that tradition. It will also incorporate in an important way the insights of scholars who are neither economists nor explicitly of the Austrian tradition, such as Charles Murray, Nathan Glazer, and James Q. Wilson, much of whose research in social policy and bureaucratic organization is nonetheless highly germane and complementary to the issues addressed here.

This updating, I believe, itself extends Mises's framework by advancing new avenues of inquiry. For while Mises's general approach to the analysis of interventionism provides a fruitful beginning, in its present form it is less than ideally suited for combining the dynamics of both traditional regulation and those of the welfare state into a unified framework.[6] I will therefore attempt to demonstrate the relation between the analysis of interventions that more directly affect market prices, the dynamics of which I maintain are central to Mises's critique, and those that are intended primarily to transfer income and wealth, the dynamics of which I believe unfold in a parallel yet somewhat different manner. These two kinds of intervention, and the dynamics to which they give rise, have thus far been inadequately contrasted and compared.[7] Hence, one of the goals of this study is to take the first steps toward unifying the price-dynamics of Mises's critique with the transfer-dynamics that underlie the welfare state. Although my efforts here represent only a beginning, I try to indicate the direction in which a general *theory* of interventionism, in contrast to a mere *critique* of the regulatory state,[8] should proceed.

Finally, I will re-interpret and revise Mises's critique in a manner that is both more consistent with developments in the modern Austrian theory of markets and more fruitful analytically. This will be especially true with regard to the analysis of the welfare state, state-sponsored monopoly, and the stability of the minimal state.

In this way I hope to provide an outline of a general framework that will help us better to understand all mixed economies and the dynamics that drive them. While, of course, each really existing mixed economy differs from all others owing to cultural, institutional, and ideological factors, I hope to isolate the essential similarities that make efforts in the direction of such a general framework worthwhile. Drawing on Hayek and Kirzner I show that interventionism is really a process of entrepreneurial adjustments in both the private and public sectors, where these adjustments tend to be both unanticipated and undesirable (from the viewpoint of the interveners) owing to radical ignorance, complexity, and dispersed information.[9] This framework helps to explain not only why states expand, but, equally important, the factors that contribute to and shape the dynamics of the *contraction* of state activities and the characteristics of the contraction process. It also yields potentially observable implications (or "pattern predictions") that help to explain, among other things, why in practice nearly all economies in the world are and have been mixed economies and why examples of pure collectivism or capitalism are and have been so rare.

With the collapse of really existing communism we are forced to bring our attention to bear more intently on the range of economic systems that comprise the middle ground between pure capitalism and collectivism – the mixed economy – and away from constructs such as complete central planning that are, at least for the time being, far removed from reality.[10] This is not to deny that the debate between the advocates of capitalism and collectivism has provided extremely useful insights for the analysis and critique of mixed economies. On the contrary, this debate has illuminated the basic forces within each that, when brought together in the attempt to form a compromise system or "middle way," generate instability. Indeed, close attention to these dynamics is particularly timely and important because it is toward the middle of the politico-economic spectrum that failed and failing communist governments appear to be groping in search of a new paradigm to guide their social and economic policies. That is, if "really existing capitalism" – the interventionist mixed economy – rather than laissez-faire capitalism is likely to become, after the demise of really existing communism, the ruling doctrine of our times, it behooves us to devote greater attention to understanding the way it works. The primary objective of this study, therefore, is to examine the nature and causes of the processes that emerge in mixed economies as an unintended consequence of limited government intervention.

The remainder of this chapter provides an overview and critique of current economic explanations of the scope of state activity (for a more detailed discussion of the differences between the various approaches see Appendix A). It first examines the *general* contributions of the so-called "public choice" approach to the analysis of political processes and institutions in comparison with traditional regulation economics. It then assesses the suitability of public choice, in its present form, for addressing the concerns of this study – the analysis of the dynamics underlying state expansion and contraction. Next, it reviews and evaluates *specific* models of government growth,[11] both public choice and non-public choice, again from the viewpoint of whether they embody an appreciation for these issues. A final section summarizes the conclusions of this chapter, more explicitly defines the scope and method of this book, and then provides an overview of the remaining chapters.

THE ECONOMIC THEORY OF REGULATION AND PUBLIC CHOICE

Narrowly defined, the "economic analysis of regulation" refers to the use of neoclassical economic theory[12] to examine the positive and normative effects of specific kinds of government-imposed constraints on economic activity with respect to particular markets in the economy. Traditional regulation economics is concerned with tracing the effects, for example, of legal constraints on rates of return on capital in public utilities, of controls on prices or entry conditions in particular industries, or of regulations that are intended to address health, safety, and environmental concerns.[13]

Another approach to economic regulation, however, is to recognize that public authorities, for whatever reason, may frequently fall short of or even fail to achieve their declared aims, and then to inquire into why this might be the case.[14] Now, there are basically two ways to think about why the programs and policies of modern governments might not achieve their goals. First, public authorities may lack the necessary knowledge to execute their plans successfully, creating a gulf between the actual outcomes and the ones they intended to produce. Second, public authorities may possess or have the capacity to possess the necessary knowledge, but actually follow a less open agenda by making their actual intentions different from the ones that they announce. Hence, perceived policy failure can result from an inconsistency between actual and intended outcomes or from a discrepancy between announced and actual intent. (It can also, of course, result from a combination of the two.) A growing body of scholarship originating[15] from seminal studies by alumni of Aaron Director's workshop at the University of Chicago,[16] political economists at the University of Virginia,[17] and others,[18] now known collectively as "the new political economy," or as we will refer to it here "public choice,"[19] has greatly increased the scope of traditional regulation economics largely by following the second course and differentiating between the announced and the actual intent of public policy. Austrian political economy has for the most part followed the first course.

In his outstanding survey, Dennis Mueller broadly defines public choice as "the economic study of non-market decision-making, or simply the application of economics to political science" (Mueller 1989: 1), in which "the basic behavioral postulate ... is that man is an egotistic, rational, utility maximizer" (ibid.: 2). Public choice, then, differs from the traditional view of regulation, first in its subject-matter – the *incentives* facing persons in their "public choice roles," i.e., "in their various capacities as voters, as candidates for office, as elected representatives, as leaders or members of political parties, as bureaucrats" (Buchanan 1979: 13) – and, second in its postulate that these persons are just as likely to pursue *selfish interests*, *à la* utility maximization, in their roles as public servants, as they are in their "private choice" roles. The advent of public choice has provided economists, political scientists, and the general public with a scientifically rigorous alternative to the "public interest" view of public policy,[20] which in effect treats persons who have moved from the private sector to government employment as having been thereby transformed from self-interested profit-seeking actors into public-spirited and selfless public servants. In public choice, regulators and regulated alike are liable to use any means open to them, including state-sanctioned compulsion and coercion, to achieve their selfish goals. Public choice, as Buchanan aptly puts it, is "politics without romance" (Buchanan and Tollison 1984: 11).

While public choice recognizes that not all political ends people pursue, acting alone or in groups, have a *narrowly* self-interested focus, it does claim that the postulate of utility maximization that underlies this perspective enables theorists, by including narrow self-interest as a choice variable, to explain a great deal of what happens in the political process. One way it can do this is by drawing attention away from the idiosyncracies of the particular personalities involved in the political process and directing it toward the incentive structures built into the political institutions within which these persons operate. Thus, for example, because representative democracy often imposes relatively high costs of information for some persons or groups compared to others, excessive growth in the budgets of bureaucracies is hard to detect, politicians engage in misleading political campaigns, and special-interest groups seek to install government-sponsored programs that concentrate benefits on themselves while spreading the costs among all taxpayers. Because of the power of the median voter under majority rule, wealth from the rich (and sometimes the poor) is transferred to the middle class, political parties become more alike, and extremist candidates lose elections. And because the state discriminates among beneficiaries according to its own criteria when it hands out favors, individuals and groups have an incentive to expend valuable resources to qualify, thereby increasing their chances of prevailing over rivals competing for the same rewards.[21]

Rascals all?

Since these phenomena typically reduce social welfare – through the deadweight losses resulting from the redistributional aspect of all these activities – much of the normative theory of public choice points toward the desirability of reform. Reform of the political process, however, is somewhat problematic from the public-choice perspective. For one thing, a concerted effort to "throw the rascals out" is difficult for the same reason that rascals are able to abuse their positions in the first place – high or asymmetric transaction costs – and only when the per capita loss to the public from letting them stay in office is greater than the per capita cost of throwing them out will it be rational for citizens to do the latter. More fundamentally, reducing waste in government and making it less vulnerable to interest-group pressure is, from the standpoint of public choice, more a matter of altering the *incentive structure* in the political process by reforming political institutions and, if necessary, altering the constitutional foundations of government, than of replacing incumbents with public-spirited persons who idealistically place the collective interest above their own and their immediate constituents' interest. Throwing out the rascals, therefore, would solve very little in the long run, unless this were a step toward more dramatic institutional reform.

But this is so largely because public choice assumes that *all* public choosers are, in a sense, rascals, be they private-interest groups that have captured passive bureaucrats and legislators or powerful public agents increasing their wealth at the expense of a docile legislature and general citizenry. Thus, in an early contribution to public-choice theory, *The Politics of Bureaucracy*, Gordon Tullock announced: "*I propose, therefore, to give special emphasis to the behavior of an intelligent, ambitious, and somewhat unscrupulous man in an organizational hierarchy*" (Tullock 1965: 26; emphasis original). In so doing, Tullock set an early and important precedent in the public-choice research program.

Not surprisingly, some, perhaps a great many, remain unconverted to the public-choice view. Steven Kelman, for example, argues on the contrary that "public spirit is widespread enough so that the role the government plays in our lives is more worthy of admiration and faith than of dislike and cynicism" (Kelman 1987: 10), and so "when people try to achieve good public policy, the result tends to *be* good public policy" (p. 209; emphasis original).

7

Similarly, James Q. Wilson observes: "What is surprising is that bureaucrats work at all rather than shirk at every opportunity" (Wilson 1989: 156).[22] But dropping the postulate of narrow self-interest would severely reduce the explanatory power of public choice. While it might still retain some power – much of the work on cycling and rational voter ignorance might perhaps remain, for example – certainly a great many other interesting implications would vanish, especially the insights that issue from the concept of rent-seeking.[23]

The overall *normative* thrust of public choice, based on standard neoclassical efficiency grounds, is that, under current conditions in the United States for instance, less government would be preferable to more government. This follows from an analysis of the deadweight losses that ensue from rent-seeking of various kinds, the logic of organized interest-group activity, bureaucratic budgetary expansion, etc. These normative implications would disappear, however, if public choice's basic behavioral postulate were jettisoned.

There are at least two good reasons why public-choice theorists would strongly resist this. First, as mentioned earlier, the utility-maximization approach permits them to bring to bear on complex political phenomena an array of sophisticated analytical tools developed within the paradigm of neoclassical economics. Second, the evidence on this postulate's descriptive accuracy, in the opinion of most (though as we have seen not all) observers today, would seem to favor the public-choice rather than the public-interest viewpoint, especially if one interprets utility maximization somewhat loosely to refer simply to self-interested behavior (since, strictly speaking, action in the real world would never be able to meet the stringent informational conditions necessary for genuine utility maximization – see below).

The position of Kelman *et al.*, however, poses an interesting theoretical challenge. What would happen to the normative implications of public choice were we to postulate public-spiritedness or a "do-gooder" mentality among public choosers? Would making the shapers of public policy benevolent and primarily concerned with promoting the general interest really produce good public policy?[24] The answers to these questions do not follow from my earlier statements about the consequences for the positive theory of public choice of dropping its central behavioral postulate. Certainly, as mentioned earlier, little would be left of public choice without it, but there may be reasons for remaining skeptical of public policy that extends the reach of government authority – reasons relating to an aspect of the political process, other than those provided by public choice, that has been largely taken for granted and, for that reason, typically neglected by political economists. Indeed, I maintain that an essential aspect of this process has been frequently overlooked in theoretical discussion in political economy even though it is a commonplace to those knowledgeable in the practical operation of public policy – i.e., the centrality of unintended consequences in the development and implementation of public policy, owing to a lack of relevant knowledge on the part of public choosers. Thus, this idea gives rise to the second approach to political economy mentioned earlier that regards policy failure as the result of a conflict between actual and intended outcomes. As I hope to show in the course of this book, a better appreciation of the causes and implications of these unintended consequences would reach many of public choice's normative as well as positive conclusions, though by a very different route. Hence, one should not interpret this challenge as one to put the "romance" back into politics, but rather as an opportunity to introduce a perspective that can shed significant new light on the political process.

Limitations of a neoclassical approach to political economy

Obviously, the choice of theoretical framework is important. If public choice, or more generally political economy, is the application of economics to political science, it would certainly matter which paradigm of economic theory one applies. The postulate of self-interest in its "rigorous" form, utility maximization, is part of the paradigm of neoclassical economics, whose foundations consist of equilibrium analysis, optimization, and perfect knowledge.[25] One need not limit the economic explanation of the political process, however, to that of neoclassical utility maximization. Since I treat this topic at greater length in Chapter 3, it is enough to say here that I believe the same heterodox method that inspired Mises, Hayek, and more recently Kirzner to focus on the dynamic nature of the market process can also enrich our understanding of the nature of the political process. To say the least, this Austrian, or "market-process," approach tends to give the roles of equilibrium, optimization, and especially perfect knowledge a great deal less importance than does neoclassical theory.[26] Austrian political economy, like Austrian market process theory, rests squarely on the idea that an essential aspect of all really existing social processes is the effort of actors to cope with a lack of relevant knowledge.

It is, of course, not strictly necessary to reject utility maximization in order to relax the postulate of self-interest. One could conceivably modify the utility functions of public choosers to include an argument representing the expected utilities of persons other than themselves and still retain the neoclassical paradigm in political science. Yet this would also retain another limitation of public choice.

Public-choice scholar, Richard Wagner, interprets the public-choice perspective on "government failure" in the following terms:

> Policy failure has often been attributed to mistakes and ignorance, but it might rather be the result of the *rational pursuit of interest* and not really a failure from the perspective of those whose interests are controlling the choice at hand.
>
> (Wagner 1989: 56; emphasis added)

I have suggested that one of the pillars of neoclassical economics is the concept of *perfect knowledge*. One may define this concept in various ways depending on the problem at hand, but its essential meaning is that agents possess the amount of information that is optimal for forming their plans – i.e., information sufficient to remove the possibility of *ex post* regret. Owing to their optimal foresight, these agents tend to be *successful* in achieving the ends they seek; in public choice this is usually some form of income redistribution (a matter I will take up separately in a moment), which is precisely the reason their activities are a cause for concern in normative public-choice analysis. Thus, perfect knowledge translates into the rational pursuit of interest, which in turn implies in the political context that public choosers are successful in executing and fulfilling their plans.

Assuming perfect knowledge also gives rise to the public-choice idea that actors must have deliberately aimed for the actual outcomes of their political actions. That is, public choice reveals a form of the perfect-knowledge assumption in its emphasis on the *intended* outcomes of the agents who drive the political process. Thus, for example, Wagner (1989) cites George Stigler approvingly when the latter states, in the context of explaining the purpose of empirical studies in economics, that economists should scrutinize

10

public policy in such a way that "the *truly intended effects should be deduced from the actual effects*" (ibid.: 56; emphasis orginal). Indeed, Wagner plainly asserts that "Public choice theory is a proposition about inferring intentions from outcomes" (ibid.: 46–7). Yet strict adherence to the dictum of inferring genuine intentions from actual outcomes could oblige practioners of public choice to make inferences that most of them would no doubt find disagreeable. Thus, for example, according to one interpretation of that dictum they would have to conclude that all of the recent social ills that social scientists have linked to failed public policy – the decay of the inner cities, inter-racial enmity, the increase in divorce and the breakup of the family, the decline of state-school education, and the rise in immorality, violence, and narcotics consumption to name but a few – are the deliberately-sought-after goals of social planners of the last generation.[27] While it might be unfair to corner public-choice theorists into such an extreme position, still it is not obvious how they would differentiate themselves methodologically from some political economists who might indeed see some or all of these social problems as the intended outcome of a veiled political agenda.

I do not claim that public choice completely neglects the unintended consequences of political action, such as deadweight losses, but that these tend to play only a marginal role in its positive analysis.[28] Indeed, that redistributional activities produce deadweight losses and other unintended effects is often completely irrelevant from the viewpoint of the decision-making agents in public-choice models, in which *incentives* are nearly always the central focus. Once again, this concentration on incentives arises from the fact that it is the very success of public choosers in achieving their intended, though veiled, objectives (e.g., erecting barriers to competition, qualifying for income transfers, misrepresenting bureaucratic budgets) that drive the results of these models. To the extent that unintended consequences (i.e., deadweight losses) are important in public choice, they are usually a part of the normative evaluation of the political process rather than an aspect of a positive theory of the dynamics of that process.

In contrast, in the Misesian critique of interventionism, unintended consequences are as important in the positive theory as in the normative evaluations.[29] The Austrian emphasis on system-wide processes here, I believe, is central to its method. Rather than critically assessing only the results of particular interventions, the

Austrian approach is equally concerned with the far-reaching and unforeseen consequences of interventions that, for this approach, fuel the political process. Again, this is not to say that public choice ignores entirely the process underlying expansion of state activity (which is addressed in the next section), but that it tends to emphasize the intended effects of agents using political means over the unintended effects, while the Misesian critique treats unintended effects as a central force.

In summary, public choice is an extremely valuable approach to the analysis of political institutions and processes and it possesses impressive explanatory power. Although these are important attributes for any theoretical framework to have, public choice's reliance on the paradigm of neoclassical economics leaves it open to Kelman's objection and tends to limit its focus to those parts of the political process having to do with intended outcomes. Moreover, insofar as it adopts a neoclassical approach to analyze the unintended consequences of the political process, the central aspect of this process, the existence of radical ignorance, would be completely disregarded. (The significance of this last point is discussed in Chapter 3.)

Are all interventions intentional transfers? Does the state ever shrink?

There are two other related points that need to be made concerning the current practice of public choice. First, the assumption of narrow self-interest tends to result in models of political behavior in which the principal concern of public choosers is the transfer of income or wealth from others to themselves. Consequently, public choice seems to have a comparative advantage in addressing the political process underlying intentional wealth transfers, which are most often found in, though not limited to, the kind of mixed economy known as the welfare state. In addition, the insights public choice gains from its analysis of intentional transfers have also been applied to other forms of government intervention, since all interventions into interpersonal exchanges directly or indirectly transfer wealth or income from one party to another. Thus, for example, health and environmental controls, civil rights directives, and commercial regulation involve wealth transfers and have this much in common with interventions in pursuit of welfare-state goals. However, this does not imply that, *for the purpose of better*

12

understanding intervention as a process, the most important thing is the intentional redistribution of wealth;[30] and while there are benefits from analyzing unintentional transfers in this way, it also blurs important differences between what might be termed "transfer dynamics" and "regulatory dynamics," as exemplified in the interventionist processes underlying the welfare state and the regulatory state, respectively.[31] While the premise of political self-interest makes public choice a powerful tool of analysis, I maintain that one should resist the temptation to assume that intentional transfers are the only, or nearly the only, aspect of the political process worth talking about.[32]

Second, narrow self-interest may be better suited for explaining the growth of government than the sort of decentralization and contraction of state activity that has been taking place recently in various parts of the world.[33] Most likely this is once again a direct consequence of public choice's emphasis on the *incentive structures* of political institutions that encourage politically self-interested behavior. As mentioned earlier, public-choice explanations of how and why government grows seem to presume for the most part that agents are able to predict accurately the outcome of specific policies, programs, legislation, or bureaucratic processes. Hence, growth in regulation is seen largely as the intended result of deliberate, narrowly self-interested actions. To repeat, to the extent that public choice regards the growth of government as no more than the desired outcome of political agents, it may be overlooking the dynamic associated with the *unintended* consequences of intervention, which push the mixed economy toward or, just as importantly, away from collectivist central planning. To borrow a phrase from the so-called "socialist calculation debate,"[34] the problems of government intervention emerge not only from a *lack of proper incentives*, but, just as significantly, from a *lack of knowledge*.

Public choice and Austrian political economy

Excluding for the present the notion of political self-interest from the analysis of interventionism is purely methodological, i.e., it is done to show how very similar conclusions regarding the operation of the political process can be derived from a very different positive framework – one that eschews perfect information and equilibrium-based neoclassical economic theory. Indeed, in Chapter 4 I argue that in terms of their usefulness in analyzing public policy, public choice and the theory of interventionism are *complements* rather than substitutes that share such important normative conclusions as the need for strong constitutional constraints that make the state, the "guarantor" but not the "creator" of rights of person and property (Wagner 1989: 15).[35] Mises himself well appreciated the basic message of what later became public-choice analysis. To cite just one example,

> As soon as something happens in the economy that any of the various bureaucratic institutions does not like or that arouses the anger of a pressure group, people clamor for new interventions, controls, and restrictions.[36]
>
> (Mises 1966: 859)

It is probably safe to say that most Austrian market-process theorists today share a sense of intellectual kinship with the public-choice approach to political economy.[37] To market-process theorists, one of public choice's most important contributions to the overall critique of interventionism is precisely its penetrating analysis of the pernicious effects of narrowly self-interested behavior in the political process, the waste associated with the use of coercion and compulsion to redistribute wealth, and the forces that influence the size of government. Although the method the majority of its practitioners use at present is equilibrium-oriented, market-process theorists can appreciate public choice's fundamental insight that purposeful human behavior in the context of the political process tends to produce unintended consequences for the system as a whole, even if, from the viewpoint of this study at least, it is possible to carry this insight much further than it has so far.[38]

THEORIES OF GOVERNMENT GROWTH AND THEIR LIMITATIONS[39]

Based on what has been said up to now, a theory of intervention should (1) be able to combine the regulatory and transfer dynamics of the mixed economy into a single framework that does not assume redistributive motives on the part of public choosers, (2) be concerned with the dynamic process underlying both the expansion and contraction phases of state growth, and (3) be able to explain this process in terms of endogenous economic forces. As I hope to show in Chapter 4, a theory capable of addressing all

14

three of these considerations would at the same time have to regard the process resulting from a policy of interventionism as a self-regulating and self-maintaining or "spontaneous" order, which is defined more fully in Chapter 3.

Let us now examine several recent and fairly representative models of government growth to see the degree to which each fulfills the above criteria. While the previous section concentrated on the *general approach* of public choice, this section examines specific public-choice models of state expansion, as well as several that are not in that tradition. First, I briefly examine models that merely address the question of why the state attains a given size. Next, I discuss some that try to explain directly what causes the growth of government and classify them as either endogenous or exogenous, based on the origin of the force driving the system to expand or contract. Among these are some that have "ideology" as a motive force, and they are treated separately.

To reiterate, the following is not meant to be a full survey of the literature. For present purposes, a detailed critique and comprehensive survey would be unnecessary. My concern here is with the extent to which standard approaches to the questions of government growth embody the three criteria stated above: an integrated framework in which public choosers eschew narrow self-interest; a concern with state contraction as well as expansion; and endogenous forces of government growth. I will therefore focus only on those aspects of the following models that pertain to these concerns.

The size of the state

Strictly speaking, I am interested not with what determines the size of government *per se*, but with the reasons why government grows or shrinks. While related they are not the same thing. Nevertheless, for the sake of completeness, and also because it will place the discussion of subsequent models in proper context, I will first examine some analyses of the equilibrium size of government.

The most common textbook rationale for state activity in general is based on the notion of social optimality. A state of socially optimal size performs functions for which it has a comparative advantage over the market, and for which social benefits exceed social costs. The state is optimally sized when there is an equality in the social benefits and costs of an additional increment in each such function. The most typical examples are those connected with the existence of so-called pure public goods and externalities. Non-rivalrous, non-exclusive goods such as television broadcasts and national defense are typical examples of pure public goods, while pollution and technical innovation are common examples of negative and positive externalities, respectively. Voluntary exchange on the market is said to be incapable – and presumably the government capable – of providing the optimal amount of goods or services that generate externalities to a significant degree. That is, the property of externality, in both public goods and externalities proper, creates incentives for private agents to free-ride on the contributions of others. (In this sense, a polluter free rides on the "contributions" of those who suffer the cost of pollution just as national defense protects even those who do not pay for it.)[40] It is argued that under these circumstances state coercion and compulsion is necessary overcome the free-rider problem.[41]

Other models, however, purport to show that we would tend not to see optimally sized states. For example, the so-called "fiscal illusion" hypothesis put forward by Tanzi (1980), posits that government will grow beyond the size its citizens prefer if it can increase taxes in such a way that the government appears smaller than it is. Thus, Tanzi invokes some kind of asymmetric information cost to explain how government could grow larger than its citizens want, although he leaves unanswered the questions of whether government activity would in fact expand under the conditions he specifies and from what sector, private or public, and in what form the pressure to increase intervention would come. Dwight Lee (1989) reaches a conclusion similar to Tanzi's though by a different route. He reasons that, in the context of ever-present pressure from organized interests to extend government intervention, the degree of public control over government that would keep these interests in check, and thus make the minimal state achievable, would for this very reason also make the minimal state smaller than optimal.[42]

Taking a slightly broader approach, Becker (1983) tries to include the provision of public goods within a conception of government activity that is still, however, essentially redistributive. He hypothesizes that if all government activity were redistributive, then government would provide public goods and reduce externalities wherever the collective gains from doing so exceeded the collective costs. Pressure groups serve as the motive force behind this result since they will seek subsidies (or tax reductions) until the state achieves an equilibrium size at the point where the marginal benefits and costs from applying pressure on public authorities are equalized. Because the state can subsidize more efficiently, or tax less efficiently, groups whose interests have public goods or positive-externality attributes will be more likely to succeed than other groups that only seek redistribution or that will impose negative externalities.

To appraise these models from the perspective of the present study, note that the Tanzi, Lee, and Becker hypotheses rely primarily on intentional redistribution or rent-seeking as a motive force. All fail to explain the process by which the state grows to its equilibrium size, whether optimal or suboptimal. Although one could infer that the equilibrium size of the state would vary as population, information costs, costs of controlling government, and the relative efficiency of pressure groups increased or decreased, depending on the model in question, this really only amounts to comparative statics rather than a description of the endogenous dynamic process by which the state expands or contracts. Thus, because of their inherently static nature these models have little usefulness to us.[43] Some of the models that follow, however, use the static externality/public-goods model as a starting point, as we will presently see.

The growth of government

It will be convenient to divide the models that deal with government growth, proper, into the categories of exogenous and endogenous explanations. As stated already, it is the latter that are of primary interest to us, although, once again, I will review the former for the sake of completeness and context.

Exogenous explanations of government growth

Increasing population density and geographic proximity are often cited as exogenous factors in government growth. They can result in a higher incidence of positive and negative externalities because as larger numbers of people begin to live closer together this increases the likelihood that spill-over and neighborhood effects will occur. For example, a given amount of air pollution (or air-pollution abatement) is more likely to harm (or benefit) a greater number of persons as population density and proximity grow. As has just been seen, externality is the basis in standard economics for the rationale behind government provision of certain goods and services, so that growth in population size and density may stimulate the demand for more intervention. Assuming that the amount of intervention the state is willing and able to supply is responsive to changes in demand, then *ceteris paribus* the state will expand when population size and density increase and contract when they decrease.

Next, let us examine three different explanations of the impact of income on government growth. The first, and simplest, is based on the bald assertion that government services are normal (or luxury) goods in the standard economic sense. Hence, as economies expand and median income rises, demand for government services will also tend to rise. Again, assuming that proper supply conditions obtain, government should grow and shrink with median income.

Each of the next two income-based models applies the median-voter theorem, though they reach very different conclusions about the impact on government growth of variations in income across the voting population.

Meltzer and Richard (1978), for instance, demonstrate that either growing income *inequality* or greater suffrage can result in a growing demand for government. Their model assumes, consistent with public-choice analysis, that government activity consists solely of income redistribution by means of a per capita lump-sum subsidy financed through a proportional tax. They argue that if growing income inequality is accompanied by a decline in the median voter's income relative to the mean income level, then median voters will demand and get a redistribution of income in their favor. They claim that a similar result would obtain were suffrage rights broadened and those who were added to the voting rolls had incomes below the median.

In the context of representative government engaged, once again, solely in income redistribution, Peltzman (1976) argues that a rational candidate for office will compete for votes by promising income transfers to those who join his coalition in order to secure their loyalty. He demonstrates that, under these circumstances, government will tend to grow as pre-transfer incomes become more *equal* because the greater the equality of the initial distribution of incomes among a candidate's potential constituents, the greater will be the degree of substitutability between himself and his rivals, and therefore the more redistribution he must promise voters to keep them in his coalition. Peltzman claims that an important factor in both raising income levels and lowering income variance is an increasing stock of human capital brought about through education. Thus, he argues, greater investment in education will tend to increase the size of government.

According to Baumol (1967), if the price of government-provided goods increases when the price-elasticity of demand for such goods is inelastic, the expenditure on government, and thus its size, will also increase. He claims that the price of government-provided goods has indeed risen relative to other goods because the former tend to be in the form of services, which in turn tend to be less capital intensive than manufactured goods. This is significant because, compared to the governmental sector, capital-embodied productivity increases would then have a greater impact in the private sector because there production is relatively more capital intensive owing to the lower proportion of output in the form of services. Relatively low rates of productivity in the governmental sector, then, would raise the price of government-provided goods relative to goods produced in the private sector.

Of these models, only those of Meltzer and Richard and of Peltzman depend on redistributive motives. All, however, rely on changes in parameters to explain changes in the size of government. But we may well ask, Why does population grow? What makes incomes rise? Why do greater income inequality or suffrage take place? What induces investment in education to rise? Why should capital-embodied productivity increases occur? Like the explicitly static models discussed earlier, at most these models seem able only to perform comparative-statics analysis, and thus fall short, from our perspective, of satisfactorily explaining why government grows.

Endogenous explanations of government growth

Let us now examine a pair of models that do incorporate endogenous forces of some kind, or that at least (as in the case of the first model discussed) have an aspect that may be helpful in understanding endogenous change. Our earlier discussion of the strengths and limitations of public choice might lead one to believe that at present theorists working in that tradition seldom if ever address the kinds of questions that are central to the present analysis, and that even when they do so it is from a rather narrow neoclassical perspective. While there is a strong element of truth to this with respect to the current state of public choice in general, there have been some notable exceptions whose work can shed considerable light on our analysis.

Niskanen's seminal essay on bureaucracy (1971), which is squarely in the public-choice tradition, assumes the objective of bureaucrats is to maximize their own utility subject to an oversight constraint. While raising salaries and perquisites for a given rate of bureaucratic output would appear to accomplish this objective directly, the legislature to which bureaus are answerable can monitor and control such activity at relatively low cost. Niskanen therefore hypothesizes that bureaus may instead maximize utility by raising their output beyond that level the legislature, and indirectly the median voter, finds desirable, and then demand larger budgets to cover their additional activities. As a result of this constrained budget maximization the bureaucrat enjoys non-pecuniary rewards (e.g., larger staffs, more influence and political clout).

Up to this point Niskanen's analysis is purely static. It does, however, indirectly offer an endogenous explanation for government growth. Niskanen posits that the ability of the bureaucracy to fool the legislature is itself a function of the size and complexity of the budget, and so monitoring becomes more difficult the bigger the absolute size of the bureaucracy. This means that if initial conditions permit bureaus to fool legislatures into giving them larger budgets than necessary, then bureaucratic growth can take on a life of its own. That is, when such conditions permit bureaus to increase their budgets, they thereby raise the level of bureaucratic complexity that makes them harder to monitor, which in turn will make it easier for them to increase their budgets in the next round, leading once again to greater bureaucratic complexity, and so on. Thus, in Niskanen's model, bureaucracy grows over time so long as monitoring costs at the margin are sufficiently high, but where the latter are themselves a function of the size of the bureaucracy.

The discussion later in Chapter 4 on the fundamental dynamics of the interventionist process draws in part on this concept of growing complexity, as well as Herbert Simon's concept of bounded rationality, to help explain the failure of public authorities to learn from past mistakes. Perhaps even more significant from the viewpoint of the present study, however, is Mancur Olson's analysis of the rise and decline of nations. In an important sense, Olson's approach to explaining government behavior is still well within the paradigm of public choice, the power as well as the limitations of which I have already examined. Thus, the motive force in his model of the rise and decline of nations consists of the activities of quite well-informed interest groups, or "distributional coalitions," whose principal concern is the redistribution of income. What sets Olson's model apart from, say, Pelzman's model, and what he has partly in common with Niskanen's, is his focus on the dynamics resulting from the *unintended consequences* of human action.

Olson (1982) discusses the conditions favoring the growth of interest groups and their impact on the macroeconomic perform-ance of different countries at different times in history. Growth in the scope and magnitude of interest-group activity – conditioned by, among other things, whether a given society has remained economically and politically stable for a long period of time with unchanged boundaries and a homogeneous population – generates various kinds of inefficiencies. But so long as the per capita costs of engaging in wealth-producing activity for those sharing a common interest are high relative to the per capital benefits they receive from it (owing to large external effects) and the per capita costs of output redistribution are low relative to the per capital benefits, there will be a strong tendency for scarce resources to go into redistribution rather than wealth production – i.e., where the rate of return on the resources invested is higher. The value of resources so expended are deadweight losses to society because they produce nothing of value to consumers, *qua* consumers.

> In short, the typical organization for collective action within a society will, at least if it represents only a narrow segment of the society, have little or no interest to make any signifi-cant sacrifices in the interest of the society; it can best serve its members' interests by striving to seize a larger share of a society's production for them. This will be expedient, more-over, even if the social costs of the change in the distribution exceed the amount of redistribution by a huge multiple; there is for practical purposes no constraint on the social cost such

an organization will find it expedient to impose on the society in the course of obtaining a larger share of the social output for itself.

(ibid.: 44; emphasis omitted)

Continued long enough, expanding regulation and political rent-seeking could eventually generate inefficiencies due to complexity and deadweight losses so enormous that the per capita costs of redistribution will begin to outweigh the per capita benefits. When this happens there is an incentive for even rent-seekers to do away with or at least severely constrain distributional coalitions, although coalitions that continue to prosper will still have strong incentives to push in the opposite direction. If there is an accompanying economic upheaval, this could serve to tip the balance in favor of radical reforms. According to Olson, however, it is more typical that some sort of exogenous change, such as a foreign invasion, will lead to the breakdown of distributional coalitions. (Hence, this portion of Olson's thesis could be classified as an exogenous explanation.)

Some of the implications Olson draws from what he terms the "logic of collective action" not only parallel the concerns of the present study, but also have direct relevance for it. For example, he notes that "The accumulation of distributional coalitions increases the complexity of regulation, the role of government, and the complexity of understandings, and changes the direction of social evolution" (ibid.: 73). To derive this conclusion he relies, in part, on Charles Schultz's description of the evolution of regulatory complexity as a dynamic process. In this process, regulations intended to close one set of loopholes not only make the framework of regulation more extensive and complex, but also create opportunities for political entrepreneurs to find unexpected ways of profiting from them. This then provokes the interests behind the original regulations to amend or extend them still further in order to close these loopholes, which increases the complexity of the regulatory framework even more and once again offers fertile ground for political entrepreneurship (ibid.: 70).

As mentioned above, I will have occasion in Chapter 4 to refer back to the process that Niskanen and Olson describe here, for the underlying dynamic presumes the existence of unforeseen and unanticipated consequences, which depend in turn on difficulties in knowledge acquisition of some kind. In this respect, it is significant that Olson explicitly eschews perfect competition as a frame of reference (ibid.: 59), and adopts what he terms an "evolutionary" approach to macroeconomics. Of the two senses in which one could characterize Olson's model as reflecting an appreciation of the unintended consequences of intervention – the unintentional deadweight losses from attempts to redistribute output and the unintended complexity and regulatory growth that follow an initial intervention – the latter much more than the former resonate with the concerns of the present study.

Olson is careful not to claim monocausality for his model of government growth.[44] He notes for example that

> The interwar depression, World War II, and other developments led to profound ideological changes that increased the scope of government, and developments like the cold war and pollution, to mention only two, also increased the demands upon governments. A great many factors have to be taken into account to explain the growth of government, and all that is asserted here is that the accumulation of special-interest organizations is one of these factors.
>
> (ibid.: 71)

Indeed, while the present study aims to explore one of these other factors, it will hopefully reach, by a different route, positive as well as normative conclusions similar to Olson's.

Both Niskanen and Olson incorporate endogenous dynamic processes into their analysis, at least at some level. Both invoke to a degree the idea of increasing complexity in order to explain these dynamics, although, of the two, Olson's treatment may be somewhat more satisfactory from the perspective of the present study for two reasons. First, his analysis suggests to a slightly greater degree that knowledge problems are at work that are more fundamental in some sense than the Simoneon "bounded rationality" problems that one might with some justification associate more with Niskanen's analysis. Second, Niskanen's model is unable to explain the phenomenon of bureaucratic and, more generally, state contraction, of which there is considerable recent evidence. Olson's model, on the other hand, does include some discussion of the causes of the end to and reversal of state expansion.

There is another class of hypotheses that purport to explain the size of government. They will receive a separate treatment, however, since, unlike the models in this section considered up to now, they focus on a factor outside the traditional scope of economic analysis – namely, ideology.

The role of ideology in the size of government

I hope to show in the next chapter the importance Mises explicitly attached to ideological factors in his critique of interventionism.[45] Likewise, ideology, in the sense of one's attitude toward the proper scope and magnitude of government, also has an important place in the present analysis – one that I examine more closely in Chapter 4. To prepare the ground for future discussion, let us continue our distinction between exogenous and endogenous explanations.

Exogenous explanations of ideological change

In exogenous explanations, ideology impinges on the interventionist process in ways that are, in the construct of the analyst, largely independent of that process. It is possible to characterize Mises's use of ideology in this way, since, while he strongly emphasized the importance of the public's attitude toward state expansion, he devoted little space to explaining what causes and conditions arising out of the interventionist process itself might shift this attitude away from interventionism and toward either collectivism or laissez-faire capitalism. Regarding the possibility of a turn-around at the point at which interventionism can no longer afford to finance greater intervention Mises states,

> But neither a low standard of living nor progressive impoverishment automatically liquidates an economic system. It gives way to a more efficient system only if people themselves are *intelligent enough* to comprehend the advantages such a change might bring them.
>
> (Mises 1966 [1949]: 860; emphasis added)

Unfortunately Mises does not elaborate on what might cause people suddenly to become "intelligent enough" to discover the error of their ways or on the possibility of endogenous forces leading to this outcome. However, incorporating the insights of later market-process scholarship, especially from the work of both Hayek on the use of knowledge in society and Kirzner on the nature of entrepreneurship, could shed new light on the above

24

statement. Not until the end of Chapter 2, however, will we be ready to consider more specifically what these insights consist of.

Endogenous explanations of ideological change

Ideology becomes an endogenous force in the present analysis to the extent that we are able to explain how it changes depending on the causes and conditions operating in our construct. One can find examples of the kind of endogenous explanations of ideological change that are relevant here, to one degree or another, in the works of Higgs (1987), Glazer (1988), and Hayek (1972; 1976).

Robert Higgs, in his masterful history of government growth in the United States after the Civil War, *Crisis and Leviathan*, argues that "ideology becomes most prominent during social crisis" (Higgs 1987: 47), and that available evidence substantiates his thesis that each period of dramatic political and economic change in recent American history "altered the ideological climate" in such a way that it made acceptable a larger role for government with respect to civil and economic liberties than would otherwise have been possible (ibid.: 59). He contends that crises can permanently expand limits on the tolerable size of the state by breaking down ideological resistance to "big government." This is achieved by

· (1) providing occasions for the improvement of command-and-control mechanisms, which render them less obnoxious; (2) discrediting the conservative's domino theory, with its implication that all civil and political liberties will be lost in a mixed economy; and (3) creating opportunities for many people both within and without the government to do well for themselves and hence to look more favorably on the new order.

(ibid.: 73)

While Higgs does not claim that all government growth arises from crises (ibid.: 61), he does hold that crises produce a "ratcheting-up" effect with respect to the secular course of government growth. That is, while government may grow at a constant rate both before and after a crisis (presumably for reasons not directly related to any crisis), he argues that the post-crisis size of government is significantly larger than it would have been had the crisis never occurred, even after a period of post-crisis retrenchment (ibid.: 61). However, his thesis is intended to explain neither the source

25

of the secular trend in government growth between periods of crisis nor the source or sources of these crises themselves. Moreover, it is unclear from his analysis what forces might result in state contraction. Thus, like so many other treatments of this topic, Higgs's is regrettably one-sided.

The sociologist Nathan Glazer in his careful analysis of the limits of social policy traces the often destructive effects of well-intentioned social policy on the "fine structure of society," a self-regulating structure of beliefs, attitudes, and customs that connects and supports a social network consisting of family, community, and other informal associations. If the government attempts to replace formal (interventionistic) with informal procedures (based on the fine structure of society), for example, this "contributes to the undermining of confidence in and acceptance of informal social controls" (Glazer 1988: 148). What is important from our perspective are the implications of Glazer's argument that intervention in these matters tends to substitute the judgment of public authorities for traditional arrangements.

> In doing so, social policy weakens the position of these traditional agents and further encourages needy people to depend on the government for help rather than on the traditional structures. This is the basic force behind the ever growing demand for more social programs *and their frequent failure to satisfy our hopes.*
>
> (ibid.: 7; emphasis added)

He makes no attempt, however, to describe or explain the dynamics of the reversal of this process. Nevertheless, Glazer's insights into the perils of social-welfare policy are not only relevant to the present analysis by themselves, but, as I argue in Chapter 5, they acquire additional value from the way in which they significantly clarify the commonality between transfer and regulatory dynamics.

Both Higgs and Glazer describe the "psychological" or "moral" impact of intervention on the regulated public in broadly similar terms. Their analyses represent a type of endogenous ideological explanation that I will term the *gradual-acceptance thesis*. Each in different ways describes a process in which every act of intervention makes the next seem less onerous in the minds of all those involved, fostering on the part of the affected public a predisposition to accept, and on the part of the government a proclivity to create, further intervention.

26

Friedrich Hayek has provided a related though quite distinct ideological argument, which we will term the *self-fulfilling thesis*. According to Hayek, within the context of something approaching a minimal state, the concept of "social justice" is meaningless because the outcomes of impersonal market processes are neither foreseeable nor deliberately aimed at, and therefore cannot be meaningfully attributed to any agent or will. But once the state undertakes to implement "social justice" by deliberate redistribution, the concept becomes coherent and a very real object of political contest.[46] Thus,

> "Social justice" can be given meaning only in a directed or "command" economy (such as an army) in which the individuals are ordered what to do; and any particular conception of "social justice" could be realized only in such a centrally directed system.
>
> (Hayek 1976: 69)

In an earlier work, Hayek advanced a similar thesis, which deserves to be much more widely known. It addresses in a highly original way the familiar trade-off between measures that protect individual freedom and those that promote personal security. He argued that if the state hands out the privilege of security in a piecemeal fashion, it creates conditions in which individuals will tend more and more to value increments in security over decrements in freedom.

> The reason for this is that with every grant of complete security to one group the insecurity of the rest necessarily increases. If you guarantee to some a fixed part of a variable cake, the share left to the rest is bound to fluctuate proportionately more than the size of the whole. And the essential element of security which the competitive system offers, the great variety of opportunities, is more and more reduced.
>
> (Hayek 1972: 128)

What is novel about both of Hayek's arguments, and sets them somewhat apart from Higgs's and Glazer's theses, is that they present the *logic* underlying the incentives that drive the processes he describes, which transform the love of freedom to a desire for security, and an effort to achieve social justice to the creation of a greater demand for it. Higgs and Glazer simply assert that the ideological transformations they describe somehow take place

27

under a certain set of conditions without providing the logical connection. This, at least from the political economist's perspective, lacks theoretical force.

Since what Hayek describes in the last passage quoted is the dynamic of the ideological tension between freedom and security, let us call it the *dynamic trade-off thesis.*

To make a point that will have greater relevance in the next chapter, both of Hayek's arguments seem to be aimed specifically at the welfare state because it is ultimately concerned with the provision of security or social justice even if it means the loss of a considerable degree of individual liberty. In Chapter 5 I take up and elaborate upon the manner in which Hayek applied this argument specifically to what in the next chapter I term the "regulatory state."

SUMMARY AND CONCLUDING REMARKS

The arguments presented in this book derive from an approach adapted primarily from Mises's critique of interventionism, updated and extended to include relevant insights from other scholars both within and outside the tradition of Austrian economics. This approach, properly formulated, will isolate and identify the common ground between the dynamics that underlie the two prevailing forms of mixed economy today – the welfare state and the regulatory state. Based on this approach, I will argue that the mixed economy represents a self-ordering and self-sustaining process embodying a powerful internal dynamic that tends to cycle the system between relatively free markets, on the one hand, and collectivist central planning and inevitable crisis, on the other. Furthermore, these crises can signal turning points at which the widespread realization of the inner contradictions of what Hayek has called "constructivism" generate pressure for dramatic and perhaps radical change.

In writing this book about the dynamics of the mixed economy from an Austrian market-process perspective, I am making no claims about the monocausality of the forces identified here. My goal is to use an important though relatively neglected aspect of mixed economies to better our understanding of their evolution, and not to diminish the importance of other forces that have been discussed elsewhere in the literature. In distinguishing in this chapter, for example, between what I have called Austrian political economy and public choice my intent has been only to isolate and develop what I believe are the unique contributions of the former to our understanding of political processes and institutions, and not to diminish in any way the importance of the contributions of the latter. If this has meant pointing out in the starkest terms what are, from the perspective of Austrian political economy, limitations of public choice, my sole aim has been to promote expositional clarity and to reduce misunderstanding, and certainly not to suggest the absence of significant limitations in the present study (some of those which I believe to be the most important are addressed in the final chapter).

Nevertheless, I believe this study represents a *step toward* the creation of a theoretical framework, a theory of interventionism, within which subsequent historical research can be analyzed. Indeed, throughout this book I will be drawing liberally from case studies by other scholars and historians that to some extent already reflect the considerations to be identified here, and can thus serve to illustrate and flesh out the patterns emerging from the framework of analysis that I will be outlining. Nevertheless, this study tends to be more abstract than applied – heavy on theory, and rather light on history – although I hope to make clear in which direction empirical work based on (or theoretical extensions of) this analysis might go.

The next four chapters present the essential elements of this framework. Chapter 2 defines the meaning of interventionism in relation to alternative politico-economic systems, then presents Mises's critique of interventionism and subjects it to close scrutiny. Chapter 3 compares and contrasts two spheres of human action, the market process and what I call the governmental process, in order to isolate important forces that determine the character of the interventionist process proper. This chapter also reviews the Austrian critique of collectivist central planning, which, because it contains insights that are relevant to the analysis of interventionism, are then employed in Chapter 4 to help explain the core ideas that comprise the logic of the interventionist process. Chapter 5 elaborates on these ideas to investigate the alternative paths that a mixed economy might take on its sojourn between laissez-faire capitalism and collectivism. In so doing, it compares and contrasts the dynamics that underlie the welfare state with those of the regulatory state.

In Chapter 2 we see how Mises presumed in his critique of

interventionism that the so-called minimal state is immune from the forces that act to destabilize mixed economies. Chapter 6 directly challenges this presumption by arguing not only that the minimal state is subject to the same destabilizing forces as the mixed economy, but that under certain plausible conditions these forces will cause it to expand beyond its minimalist bounds and drive it into the interventionist process. Having by this point reviewed the inherent weakness of collectivism in Chapter 3 and argued for the instability of both the mixed economy and the minimal state, we are left with a set of propositions on and insights into the political process that I hope to show in Chapter 7 we can use to derive several pattern predictions about the behavior of mixed economies. This chapter closes with examples at the micro and macro level of historical episodes consistent with these predictions, but they do not constitute a test of these implications, at least not in the standard sense of this term. Chapter 8 offers some final thoughts.

2

THE MEANING OF
INTERVENTIONISM

Interventionism, as a system, is more than a set of relations between the market and government, it is a social process.

There are at least two ways to approach the study of interventionism as a process. One is to investigate what happens "behind the scenes" of the political process – i.e., on the political incentives and actions that beget a particular outcome – at the level of a single program or of public policy in general. The subject-matter of such a theory would include the redistributive strategies that emerge from the incentive structure of political institutions and that are intended to favor or harm particular persons and groups. Clearly, this is the territory of public choice, into which for the moment we do not trespass. Another approach takes as its subject-matter the unintended consequences both of government intervention into a single market or set of markets[1] and of adopting and implementing the doctrine of interventionism for the market order as a whole. Interventionism in this view generates within the mixed economy a social process that is not entirely the result of deliberate human design, but rather one driven to a large extent by its own internal dynamic. This latter approach is the one adopted in the present study.

Understanding the nature of interventionism, however, does presuppose a knowledge of its relations to capitalism and collectivism in their various forms. This chapter begins, then, with definitions of these and related politico-economic systems. The goal here is merely to clarify the exposition of the ideas presented in this book, rather than to render definitive interpretations of these terms.

Following these preliminaries is a detailed examination of the nature of interventionism, both as a doctrine and as a politico-economic system. While the starting point of this study is Mises's critique of interventionism, in order to update and extend his analysis in the manner described in the previous chapter it will be necessary to indicate its limitations and inconsistencies, as well as to assess critically subsequent attempts to address them.[2] The final part[3] of the present chapter discusses possible ways in which to deal with what I believe is a serious theoretical gap concerning knowledge acquisition that remains in Mises's critique.

CAPITALISM, COLLECTIVISM, AND THE MIXED ECONOMY

To begin, let us define *government* as the administrative apparatus of the state having an effective monopoly over the legitimate use of violent aggression (i.e., *political means*).[4]

A *limited government* observes (written or unwritten) constitutional limits on the scope and magnitude of its activities in the sense that it strictly obeys the *rule of law*, under which "government in all its actions is bound by rules fixed and announced beforehand" (Hayek 1972: 72).[5] Although the presumption is usually that the domain of a limited government is small relative to the *market* or *catallaxy* – i.e., the realm or order of social cooperation based on voluntary exchange – it is quite possible to imagine a government that displaces voluntary activity in most areas of the market – and whose scope and magnitude are therefore quite large – but still strictly observes the rule of law. For this reason I will distinguish the general concept of limited government from one of its specific forms, the minimal state. In the *minimal state* the scope and magnitude of state activity are restricted to a relatively small but "essential" domain; typically, to the protection of citizens against unsanctioned aggression and fraud and, perhaps in addition, to coping with some externalities and the provision of some public goods.[6]

Collectivism

In contrast, under *unlimited government* the state recognizes no principled limits to its power to intervene into catallactic affairs. State authorities in an unlimited government could arbitrarily intrude into any area they wished, though they might just as arbitrarily refrain from doing so in a particular instance. According to Mises, however,

> If it is in the jurisdiction of the government to decide whether or not definite conditions of the economy justify its intervention, no sphere of operation is left to the market. . . . That means the market is free so long as it does precisely what the government wants it to do.
>
> (Mises 1966: 723)

This suggests the possibility that just as a limited government could in principle displace a considerable range of catallactic activity, an unlimited government's scope and magnitude of *actual* operations might be relatively modest – conceivably even less than that of a limited-government regime – owing to, say, high transactions costs of governance. Hence, as in the case of limited government, it is possible to distinguish between the general concept of unlimited government and one of its specific forms. One of the more familiar of these is the system known as *collectivism* based on the *maximal state*, in which the state concedes no "autonomous spheres in which the individuals are supreme" (Hayek 1972: 56), and in fact controls and directs all means of production toward ends over which effectively it alone has ultimate approval.

Moreover, according to Hayek a feature common to all varieties of collectivism is "the deliberate organization of the labors of society for a definite end" (1972: 56). In this sense, socialism and fascism are but two varieties of collectivism, which differ mainly in the character of the ends toward which each aims. The various ideals of *socialism*, for example, typically reflect an "internationalist" outlook[7] and embrace such values as greater economic equality, popular democracy, widespread political empowerment, and assorted versions of social justice. *Fascism*, on the contrary, tends in theory to appeal to more nationalistic sentiments and to exhibit a proclivity for military governance structures. Because of its nationalistic orientation, it is difficult to attribute specific values to fascism;[8] there are conceivably as many kinds of national socialisms as there are national interests.

Another form of collectivism is what Mises (1966: 717) referred to as socialism of the "German or Hindenburg pattern," and elsewhere (1981: 485) more succinctly though perhaps more forbiddingly as *Zwangswirtschaft*. It is an arrangement under which private citizens act as the nominal owners of the means of production, but where the real control of resources is vested in a government bureau of production management of some kind. This bureau fixes, for example, all wages, prices, and interest rates in the catallaxy, hence "they are wages, prices, and interest rates in appearance only." In practice the government "directs all production activities" (Mises 1966: 718). Because this form of collectivism is the result of regulatory-state capitalism having been taken to an extreme, it operates "under the outward guise of the terminology of capitalism" (ibid.). In the limit only the appearance of capitalism remains, the government having suppressed all essential elements of the market economy, especially the expression of consumer demand via the price system, and transferred *de facto* control over factors of production from the *de jure* private owners to itself.

Market socialism in theory is also a species of collectivism. In one of its original versions, the state controls the means of production in order to "assure to the citizen a given money income and . . . would authorize the citizen to spend that income as he chose in buying commodities produced by the state" (Lange and Taylor 1964: 42). In theory this is supposed effectively to "authorize the citizen to dictate just what commodities the economic authorities of the state should produce" (ibid.). Market socialism as actually practiced, however, as in perhaps such "communist" countries as the former Soviet Union, deviated considerably from any form of pure socialism. As Peter Boettke observes in the case of the Soviet experience under Lenin's "New Economic Policy" in 1921,

> The quest to abolish the anarchy of the market and substitute for it a settled plan was forgotten. Economic planning was transformed into interventionist fine tuning or steering the economic system in the desirable direction, leaving the market system as the major method of resource allocation.
>
> (Boettke 1990: 118)

Michael Polanyi has described the famed central plans of the former Soviet Union as nothing more than "a meaningless summary of an aggregate of plans, dressed up as a single plan" (1951: 134), in which the individual plans that comprise the aggregate are the result of planning that is more decentralized or "polycentric" (ibid.: 171) in nature than a centralized planning system.[9] Such economies usually practice a form of interventionism that includes elements of welfare statism, regulatory statism, and political capitalism (see below), although just where they lie on the politico-economic spectrum would, of course, depend on the particulars of the case.

Capitalism

Near the opposite pole from pure collectivism on the politico-economic spectrum, *laissez-faire capitalism*, known colloquially as "the free market," is the system based on the principles of strict private control over the means of production and minimal statism. In this form of capitalism, privileges granted to or penalties imposed upon particular groups or persons, i.e., exceptions made to the rule of law, are rare. For example, taxes and rules that arbitrarily discriminate, as well as subsidies and gifts to special interests of any kind, are inconsistent with laissez-faire capitalism as defined here. The basic feature of *capitalism per se*, however, is simply the "predominance" within the social order of private property ownership and voluntary exchange. Yet, apart from lais-sez-faire, the alternative forms of capitalism all depart from the principle of minimal statism to some degree. And because most of these forms tend in the direction of maximal statism,[10] they are better categorized as "mixed" economic systems, and will be treated as such, below.

The mixed economy

Interventionism is the doctrine or system based on the principle of the limited use of political means to address problems identified with laissez-faire capitalism. For the reasons given in Appendix B, I will follow Rothbard (1977: 10–11) rather than Mises in defining an *intervention* as violent interference with voluntary action, usually though not exclusively through the use of political means. Thus, criminals and gangsters may practice intervention in this sense when they aggress against the person or property of others and thereby intrude into otherwise voluntary actions and exchanges. Moreover, this concept of intervention is broad enough to encompass even the interference with voluntary actions and exchanges within the political sphere (e.g., a congressional rule that restricts log-rolling).

Proponents of interventionism, on the one hand, recognize in capitalism a dynamic system far more productive of material welfare than collectivism. On the other hand, they are sharply critical of certain outcomes and practices, such as for example a highly unequal distribution of income or racial discrimination, which they rightly or wrongly believe are the undesirable but inevitable side-effects of an otherwise appealing system of production. Thus, while unwilling to reject capitalism completely, they would favor a significant expansion of state activity beyond that of the minimal state in order to correct the alleged excesses of unhampered capitalist production.

Because interventionism assigns to government discretionary powers to intercede into the market process[11] that go beyond those of the minimal state, it is distinct from laissez-faire capitalism, in which the primary objective of government is to protect the integrity of the private-property, market order. And because under interventionism public choosers do recognize some limits (at least initially) on the use of political power, it is also distinct from collectivism. I argue in Chapter 4, however, that as the process of interventionism unfolds, public choosers will tend to observe these limits, if they do so at all, more for pragmatic than for principled reasons. Thus, the very nature of interventionism, in its expansionary phase, gradually releases the tension that exists in the mixed economy between the principles of limited and unlimited government. If it transpires that the state eventually acquires the power to determine, as Mises says, "whether or not definite conditions of the economy justify its intervention," unlimited government will then have completely displaced limited government in principle if not in deed. By the same token, in its contractionary phase, this tension is reintroduced as public choosers impose constraints on political power.

Interventionism begets the mixed economy.[12] Given the many and varied ends for the achievement of which actors, presented with the opportunity, would be willing to use political means, there are naturally many varieties of mixed economy. Here let us examine a few that will both reflect this diversity and at the same time be quite germane to the discussion in later chapters. These include political capitalism, regulatory-state capitalism, and welfare-state capitalism.

In *political capitalism*, public choosers use political means to attain the ends of particular public choosers or organized interest groups (e.g., corporate, community, ethnic, and class interests). By contrast, in *regulatory-state capitalism*, government uses its coercive powers to alter directly the course of competitive processes in order to promote economic efficiency, broadly construed. Some of the more common types of government intervention under the regulatory state are wage and price controls, monetary and fiscal policy, profit ceilings, tariffs and quotas, subsidies, entry restrictions, product-quality rules, hiring and safety regulations, environmental and health directives, and restrictions on certain business practices that are considered anti-competitive. The relation of the regulatory state to political capitalism depends on whether market participants use regulation to serve ends that are narrowly self-interested or more public-spirited (i.e., efficiency oriented in this context). If self-interest outweighs public-spiritedness, the regulatory state becomes transformed into political capitalism. Public choice, as I argued in the previous chapter, tends to assume that this is indeed the case.

Similarly, *welfare-state capitalism* differs from political capitalism primarily in the ends sought rather than in the means used or in the overall institutional context. The pure welfare state employs political means (such as confiscatory and discriminatory taxation of individuals to provide in-kind and cash payments to others) mainly to redistribute income or wealth directly in order, for example, to attain greater equality of outcomes among individuals and groups or a larger measure of security from the vicissitudes of capitalism. In contrast, as we have just seen, political capitalism would redistribute in order to achieve more narrowly self-interested ends. Clearly, however, actors may use the lofty rhetoric of welfare-state ideology as a ruse, while in reality pursuing and promoting more immediate and selfish ends. From the previous chapter we know that the divergence between announced and actual intentions is the chief proposition of public choice. Thus, public choice is generally concerned with the regulatory state and the welfare state to the degree that the public choosers in them adopt the motives that characterize political capitalism.[13]

The relation between the welfare state and the regulatory state is, of course, one of the main concerns of this book. For the purpose of distinguishing between them conceptually it is necessary only to say that, while either system may contain elements of the other (as well as, as we have just seen, political capitalism), the focus of the welfare state is primarily on explicit redistributions of income and wealth, and that of the regulatory state is primarily on redressing more traditional varieties of "market failure," typically by intervening into the operation of the competitive process, itself. (I explore this distinction further in the next part.)

THE ECONOMIC CASE FOR INTERVENTIONISM: REGULATION AND REDISTRIBUTION

To the supporters of the "middle way" of interventionism, it represents an alternative politico-economic system that lies optimally between the extremes of laissez-faire capitalism and pure collectivism – an ideal blend of both systems that manages to avoid the shortcomings of each. They view capitalism as an unparalleled engine of material wealth that unfortunately generates a number of problems that voluntary exchange in the market, alone, is incapable of solving. There is for them an unavoidable trade-off under capitalism between wealth production and occurrences of "market failure" and injustice, the so-called "efficiency versus equity" dilemma of traditional political economy.[14] They therefore advocate the judicious use of limited intervention to preserve capitalism's best features (e.g., wealth production and the effective adjustment in the use of resources to changing economic conditions), while at the same time realizing the ideals of collectivism (e.g., in the case of socialism, an emphasis on social justice and income equality).

In standard microeconomic theory, the case for government intervention is predicated on the presence in markets of substantial monopoly power, economies of scale, externality, and information asymmetry. In macroeconomic theory, business fluctuations, excessive labor unemployment, and price inflation, are all ills to which supporters of intervention believe capitalism is prone, and for which they urge extra-market correctives. Some also recommend adding extreme income inequality to this list of more traditional instances of market failure.

The normative economic basis for regarding the above microeconomic phenomena as market failures is the waste of valuable resources and loss of social surplus (i.e., deadweight loss) that accompany them. The existence of monopoly power, economies of scale, externalities, and information asymmetries can cause equilibrium rates of output, for example, to diverge from their Pareto optimal values.[15] These are then said to require microeconomic intervention – i.e., "regulation" in the narrow sense – to correct them and to eliminate the deadweight losses.[16] Moreover, for each kind of market failure there is said to be an appropriate public-policy response. Thus, antitrust laws are needed to discourage anti-competitive practices that establish monopoly power; natural monopoly owing to economies of scale requires regulatory ceilings on rates of return; government can address the problems of positive and negative externalities in the form of public goods and environmental pollution through granting subsidies, imposing taxation, or more clearly specifying property rights; and information asymmetry that manifests itself in principal–agent problems, signalling behavior, adverse selection, and moral hazard, might require government provision of certain services, such as health insurance for the very poor and the chronically ill.

Similarly, such macroeconomic market failures as the business cycle, unemployment, and inflation are said to call for the appropriate balance of monetary and fiscal policy, unemployment insurance, and wage and price controls. Finally, extreme disparities in income levels and widespread poverty that some believe inevitably attend capitalist production give rise to the redistributive income- and in-kind transfer programs characteristic of the modern welfare state.[17] The welfare standards for macroeconomic market failures are rather less well established than their microeconomic counterparts. One possibility for evaluating deviations from optimal unemployment, for example, is the so-called "non-accelerating inflation rate of unemployment," although there is no strong consensus on this as a benchmark. The other macroeconomic market failures seem to be even less grounded in normative economic theory *per se*, and perhaps rely more on community or political beliefs about what constitutes a stable economy, acceptable levels of inflation, and tolerable differences in living conditions, although philosophical constructs, such as John Rawls's "difference principle" (Rawls 1971: 75–83), are also possible normative bases for macroeconomic intervention.[18]

From this brief look at the standard market-failure case for government intervention it is possible to discern two rationales for interventionism, which can be used to distinguish between the regulatory and welfare states. Specifically, income inequality can serve to justify the transfer policies of the "pure" welfare state (i.e., untainted by either political capitalism or the regulatory state), while the more traditional macro- and microeconomic market failures can provide the intellectual support for the "pure" regulatory state. The present study will indeed define the *modus operandi* of each of these systems in just this manner.

In addition to representing different versions of the mixed economy, these systems have two other things in common. First, as I hope to show in Chapter 5, the interventionist dynamics that underlie these systems – which I will term *transfer dynamics* for the welfare state and *regulatory dynamics* for the regulatory state – are fundamentally the same, although subtle yet important differences between them exist. Second, all forms of intervention, including regulation, entail income transfers of some kind (Rothbard 1977; Posner 1971). These transfers may be either direct, as when one income group is explicitly taxed to pay for benefits going to other income groups, or indirect, as with the "forced savings" that accompany inflationary expansions of central-bank credit.

Some additional illustrations of indirect transfer may be helpful here. For example, a public policy that raises the quality standards of prescription drugs transfers income away from those pharmaceutical companies that have a comparative advantage in manufacturing drugs of less-than-average quality (which may still be quite high) in favor of those companies whose comparative advantage lies in producing drugs of better-than-average quality. Moreover, those who favor laws mandating that drugs be of a quality higher than what the unregulated market would have dictated are benefited at the expense of those who must now pay increased prices for prescription drugs owing to the higher costs of producing the higher-quality drugs. Decrees restricting the sale or development of certain areas the government deems environmentally sensitive favor those who prefer additional pristine wilderness at the expense of those who must now pay more for housing and office space built on real estate whose prices are now higher than they would have been owing to the decreased supply of developable real estate. Ordinances forcing cars to park on alternate sides of city streets on different days of the week to ease street cleaning favor those who prefer cleaner streets at the expense of those who prefer more convenient parking. In short, because every intervention represents an interference with voluntary action of one kind or another, the gain to some comes at the expense of lower incomes or smaller subjective benefits to others. In this sense, all interventions entail income transfers. (In Appendix C I discuss Rothbard's taxonomy of intervention, which makes even clearer the income-transfer nature of all government intervention.)

Transfers may also be either unintentional or intentional. This could relate to the difference between *ex ante* intentions and *ex post* outcomes owing to sheer ignorance,[19] on the one hand, and, somewhat more sinisterly, to the distinction between announced and actual intentions, on the other. Once again, however, whether intentional or not, income transfers and their associated dead-weight losses are not the main focus of the part of this study having to do with explaining the dynamics that drive the interventionist process. There the chief interest is in examining the unintended consequences of the public policies of both the regulatory and welfare states, in the hopes that doing so will shed new light on the process of state expansion and contraction. As we will see in Chapter 4, however, the income-transfer aspect of intervention plays a central role in explaining why mixed economies must inevitably confront system-wide crises.

THE CRITIQUE OF INTERVENTIONISM

Practitioners of the dismal science are seldom happier in their work than when pointing out the unexpected results of a public policy. Indeed, since the days of Adam Smith, the traditional preoccupation of the economist has been to reveal the unintended and frequently unwanted consequences of particular instances of government intervention. Thus, an important goal of economic analysis today remains to trace the often obscure effects of a given public policy on market behavior. The Austrian contribution to the analysis of the mixed economy, however, goes beyond the mere scrutiny of the effects of specific public policies to an overall critique of the doctrine and practice of interventionism, in general. The following passage from Mises conveys the gist of that critique:

> The middle system of property that is hampered, guided, and regulated by government is in itself contradictory and illogical. Any attempt to introduce it in earnest must lead to a crisis from which either socialism or capitalism alone can emerge.
>
> (Mises 1977: 37–8)

Upon reflection, the case for interventionism rests on four assumptions. The first is that interventionism is a logically consistent and intellectually defensible economic system. Second, the state is able to identify market failures when and where they occur, determine the relative importance of these failures, and construct a coherent program of limited intervention. Third, interventionism will achieve, from the point of view of its sponsors, an outcome more desirable than the failures it was meant to address. And fourth, the state is free from the influence of redistributive coalitions and the self-interested behavior of agents operating within the political process. Mises, by questioning the logical consistency of interventionism and pointing out the undesirability of its consequences in the above passage, attacked the first and third assumptions explicitly, although as I explain later in this chapter his assault on the second (perfect knowledge) assumption was mostly implicit. Mises also addressed the fourth (public interest) assumption, and was well aware that the actions of self-interested public and private agents could pervert public policy. He derided, for example, the position of the advocates of the public-interest viewpoint as "the welfare cliché that contrasts the selfish and narrow-minded individual ... and the far-sighted benevolent government, unflaggingly devoted to the promotion of the lasting welfare of the whole of society" (Mises 1966: 845). Nevertheless, the strength of the Austrian contribution lies in the way that it shows how the interventionist state will tend to expand (contract) in the direction of pure collectivism (laissez-faire capitalism) even when public choosers do not deliberately aim to do so, and are in addition intelligent, well intentioned, and act only in the interests of the whole of society.

Unlike either pure collectivism or laissez-faire capitalism, Mises argued that interventionism is untenable as a doctrine and inherently unstable as a system because it is at odds with fundamental market forces. In a classic example, Mises describes the nature of the interventionist dynamic that lies at the heart of the Austrian analysis of interventionism, and, for that reason, it will serve as a paradigm for the present study. In that example, Mises (1977) traces the ramifications of imposing a price ceiling on the suppliers of a commodity that the government wants to make more widely available at a lower price. The initial market response, which should be familiar to any first-year undergraduate in economics, is a shortage of the regulated product. To the extent that the government effectively enforces its ceiling, suppliers will have no incentive to respond to the shortage by increasing production, leaving some buyers disappointed. To avoid this consequence of its policy, the government will have either to abandon the price control or to supplement it with rationing.

If it chooses to do the latter, things become more complicated once buyers have consumed the current quantity supplied. Since marginal suppliers will no longer find it profitable to produce at the regulated price, the shortage will become even more chronic and long-term unless the government takes further action. It will have either to give up its price-control/rationing scheme, or to try somehow to induce suppliers to produce more. If it remains steadfast to its original aim, the government might threaten to coerce suppliers into producing more, but this would likely be seen (at least at this stage) as an overly harsh response, and would be in any case only a short-term "solution." Alternatively, it could subsidize suppliers, either with a direct transfer financed through taxation or by imposing controls on the prices of inputs. A tax-subsidy scheme (which Mises did not consider in this particular example) would only succeed in reducing the output of suppliers in those parts of the catallaxy subject to the tax and call forth further intervention there, as would extending price controls to the suppliers' input markets in order to lower their production costs, as we will see.

The basic policy choice confronting the government here is the same as before but starker – i.e., either completely dismantle the expanding structure of price regulation or press on with even more extensive regulation. If the government chooses to extend price controls, it would not be able to stop at the producers' own immediate suppliers, since shortages would soon develop at that stage of production. That is, controls would have to extend not only to the producers' suppliers, but also to the suppliers of their suppliers, to *their* suppliers, and so on. Eventually, unless the government completely abandons its attempt to manipulate prices and quantities, "The controls must encompass all branches of production, the prices of all goods and all wages, and the economic actions of all entrepreneurs, capitalists, landowners, and workers" (ibid.: 25). This must be so because "If any industry should remain free, capital and labor will move to it and thus frustrate the purpose of government's earlier intervention" (ibid.). Moreover, anything less than a complete abandonment of the policy would, to the degree that intervention remained beyond the level necessary to sustain the market in question, leave in place the fundamental tension between catallactic and political forces.

From the perspective of the government's original intent – i.e., to lower the price and increase the availability of the initial commodity – the policy of price regulation must be judged a failure. The government can only hope in vain to expand controls quickly enough to keep pace with the more nimble forces of the market as long as its agenda includes only *piecemeal* intervention. This is why Mises argues that "it may be said that limited intervention is illogical and unsuitable, that the economic system that works through such interventions is unworkable and unsuitable, and that it contradicts economic logic" (ibid.). Expanding government control crowds more and more private activity out of the catallaxy, political relations replace catallactic ones. There is once again fundamentally only one choice consistent with economic reality and reasoning: "government either abstains from limited interference with the market forces, or it assumes the total control over production and distribution. Either capitalism or socialism; there is no middle of the road" (ibid.: 26).

Robert Higgs's account of the American experience with price controls during World War II is a striking example of observation conforming to theory, even though Mises published his narrative over a dozen years earlier (Higgs 1987: 207–11). He recounts how the original "Emergency Price Control Act of 1942," which was intended to keep down the prices government had to pay for war-related resources, led after a short time – following a series of shortages, discriminatory rationing, and political conflicts – to the more comprehensive "Economic Stabilization Act of 1942." According to Higgs, "After April 8, 1943, when the President [brought] virtually all consumer goods within the reach of the price controls ... the market system remained for the duration of the war in suspended animation ... capitalism it definitely was not" (ibid.: 210–11).

Mises's story, although it deals with a particular kind of government intervention, wonderfully illustrates the general nature of the interventionist dynamic that plays a central role in his critique and serves as the foundation for the present study. At the most general level of analysis, profit-seeking actors in both the market and governmental processes tend to respond to an intervention in ways that frustrate or circumvent it and that the authorities fail to anticipate (for reasons Mises did not make clear but which are elaborated upon later in this chapter and in Chapter 4). Because of these unanticipated responses, there is a tendency for an intervention to bring about a condition worse than that which it was intended to improve.[20] (In Chapter 4 I attempt to explain why this is the case.) Moreover, the accumulated problems of piecemeal intervention, which may trigger a series of minor crises, inexorably reach a climax – a crisis of the mixed economy itself – that forces public choosers either to push toward more coherent, thorough-going government planning (collectivism) or to abandon inter-ventionism altogether in favor of less interference with the market process (laissez-faire capitalism). It is in this sense that Mises speaks of interventionism as "self-defeating."

Thus, Mises was able to conclude that interventionism is an "interlude" and must come to an end for three, apparently independent, reasons.

> First: Restrictive measures always restrict output and the amount of goods available for consumption... [and] can never constitute a system of production.... Second: All varieties of interference with the market phenomena not only fail to achieve the ends aimed at by their authors and sup-porters, but bring about a state of affairs which – from the point of view of their authors' and advocates' valuations – is less desirable than the previous state of affairs they were designed to alter .. Third: Interventionism aims at confiscat-ing the "surplus" of one part of the population and at giving it to the other part. Once this surplus is exhausted by total confiscation, a further continuation of this policy is impossible.
>
> (Mises 1966: 858)

The first and second[21] reasons given above ("output restriction" and "contrary outcomes," respectively) clearly pertain mainly to what I have termed pure regulatory statism. The third reason ("confiscated surplus") may also apply to regulatory statism in the sense that, in effect, all regulations transfer income. In this case, the policies that give rise to the first and second reasons may also be viewed as indirect methods of confiscation. As mentioned earlier the confiscatory or redistributive aspect of all government intervention will be important in the present study's explanation of how crises arise in mixed economies. But if Mises had intended these three reasons to be inter-related in this manner, i.e., as parts of an integrated framework, he does not appear to have explicitly linked them in his writings.[22] Therefore, I believe it is fair to say that, to the extent that Mises saw the deliberate aim of public policy as the transfer of income, he considered his third reason (confiscation of "surplus") as strictly a feature of the welfare state.

Thus, it appears that Mises maintained separate and distinct explanations for the failure of the regulatory state and the welfare state, although he plainly believed them to be part and parcel of a single concept of interventionism and that actual interventionist economies practice a combination of regulation and redistribution. We should not criticize Mises for declining to integrate more completely two of the driving forces of the mixed economy – transfer and regulatory dynamics – by introducing insights on the nature of knowledge-related problems that only more recent research has brought to light. It is, however, incumbent upon anyone today attempting to offer a theory of the mixed economy not to shy from this task. A challenge for modern Austrian political economy, therefore, is to explain more precisely the operation of the regulatory dynamics described in Mises's price-control example, and to integrate these dynamics with the transfer dynamics of the welfare state into a more general theory of interventionism.

LIMITATIONS OF MISES'S CRITIQUE

While Mises's critique represents the logical starting point for this general theory, it raises a number of questions in addition to the one just discussed.

The "paradox of interventionism"

The first of these pertains to what might be called the Misesian "paradox of interventionism." We have seen that Mises used words such as illogical, unworkable, unsuitable, self-defeating, and contradictory to describe interventionism. In addition, while he did not use the term, interventionism as a system was in Mises's estimation highly *unstable*, a mere "interlude." Among the alternative systems, therefore, one could easily come to imagine *a priori* that it would be the least enduring. Yet casual observation reveals that, among existing politico-economic systems, the interventionist mixed economy, all of its contradictions notwithstanding, is by far the most popular, widespread, and persistent of them all. I address this paradox in Chapter 7.

How stable the minimal state?

A second difficulty is a consequence of Mises's conception of interventionism in terms of state activity beyond the minimum necessary to promote social cooperation and the coordination of the market process – i.e., activity beyond that which is appropriate to the minimal state and laissez-faire capitalism. According to Mises (1977: 17), "Measures that are taken for the purpose of preserving and securing the private property order [i.e., laissez-faire capitalism] are not interventions."[23] Consequently, the minimal state's use of political means in the pursuit of its proper and strictly circumscribed functions is for Mises not interventionism. Yet, he seems not to have considered whether problems similar to those that plague intervention beyond the minimal state might for the same reasons also confront the minimal state itself. Mises apparently took it for granted that the minimal state is, in some sense, stable without explaining why this should be so. Chapter 6 investigates the stability of the minimal state at some length.

The exclusion of nationalization and price subsidies[24]

According to Mises,

> With regard to the same factors of production there can only exist private control or public control. If in the frame of a system of social cooperation only some means of production are subject to public ownership while the rest are controlled by private individuals, this does not make for a mixed system combining socialism and private ownership.
>
> (Mises 1966: 716)

Curiously, this implies that so long as *any* isolated pockets of private property remained in an economy, no matter how otherwise collectivist, it would still not constitute a "mixed system," i.e., interventionism. Thus, a third problem relates to Mises's explicit exclusion of partial socialization and nationalization from the concept of interventionism.

The failure to integrate fully the welfare state and the regulatory state within a unified theory of interventionism is also related to this problem. That is, Mises's omission of nationalization would not be surprising if it were a form of transfer, which I argue in Chapter 5 it is. (In Appendix B, I try to link this to his early denial (in 1927) that a price subsidy is a form of intervention.) Both of these problems of integration are addressed in Chapter 5.

Absence of perfect knowledge under interventionism implicitly assumed

The fourth lacuna in the Misesian framework is perhaps the most serious from the perspective of modern Austrian market-process economics. The latter places emphasis on understanding social order in terms of the consequences of human action that are unintended owing to the existence of radical ignorance and the opportunities this creates for actors in social processes.[25] Fortunately, for this very reason it is a problem that the more recent contributions of market-process theorists are ideally (though perhaps not uniquely)[26] suited to address. Specifically, a theory of interventionism should be able to explain why state authorities acting in the public interest would continue to embrace a policy of interventionism in the face of mounting problems emanating from that policy. If interventionism is in fact self-defeating, why do private and public agents, acting in the public interest, remain committed to it in the face of its accumulating negative effects? (An adequate response to these questions would partially resolve the Misesian paradox discussed earlier.)

With respect to regulatory dynamics, Mises was silent. He did not spell out the nature of the constraints that consistently hamper benevolent public authorities in mixed economies from becoming aware of the existence of intervention-related shortages and surpluses and correctly identifying their source before it is too late. Nevertheless, it is possible to use Mises's own contributions to the debate on the feasibility of economic calculation under collectivist economic planning, along with more recent research into the dynamics of learning, to fill in this gap in his critique of interventionism. Indeed, while not explicit in his critique, Mises may have simply taken for granted the problem of dispersed information and radical ignorance (to which, as we will see below, Hayek and Kirzner have done so much to draw our attention) in exposing the unstable and the self-defeating nature of interventionism.[27] In any case, explicitly integrating these insights into an Austrian critique of interventionism will, I maintain, illuminate the dynamics of the resulting process and indicate the direction that a more general theory of interventionism might take. Such an integration is attempted in Chapters 3 and, especially, 4.

In his discussion of the welfare state, on the contrary, Mises is quite explicit in underscoring the importance of *ideology* – in this case, a statist or anti-capitalist mentality.

> While vague in every other respect, it is very clear in its abomination of large fortunes. It objects to big business and great riches. It advocates various measures to stunt the growth of individual enterprises and to bring about more equality by confiscatory taxation of incomes and estates. And it appeals to the envy of the injudicious masses.
>
> (Mises 1966: 844)

For Mises, this mentality induces authorities to opt for more rather than less intervention at critical decision points in the dynamics of the welfare state and arouses the "injudicious masses" to call for even more intervention. It discourages capital accumulation and serves to "check the evolution of profit-seeking entrepreneurship" (ibid.: 836).[28]

IDEOLOGY, POLITICAL INCENTIVES, AND "THE KNOWLEDGE PROBLEM"

Thus, "ideological blindness" of some kind might explain the failure of public authorities to learn from their mistakes. Recall that, in addition to the exogenous role that Mises gave to ideology in the interventionist process, Chapter 1 examined in some detail the contributions of Higgs, Glazer, and Hayek, which were termed, respectively, the gradual-acceptance thesis, the self-fulfilling thesis, and the dynamic trade-off thesis. Any one or a combination of these exogenous and endogenous explanations might therefore account for government learning failure. In Chapter 4, however, I define a less independent, though no less critical, role for ideology in the interventionist process, while in Chapter 5 I elaborate on the dynamics of shifting ideological preferences.

A second possibility is to take the approach of public choice and focus on the problems connected with the (mainly political) incentives of agents and coalitions, whose actions produce negative unintended (but from their point of view irrelevant) consequences. Although public choice *in its present form* tends to downplay dynamic processes based on the unintended consequences of public

49

policy, its relevance to the problem of learning failure in government is somewhat greater. In particular, we have seen in Chapter 1 that certain scholars in the public-choice tradition, Niskanen and Olson in particular, have investigated questions relevant to the present study. To the extent that they have addressed the informational concerns that give rise to these questions their approach, and perhaps also their analysis, may be similar enough to the one undertaken in this book to be integrated into it, as later chapters will show.

The importance of the "knowledge problem" to a theory of interventionism

So far, ideology and perverse incentives have been considered as possible explanations of government learning failures, but there is also a third alternative. Throughout this chapter certain references have been made to informational problems and to the way in which relatively recent Austrian insights into them might serve to shed new light on Mises's critique of interventionism. Here I describe the nature of these problems and show how this helps to explain the incidence of learning failures in the interventionist process. (The next chapter deals at some length with the different forms this phenomenon takes in the private and the public sectors, and the manner in which each sector copes with it.)

What economists working today in the tradition of Austrian market-process theory refer to as "the knowledge problem," has its origins in the economic writings of Hayek in the 1930s and 1940s. While Hayek later refined his analysis of how social institutions serve to harness human knowledge and applied it more broadly to social and political philosophy, his earlier writings on economic policy issues contain perhaps the freshest statement of the problem, and so excerpts from some of these will serve as an introduction to this important area of study.

There are essentially two aspects to the knowledge problem: the first is the "setting" in which knowledge relevant to decision-making is at the same time resistant to quantification and dispersed among anonymous individuals; the second is the problem of getting this knowledge to the relevant actors. In Hayek's words,

The peculiar character of the problem of a rational economic order is determined precisely by the fact that the knowledge of the circumstances of which we must make use never exists in concentrated or integrated form but solely as the dispersed bits of incomplete and frequently contradictory knowledge which all the separate individuals possess ... it is a problem of the utilization of knowledge which is not given to anyone in its totality.

(Hayek 1948: 77–8)

The nature of this dispersed knowledge is of a rather mundane kind. Hayek describes it as "the knowledge of the particular circumstances of time and place" as, for example,

To know of and to put to use a machine not fully employed, or somebody's skill which could be better utilized, or to be aware of a surplus stock which can be drawn upon during an interruption of supplies, is socially quite as useful as the knowledge of better alternative techniques.

(ibid.: 80)

This kind of knowledge, precisely because it is *contextual*, is of a sort "which by its very nature cannot enter into statistics and therefore cannot be conveyed to any central authority in statistical form" (ibid.: 83).

Such is the setting of the knowledge problem. It becomes manifest once the need arises to harness scattered, contextual knowledge so as to promote social cooperation and the division of labor by coordinating the almost countless number of individual, and often mutually inconsistent, plans that are based on them. Thus,

the "man on the spot" cannot decide solely on the basis of his limited but intimate knowledge of the facts of his immediate surroundings. There still remains the problem of communicating to him such further information as he needs to fit his decisions into the whole pattern of changes of the larger economic system.

(ibid.: 84)

While the various solutions to the knowledge problem in the market and government are the topic of the next chapter, enough has been said to suggest that, given the complexity of the politico-economic order resulting from the regulations and transfers that characterize the mixed economy, it is reasonable to conceive of something like the knowledge problem operating in the process of interventionism. That is, it is fairly plain from Olson's (1982) and Wolf's (1990) analysis, for example, how the politico-economic order formed by the interventionist process would be a highly complex and continually changing thing. In such an environment it is not hard to imagine that a particular legislator or bureaucrat would be strained far beyond the powers of human cognition in the attempt to track the unintended (and perhaps even the intended) consequences of a particular program or command.[29] Moreover, other programs and commands would impinge on the observed success or failure of a given planner's intervention – indeed, the actions of other branches of government and the spontaneous responses of the market might even render clear observation increasingly problematic as the public sector grows in size and scope. Therefore, the delay in or absence of learning on the part of public authorities that is implicit in Mises's critique of interventionism may be the result of the existence of the knowledge problem. The problem remains, however, of determining under what circumstances public choosers are most likely to learn why interventionism chronically falls short of its goals and then reverse the process. The questions of learning failure and eventual discovery are addressed in Chapter 4.

Another aspect of the knowledge problem, one that emphasizes the yet-to-be-discovered nature of much relevant knowledge, derives from the more recent work of Israel Kirzner. Indeed, the way of viewing the interventionist process described in the previous paragraph rests crucially on Kirzner's (1985) insights into the impact of intervention, not on static markets, but on the process of finding previously unknown opportunities for entrepreneurial profit, as well as on his extensive investigations into the role of entrepreneurship in the market process, in general, and into the kinds of learning that take place within that process (1963, 1973, 1979, 1992). How they elucidate the *theory* of interventionism, however, will again have to wait until Chapter 4.

This study tends to focus on endogenous processes. For example, because ideological change plays a key role in the interventionist process, a theory of interventionism needs to explain as much of this change as possible. This concern with ideological change will therefore tend to center on its endogeneity, although, consistent with the subjectivism of Austrian economics, what decisions public choosers make when confronted with the consequences of their actions will not be viewed as completely deterministic. In addition, it will also focus on the consequences for the interventionist process of the knowledge problem, which are also largely endogenous.

As already noted, narrow political interests and exogenous ideological changes do not exhaust the range of possible explanations for government learning failure, an essential part of the interventionist process. It is possible initially to abstract to a large extent from political self-interest and exogenous ideological change in order to isolate analytically a unique Austrian method of political economy. Completely removing these two factors is, however, as we will see, neither possible nor desirable in a realistic theory of political economy. Yet, as we will also see, minimizing the influence of political interest does not preclude the possibility of a process of state expansion and contraction that will be useful for understanding really existing mixed economies. Removing ideology altogether from a theory of interventionism would be even more problematic, although any explanation of ideological change cannot perforce avoid stressing endogenous over exogenous forces of ideological change. As I argue in Chapter 5, ideology, or more precisely (endogenous and exogenous) change in ideological preferences, plays a more central role in the transfer dynamics of the welfare state than in the regulatory dynamics of the regulatory state.

CONCLUDING REMARKS

In summary, this chapter began by exploring the meaning of interventionism and its relation to other politico-economic systems. It presented and then scrutinized Mises's critique of interventionism as a basis for a more general theoretical treatment, in which the regulatory state and the welfare state can be combined into a unified framework. Four issues that emerged from this scrutiny call for further study: the paradox of interventionism; the stability (or lack thereof) of the minimal state; the integration of nationalization, the regulatory state, and the welfare state into a theory of interventionism; and the failure of public authorities to learn from their mistakes in time to avert a crisis of the mixed economy. With respect to the last issue, I reviewed the various ideological forces that might account for the lack of awareness of policy failures on the part of public authorities, and then recalled Olson's account of the power of perverse incentives to drive the system toward a possible crisis. I then introduced and briefly explained the knowledge problem, which at this stage of the analysis I could only suggest as an additional explanation for government learning failure. The chapter concluded with a restatement of the goal of producing an explanation of state expansion and contraction that is focused on the dynamics behind these phenomena, and does not depend on public-choice type assumptions about the motives of agents.

What remains to be done is to elaborate on each of the four issues that were identified as gaps in Misesian analysis – namely, the Misesian paradox (Chapter 7), the instability of the minimal state (Chapter 6), the integration of concepts (Chapter 5), and the roles of ideology and the knowledge problem (Chapters 3, 4, and 5). While the importance of ideology and the knowledge problem was addressed in this chapter, except for a few passing remarks I still have to show precisely in what way they are to be incorporated into a theory of the interventionist process. Indeed, I have not yet outlined in any detail how the interventionist process operates. That is the overall objective of the next three chapters. Chapter 3 isolates and examines the learning procedures of government and catallaxy in order to help clarify the distinct forces that then interact to generate the interventionist process. The general outline, along with some details of this process, in both its expansionary and contractionary phases, is the subject matter of Chapter 4. Chapter 5 then compares and contrasts the dynamics of the regulatory state with those of the welfare state.

3

THE USE OF KNOWLEDGE IN GOVERNMENT AND CATALLAXY

The argument of this chapter[1] proceeds from the premise that government and catallaxy alike must each cope with the problem of dispersed knowledge and radical ignorance. The dynamics of the mixed economy in fact emerge from the interaction of these two fundamentally different social institutions in the presence of the knowledge problem. Knowing the distinctive features of the learning procedures with which each institution confronts the knowledge problem should help to explain why that interaction engenders the interventionist process.

GOVERNMENT AND CATALLAXY: THEORY AND PRACTICE

The operations of government are, in principle, centered around a hierarchy of objectives, consciously chosen and rationally pursued. The catallaxy, on the contrary, is a "spontaneous order," in which social rules and the patterns of behavior based on them emerge, not from conscious design, but as the unintended though orderly consequences of an untold number of purposeful individual actions. Because governments are founded upon the principle of "organization," whereas the interactions among individual (though interdependent) actors in markets form a spontaneous order, the rules guiding action in government and market differ fundamentally.[2] That is, in principle, public authorities deliberately determine the goals and procedures of a perfectly functioning government much as a technician programs a computer to perform specific tasks. By contrast, one cannot even say that the catallaxy has a purpose. It is essentially an arena of voluntary exchange in which, through a spontaneously driven process, the private purposes of individual actors tend to be coordinated. Thus, it is sensible to speak of the teleology of government in a way that would be meaningless in reference to the catallaxy.[3]

Practical governmental organization, however, presupposes a state capable of centrally planning and coordinating the activities of public agents in conformity with its specified objectives. Whether it can actually do this depends on many factors, not the least of which is the degree to which it can overcome obstacles to the use of knowledge in government. That is, owing to the complexity of modern bureaucratic government, the state might easily pursue contradictory or incompatible policies, even with a strong executive with a clear plan or vision. For example, the intentions of bureaucrats in related agencies, facts that "frontline" agents in the field have collected, and other kinds of contextual "knowledge of time and place" within the sphere of governmental operations are typically dispersed among a myriad of anonymous public agents and are difficult or impossible to communicate to the central authority.[4] Under these circumstances, when a particular governmental agency acts, it may be impossible to tell for whom and toward what ultimate end it does so, not only for reasons relating to conflicting bureaucratic jurisdictions or the lack of strong executive leadership, but more fundamentally because the size and complexity of modern government frequently renders fanciful the very idea of a state that maintains complete control of all its parts. Unless some kind of self-correcting process or mechanism guides the plans of the many and varied public agents toward full coordination, the notion of a general blueprint or overall vision against which all governmental plans are consciously coordinated would be illusory.

It is perhaps then not too bold an assertion to claim that the existence of a "governmental knowledge problem" follows from the Austrian analysis of economic planning under collectivism.[5] Indeed, one could argue that this knowledge problem hinders the attempt to centrally plan and control complex organizations of all kinds, including very large corporations in the catallaxy. Yet it is arguably something to which government is especially prone. This is so both because governments tend to be larger, by nearly any measure, than market organizations, and because organizations in the public sector function under political constraints from which those in the private sector are largely spared. As with planning under less-than-pure collectivism, however, central planning within a less-than-maximal state might cope with the governmental knowledge problem to the extent that the market process still possesses a reasonably functioning price system. This is because public agents could still rely on the price system's signals to guide and inform many (though not all) of their governmental planning decisions. And insofar as this is possible, it might also be reasonable to describe any systematic adjustments that public agents make to unforeseen or novel circumstances within government when its activities are not yet fully coordinated as a "governmental process."

Although the systematic adjustments that take place within each sector could each be characterized as a "process" (i.e., ordered change), a basic difference between them remains in that the catallaxy functions, in a sense, because of, while government operates in spite of, the knowledge problem. That is, one can view the *raison d'être* of entrepreneurial management in the market process as precisely the existence of dispersed knowledge and radical ignorance, while governmental or bureaucratic management, much more than market entrepreneurs, must maintain a rigid rule orientation inherently hostile to the exceptions that unforeseen conditions or changes might occasion. Of course, these two spheres of action are not completely independent of each other. Indeed, the dynamics of the mixed economy arise out of the attempt of some part of the state apparatus (often without the knowledge or consent of other parts) deliberately to alter the course of the market process toward an outcome different from the one that would have otherwise emerged. Similarly, agents in the catallaxy also have an incentive (though one that I will minimize in this discussion) to manipulate some part of the governmental process in a manner that addresses their own interests. Unlike oil and water, market and governmental processes intermingle and influence each other in ways that can defy prediction, though not necessarily understanding. Before exploring the complex dynamics that emerge from this intermingling, however, we need first to isolate the unique properties of the dynamics of each process. That is the principal goal of the present chapter.

A note on method

In order to carry out even the positive analysis of public policy, however, political economists must first resolve for themselves the extent to which catallaxy and government are antagonistic or compatible. Assuming (as I do here) for the sake of argument that, at least up to a certain point, they are largely compatible, then the attempt to study the market process in isolation also typically assumes, perhaps tacitly, that government activities are fully coordinated (i.e., the governmental process has played itself out), or that any needed adjustments take place very rapidly. Otherwise, it would be necessary to account for every disturbance in government that might interfere with coordinating forces in the catallaxy. If, for example, laws regulating immigration change in response to unexpected policy shifts in social services provided to illegal aliens, private firms that hire both legal and illegal immigrants would also have to make unanticipated adjustments in their plans, which would then set into motion wider catallactic adjustments. For the same reason, studying the governmental process in isolation requires us to do so against the backdrop of a fully coordinated market, or one capable of very rapid adjustment.[6]

Kirzner (1973) has shown that the interpretation of market phenomena depends crucially on whether the approach one adopts is based on endstate equilibrium theorizing or on market processes that occur outside of equilibrium. In the same manner, as mentioned in Chapter 1, if political economy is the application of economic theory to political institutions and phenomena, then it is also crucial whether the economic theory one so applies has a neoclassical or an Austrian foundation. With this in mind, the following section first outlines the nature of the market process from the perspective of modern Austrian economics, in order to provide a frame of reference for the present discussion. Next, since the governmental process depends on the presence of a knowledge problem essentially identical to that confronting pure collectivism, those elements of the so-called socialist-calculation debate relevant to this issue are recounted. I then examine the governmental process and the manner in and degree to which it successfully copes with the knowledge problem through non-price coordination devices, including bureaucratic management. The final section offers some concluding remarks.

THE MARKET PROCESS[7]

Perhaps the greatest challenge for anyone trained in standard neoclassical economics who wants to learn the meaning of modern

Austrian market-process theory lies in acknowledging the existence of so-called *radical ignorance*. To be radically ignorant differs from being ignorant by choice, or *rationally ignorant*, because the former reflects the actor's utter unawareness of some aspect of the choice framework itself.

For instance, we can say that someone who has not read *The Wealth of Nations* is rationally ignorant of it if, given full knowledge of the value of this book to him as well as the time and effort needed to read it, he has concluded that the cost of reading it outweighs the benefit. Alternatively, he may, for example, be unaware of the book's very existence or of the benefit that would accrue to him from reading it. The latter case, in which he is not ignorant by choice, is an example of radical ignorance. Furthermore, to explain his eventual discovery of *The Wealth of Nations* as the result of a deliberate decision on his part to do so would be unsatisfactory, since this presupposes his prior awareness of the costs and benefits of making the discovery, which would raise the question of the source of this prior awareness, and so on. To avoid an infinite regress, it is necessary at some stage of the analysis to interpret the perception of costs and benefits as an act of *pure discovery* regarding information about which the actor has had no prior awareness.[8]

Similarly, market exchanges will not take place if information costs are too high relative to perceived benefits, or because actors are completely unaware of the existence of double coincidences of wants regardless of whether information costs are low or even non-existent. In the first case, leaving a trade unconsummated is consistent with *equilibrium*: Since actors are informed of all relevant constraints, alternatives, and values, they have no cause to regret their decision (for it is simply implicit in the structure of the problem) and therefore have no incentive to alter the *status quo*. In the second case, actors will have either simply overlooked or unwittingly passed over[9] a profitable exchange, and without prior knowledge of the error's existence their awareness of it will follow, if it does at all, not from a calculated choice but from an act of pure discovery. In light of their discovery, actors would then have an incentive to alter their plans to adjust to the newly perceived conditions.

Profit and loss are central to the market process. The profit-seeking of entrepreneurs is the *sine qua non* of competitive rivalry. Unexploited profit opportunities represent losses, while discovered error creates profit. Kirzner (1973) has used the term "entrepreneurship" to describe that aspect of human action that is alert to opportunities to make profit and avoid losses.[10] In the context of the market process, entrepreneurship essentially consists of alertness to instances in which, owing to the presence of radical ignorance, commodities and resources are under- or over-valued relative to their alternative uses. And in all but the most primitive market systems, market prices, emerging spontaneously from a chain of voluntary exchanges, are the media that tend to reflect these relative values, however imperfectly. Indeed, entrepreneurial discovery typically takes place with respect to market prices that are, strictly speaking, erroneous in the sense that they fail to communicate fully and accurately to the relevant actors market expectations regarding underlying preferences, resource availabilities, and technological alternatives. In the presence of radical ignorance such errors are likely to be widespread, leading to an array of non-equilibrium and Pareto suboptimal prices for any given commodity. But the resulting price differentials also serve as indicators of possible opportunities for profitable arbitrage. Hence, while in isolation non-equilibrium prices will likely mislead, the discovery of genuine price *differentials* signals to alert actors the presence of arbitrage profits owing to unrevealed error.[11]

The tendency to eliminate these arbitrage profits through entrepreneurial rivalry would lead to a more effective utilization of contextual knowledge. The initial entrepreneurial discovery of an arbitrage profit opportunity, so long as any pure profits remain in a given line of activity, does tend to increase the likelihood of further entrepreneurial discovery. Thus, a vital component of the market process is the tendency for the profit awareness of other actors to be sharpened, following an entrepreneurial discovery in a particular line of activity, which promotes the emergence of a spontaneous and competitive profit-seeking process. However, because this rivalry could take forms harmful to the general welfare, social institutions serve to define and encourage acceptable behavior (or discourage unacceptable behavior) within a market order. These institutions include laws governing property ownership, exchange, and the peaceful settlement of disputes, as well as the social rules and customs (e.g., the importance of honesty and reliability) that give context and meaning to these laws, direct their application, and foster their evolution. In addition, institutions such as money and credit, banks, insurance, the firm, and (especially as we have just seen) the price system may also have emerged, simplifying trade and advancing the coordination of plans. Indeed, these institutions, viewed collectively, are what we commonly think of as "the market."

In summary, the market process is a spontaneous order sustained by an institutional framework in which private property and voluntary exchange predominate. It emerges from the largely independent purposes of individual actors who plan, in the face of partial radical ignorance and unanticipated change, with the aid of freely adjusting relative prices.

Normative market-process theory

From the point of view of market-process theory, the usefulness of an equilibrium-based, normative construct such as Pareto optimality, long the centerpiece of neoclassical welfare economics, is severely limited as a normative benchmark for practical policy. Its chief weakness has little to do with the traditional criticisms that have been leveled against it, for example, by Kaldor, Hicks, Scitovsky, and Arrow. Indeed, most of its alternatives share the same limitation as the Pareto criterion, namely, an unhelpful focus on situations in which radical ignorance is absent and agents possess all relevant information. They fail to recognize the implications of the knowledge problem (or indeed to acknowledge that such a problem even exists), wherein decision-makers find themselves radically ignorant of relevant information dispersed among anonymous individuals across the market. The impossibility of an actor actually obtaining complete, relevant knowledge about the current and future states of the real world effectively renders irrelevant the central question of standard welfare economics of whether a change produces a Pareto improvement, at least for purposes of policy analysis.

Equilibrium-based criteria are necessarily concerned primarily with endstates in which all equilibrating adjustments have played themselves out and entrepreneurial activity has ceased. In contrast, a process-based normative criterion is concerned less with the degree to which actual conditions in the catallaxy deviate from an ideal endstate than with whether conditions exist – e.g., the market institutions previously mentioned – that facilitate the discovery of market-based errors. Such a criterion would ultimately refer to the underlying preferences of consumers, yet it would be largely indifferent to the efficiency of current resource allocation *per se*.[12]

While an individual's incentive to act entrepreneurially lies in his desire to better his perceived condition, the social function of entrepreneurship, its normative character, centers around the uncovering of plan inconsistencies and divergences between perceptions and objective facts,[13] generated by radical ignorance. In the positive theory of the market process we have seen that non-equilibrium price differentials, resulting from errors committed in the presence of radical ignorance, fuel the engine of entrepreneurial discovery. In normative market-process theory these non-equilibrium prices also play a central role, not surprisingly one quite different from that which equilibrium prices (typically, long-run perfectly competitive prices) play in standard neoclassical welfare economics. Equilibrium prices are said to reflect perfectly opportunity costs, optimally allocate factors of production and outputs among competing uses, and in some circumstances signal non-price characteristics of the commodity (often with somewhat less happy consequences). Clearly, non-equilibrium prices do none of these things very well. The normative role of non-equilibrium prices, or more precisely non-equilibrium price differentials, lies in their ability to signal to alert entrepreneurs the existence of profit opportunities that plan discoordination and error generate. To reiterate, the knowledge problem rules out the prospect that public authorities, armed with an endstate criterion such as Pareto optimality, can consistently identify, measure, and remove inefficiencies in an actual catallaxy. But to the extent that social institutions that promote entrepreneurial alertness are in place, actors within the market process who profit from discovering inefficiencies will tend to drive the system toward (though without ever actually reaching) full plan coordination and optimal resource allocation.

Finally, while the question has often arisen whether the market process is equilibrating in any meaningful sense, this is not the place to evaluate the concept of equilibrium as an appropriate tool for the social sciences. Yet, even if the competitive rivalry could be seen as equilibrating – since it tends systematically to reward the entrepreneurial perception of error – this is no assurance that the actual catallaxy or even a single market within that order will ever attain or even near an equilibrium in practice. Once again, the general normative implication of the criterion of plan coordination for policy is to promote those social institutions that facilitate the discovery of error (e.g., where plan discoordination is the result of uncertainty concerning resource ownership, legislative or judicial actions might more clearly specify meaningful private property rights).

Competition and monopoly in the market process

In market-process theory, the necessary and sufficient condition for competitive rivalry is free entry, the sole requirement of which is the absence of a monopoly over an input essential to a particular line of production.[14] Without an input monopoly, a seller remains vulnerable to competitive entry by others who will duplicate his production process as long as it is profitable to do so. This vulnerability exists because the exercise of pure entrepreneurship – i.e., alertness to profit opportunities – requires no resources (in contrast to a deliberate search for information) and is therefore costless and immune from the possibility of monopolization. Indeed, according to Kirzner, "*pure* entrepreneurship is exercised only in the *absence* of an initially owned asset" (1973: 16; emphasis original). It is this costlessness of entrepreneurial profit-seeking that renders the market process inherently rivalrous and competitive (ibid.: 17).

It follows that entry is discouraged (i.e., the opportunity for profitable entry is denied) where an entrepreneur-producer or the state monopolizes an essential input. In this case, even though the market process is on the whole a rivalrously competitive one,[15] it is possible for resources in particular lines of production to be under-utilized with respect to consumer preferences (in order to generate monopoly rents) compared to the level of use that would obtain were ownership divided among more than one independent resource owner. The absence of a profit incentive means entry that would tend to correct the under-utilization when ownership is more diffuse will not be forthcoming. Thus, in market-process theory, even though entrepreneurial discovery is costless, the possibility of monopoly and monopoly power remains.

In the market-process paradigm, however, competition and monopoly do not represent polar opposites as they do in neoclassical economics, but rather coexist in a manner quite unlike that described in standard market theory. That is, competition and monopoly in market-process theory are both creatures of forces that obtain only outside of equilibrium, and are therefore not suited to being synthesized into such hybrid equilibrium constructs as imperfect or monopolistic competition (Kirzner 1973: 112–19). One implication of their non-equilibrium nature is that practices that appear anti-competitive in a static context may actually be highly competitive when viewed from a non-equilibrium dynamic perspective. Hence, the monopoly and monopoly power that serve to reward innovation and protect it from rivalry are competitive in the context of a dynamic process.[16] In addition, so long as there is no monopoly over such inputs as creative genius, the very success of a monopolist earning monopoly rents will actually tend to alert rival innovators who will over time erode the monopolist's position. And because the entrepreneurship needed to discover the profitability of innovating around a monopoly is costless, and therefore impossible to monopolize, the long-term competitiveness of the market process appears assured even in the presence of substantial monopolistic entry barriers.[17]

Should a single owner or collective gain economic control over an ever greater share of market resources, however, what would be the effect on the competitiveness of the system as a whole? On the one hand, monopolization within a single line of activity can stimulate competitive innovation by protecting an entrepreneur against imitators who would lower the expected returns on his uncertain investment (even though *ex post* those returns might appear excessive[18]). Thus, limited monopolization can to some extent promote the market process. On the other hand, monopoly in a single line of activity slightly lessens competition in the entire system, by reducing the payoff to entrepreneurial discovery in that line. Here the monopolist not only has sole control over, say, a particular production process, he ultimately has the sole interest in any new knowledge that might be relevant to that production process. If the threat of competition in this and closely related lines of production is absent, the possibilities for creative discovery and the likelihood of avoiding error, depending as they are on a single mind, will be diminished. This suggests that as the proportion of social resources under the control of a single monopolist continues to expand, the discoordinating forces of monopolization[19] will begin to outweigh the coordinating ones. From the so-called socialist-calculation debate we have learned that under monopoly ownership of all resources in the system, i.e., collectivism, competitive rivalry in the market ceases altogether. Apart from the problems that would arise from the absence of a *bona fide* price system under collectivism (which this situation resembles and which I will discuss in a moment), the difficulties emphasized here center as before on the system-wide monopolist being the only actor with the entrepreneurial incentive to discover instances of plan discoordination. And while anyone may uncover an error and attempt to sell the information for profit, it is still the case that, unlike the market process wherein anyone is a potential client, under a system-wide monopoly ultimately only the monopolist himself has the incentive to buy the information.[20] This suggests not only that the market process and complete system-wide monopoly are incompatible, but that progressive monopolization of an economy's resources, *at some point prior to complete collectivism*, must begin to degrade the market process itself. Beyond that point further monopolization will inflict net harm on the market process, in part because its stifling of entrepreneurial discovery will then have completely offset its stimulative effect on discovery and innovation. The other harmful influence stems from the dwindling availability of reliable relative-price data from the catallaxy on which government depends to guide its decision-making.[21] These two sources of discoordination are important for the discussion of the details of the interventionist process in Chapters 4 and 5. In the next part, however, I will pursue the analysis of monopoly by examining the learning procedure with which a state that has monopolized all social resources attempts to cope with the knowledge problem.

COLLECTIVIST CENTRAL PLANNING

From what I have so far argued regarding how the catallaxy operates, it would seem to follow that the state's attempt to achieve social cooperation principally through the use of political means and collectivist planning conflicts directly with the spontaneous forces of the market process. A logical way to begin to support this claim would be to outline the current Austrian position in the so-called socialist-calculation debate, which Mises initiated in 1920[22] and which has been subsequently elaborated upon by Hayek (1948: 119–208) and more recently by Kirzner (1992: 100–18, 152–62), Lavoie (1985a), and Boettke (1990, 1993). The aim here, however, is not to trace the historical development of this position,[23] but to present its essential elements in order to clarify the nature of the coordination problems that confront all degrees and levels of government planning, and in particular to provide, for the purpose of understanding the governmental process, the necessary theoretical counterweight to the previous discussion of the market process. This will help to show later that many of the problems that beset actors in collectivist systems are also endemic to the governmental process within the mixed economy.

The failure of collectivist central planning

There have been several references to the fundamental importance for the market process of clearly defined ownership rights to private property. Let us now examine more closely the fundamental role of private property rights for the discovery of error and plan discoordination, and the reasons why, when these rights are absent, as they are under collectivism, such discovery becomes highly problematic.

We have seen that the price system operates to signal entrepreneurs of the existence of plan inconsistencies, the discovery and removal of which represent opportunities for them to gain. But for the price system to function, of course, potential traders need to be reasonably sure that the exclusive right to possess, use, and dispose of the commodities (Gifis 1984: 372) exchanged will be transferred along with the commodities themselves. To the degree that property rights are thus secure and clearly defined, actors are better able to evaluate the usefulness of their own property and those of potential trading partners, either to themselves or to others. They are then in a position rationally to assess the suitability of potential trades, which, whether they actually take place or not, impinge on the relative prices at which commodities exchange. Their genuine interest, stemming from their property ownership, in such exchanges and relative prices forms the basis of the entrepreneurial alertness that enables the market process to adjust to changing circumstances.

The absence of property rights in a given area of an economic system precludes the possibility there of market exchanges, as well as the formation of relative prices that would contribute to the discovery of plan inconsistencies. A policy of partial collectivism (or an incomplete private-property order), therefore, tends to degrade the effectiveness of the market process. The question of the precise pattern of partial collectivization (i.e., whether property rights are weakened through heavy regulation, nationalization and state-supported monopoly, or coercive income transfers) and whether it makes a difference to the manner in which the interventionist process unfolds, is the main topic of Chapter 5. What is relevant here is that a weakening of private ownership of the means of production, however it takes place, compromises the ability of the market process to coordinate independent actions because actors who are uncertain of their control over and claim to the returns from their holdings – or who are aware that their control and claims are weakening or vulnerable – are less likely to act entrepreneurially. At the extreme of complete collectivism, property rights in the sense outlined above disappear from the system, so the relative prices that are so crucial in coordinating the plans of independent actors throughout society never emerge out of the voluntary exchanges of property. A vital link in the social knowledge-creation and transmission process vanishes, and with it much[24] of the scope for entrepreneurship.

In short, the absence of private property rules out the prospect of voluntary exchange based on dispersed and local knowledge. Without such exchanges meaningful relative prices fail to emerge. The absence of relative prices greatly limits the effectiveness of entrepreneurship and competitive rivalry. Finally, the dramatic decline in the entrepreneurial-competitive process jeopardizes the successful coordination of social interactions on anything but the most rudimentary scale.

Some have proposed varieties of collectivism, such as so-called "market socialism," that try to have it both ways by attempting to retain the coordinative properties of prices within a system of collective ownership.[25] Should these prices fail to coordinate plans successfully, public authorities are supposed to continue to adjust them until they hit upon the equilibrium prices that achieve complete coordination. What such schemes fail to recognize is that in the real world the significance of the price system derives entirely from the existence of the knowledge problem. That is, according to market-process theory, the price system emerges spontaneously in *response* to the knowledge problem as partially ignorant actors set exchange ratios, but the price system also *assists* the entrepreneurial-competitive process to better coordinate the independently formed plans of these actors, whose plans are inconsistent in the first place precisely because knowledge is dispersed among anonymous actors. Were the authorities to possess perfect knowledge, or possess the knowledge of how to acquire it, as they must if administered-pricing schemes are to be successful, they would be able to set commodity prices at their equilibrium levels. In this case the *sine qua non* of the price system in the real world of imperfectly coordinated plans would cease to exist because non-equilibrium price differentials are what fuel the entrepreneurial-competitive process. If the authorities lack perfect knowledge, what they administer might have the appearance of market prices, but the structure of relative prices would not signal error and reward discovery as it does in the market process. It would on the contrary disrupt social cooperation and plan coordination. From the viewpoint of market-process theory, to attempt deliberately to administer the price system in the presence of the knowledge problem is contradictory – the system of genuine market prices, while the result of human action, cannot result from human design.

Property rights under collectivism

One of the most obvious features of collectivism as a politico-economic system is the absence of the right of private persons to hold property. Here, however, let us explore two ways in which private property might still have a role even under pure collectivism.

First, property rights of a sort might exist under an *absolute dictatorship* to the extent that the dictator personally controls all resources in the economy, which he would then regard as his personal property and run like the executive of a giant firm,[26] initiating or approving all plans from the "top down." Like any property owner, he prefers, other things being equal, to employ the resources at his command in such a way that it brings him the greatest benefit (broadly or narrowly construed). Thus, he will try to invest in the various lines of activity at his disposal until he perceives that their individual returns at the margin are equal.

Unlike an investor in the market process, however, in a collectivist society there are no market prices to help guide the dictator by serving as indicators of expected benefit and expected cost *ex ante*, and enabling him objectively and meaningfully to record the benefits and costs *ex post*, of each undertaking. While the absence of market prices in this instance would not prevent the dictator from making rational decisions (since it is ultimately his preferences that directly and indirectly determine the value of the economy's resources), it would most certainly compound the complexity surrounding the evaluation of the choices facing him.

An even more profound problem, however, is one that we have already encountered earlier in this chapter. It is that in a pure collectivist dictatorship ultimately only the dictator himself has the entrepreneurial incentive to acquire information about (non-pecuniary) profits that might exist owing to plan discoordination. That is, while it is true that other, perhaps many other, actors in a collectivist regime might appear to have an incentive to acquire information that they could then "sell" to the dictator in exchange for some reward, the mere possibility of such profitable exchanges is not convincing proof that some such arrangement could substitute for the entrepreneurial-competitive process of the market. This is so because ultimately only the dictator, the sole property holder in society, would be in a position to determine whether these exchanges should actually take place. That is, while there may exist, in a sense, the possibility of an unlimited number of sellers of information under collectivism, the other side of each of these potential exchanges would always be restricted to a single buyer.[27] Thus, should the dictator, as an information monopsonist, fail to perceive opportunities to remove plan inconsistencies, citizens would have only his alertness upon which to rely for the detection of these errors.

A second instance in which limited property rights exist under collectivism occurs when planning takes place from the "bottom up," as it does theoretically under a pure *collectivist democracy*. A public chooser may be able to "sell" his vote to another (in the case of direct collectivist democracy), the value of which derives from the partial claim over scarce resources it represents; or he may be able to trade his services (in the case of representative collectivist democracy) for wealth or other political services within the political process. But these amount to private property rights inferior to those under a dictatorship because the public choosers, whether in a direct or representative democracy, do not, like the dictator, have an exclusive right to possess, use, and dispose of social resources. Rather their claims are only partial and temporary. While, for example, a bureaucratic executive may have the ability to trade services for political favors, he is not entitled to sell his office for its discounted capitalized value (if this could even be calculated). Hence, his situation is really no different from that of a manager of a firm in the quasi-private sector of a collectivist system, who does not control the means of production, though he is free for the most part to buy and sell lower-order (i.e., mainly consumer) goods. This, however, does not constitute private property in the sense relevant to the solution to the knowledge problem.

Unlike an absolute dictatorship, under a collectivist democracy there are no permanent encompassing interests (the limitations of which have already been discussed) that might even partly offset the incentive problems (though not the knowledge problem) that accompany collectivism *per se*. This is because the locus of power under democratic systems is subject to unpredictable shifts. A democratic national government capable of maintaining the kind of coherence necessary to implement a central plan or to follow a common vision, requires an unchanging locus of power that issues the orders and directives consistent with that vision or plan. An observation drawn from a capitalist democracy, the United States, would seem to be relevant here. Hedrick Smith describes political power in Washington, for example, as "fluid."

> Quite literally, power floats. It does not reside in the White House, nor does it merely alternate from pole to pole, from president to opposition, from Republicans to Democrats. It floats. It shifts. It wriggles elusively, like mercury in the palm of one's hand, passing from one competing power center to another, with the driving leadership on major policies... gravitating to whoever is daring enough to grab it and smart enough to figure out the quickest way to make a political score.
>
> (Smith 1988: 14)

As a practical matter, then, a fixed central authority under a collectivist democracy may not even exist.

In addition to the problem of a shifting locus of power, the so-called "Arrow Impossibility Theorem" would seem to imply a serious problem for the formulation of a coherent overall socioeconomic plan under democratic or "bottom up" planning. Since this theorem states that, under a set of "ethically uninspiring axioms" (namely, unanimity, non-dictatorship, transitivity, and range),[28] no process exists that satisfies all of them at once. Thus, public choosers in a collectivist democracy voting to establish a set of social priorities, a simple public policy proposal or a comprehensive plan, would face the prospect of a non-determinate, cyclical outcome of the voting procedure in which no single dominant winner emerges, or, to be more precise, in which each alternative dominates and is in turn dominated by all the others.

Finally, Hayek argues that democratic collectivism is highly unstable in the sense that forces internal to the political order tend to drive it toward complete dictatorship.[29] First of all, because of the maximal nature of the state under a collectivist democracy, the government's legislative agenda encompasses incomparably more decisions than a typical non-collectivist legislature would have to weigh and debate. The more crowded and inclusive the agenda, the greater the likelihood of disputes between factions with conflicting interests. The avoidance of endless disputes, however, presupposes "the existence of a complete ethical code in which all the human values are allotted their due place" (Hayek 1972: 57). This is unlikely given the limits of an individual human mind, whether narrowly selfish or benevolent, to comprehend more than a tiny fraction of the interests of all public choosers. Although there are probably values about which all or a majority of public choosers might agree, disputes will arise with greater frequency as the expanding agenda of government impinges on ever more values outside of this relatively limited set (ibid.: 57). Hayek likens the situation in which there is a general popular agreement under a democratically collectivist regime about the desirability of central planning without at the same time an agreement on specific ends, to that of a group of people who "commit themselves to take a journey together without agreeing where they want to go; with the result that they may all have to make a journey which most of them do not want at all" (ibid.: 62). Thus,

> planning creates a situation in which it is necessary for us to agree on a much larger number of topics than we have been used to, and . . . in a planned system we cannot confine collective action to the tasks on which we can agree but are forced to produce agreement on everything in order that any action can be taken at all.
>
> (ibid.: 62)

To work as it is supposed to, a collectivist democracy has to decide from among a growing number of conflicting and competing ends. Those in the best position to view the alternatives, those with knowledge of (or who believe they know) all the relevant facts, will have a comparative advantage in political decision-making.

71

Hayek maintains that, for these "experts," the temptation to impose their own (putatively better informed) choices on the community will usually be too great to resist (ibid.: 65). Public choosers, under pressure of political indecision, begin to manifest an attitude of accommodation toward such experts. That is, because of the paralyzing effect these disagreements will have on government operations, public choosers both within and outside of government will tend to agree to, and even welcome, the delegation of their political authority to these experts in order to break the "logjam" (or "gridlock" to use a more contemporary term) in the democratic process. Indeed, given the crowded and disputatious nature of the agendas confronting a collectivist administration, democracy would seem the least efficient form of government and the rule of one mind, able rationally to order "social" priorities, the most effective at getting things done. Thus, the logic driving the instability of a collectivist democracy points inexorably toward collectivist dictatorship, the limited effectiveness of which we have already examined.

In summary, we might regard collectivist dictatorship as a highly abridged form of private-property ownership. Although the encompassing interests of the dictator might perhaps to some extent overcome the incentive problems associated with collectivist regimes (severely limited as he is by the lack of a price system and other methods of rational calculation), it does not overcome the limitations, in the face of the knowledge problem, of the monopsonistic nature of the market for exchangeable information. The possibility of a coordinative role for property rights is even more problematic under a collectivist democracy, which must cope with a shifting locus of control within the state apparatus. In addition, the voting mechanism under a collectivist democracy may be subject to cycling behavior, and there is a powerful tendency for a dictatorship to emerge owing to the likelihood of gridlock and widespread conflict of values under this regime.

THE GOVERNMENTAL PROCESS

Let us begin by defining the "governmental process" as the order that arises from the on-going adjustments by actors to perceived changes in conditions within the public sector alone. This definition is, on the one hand, somewhat narrow in scope because how government copes with coordination problems that emerge exclusively within the public sector is the focus here. (While problems resulting from the interaction between the public and private sectors, i.e., the interventionist process, are not.) The admittedly unrealistic separation of government from catallaxy serves to isolate some important aspects of the former that lend clarity and richness to the examination of the interventionist process in the next chapter.

On the other hand, this definition might appear to be overly broad since it encompasses some behaviors that are not strictly "governmental," narrowly defined. If in practice the state rather than the market determines what the goals of a private organization should be, or if it imposes political or other non-market constraints on a private organization to such an extent that profit-seeking is no longer its principal objective, the organization would in a meaningful sense be a part of the public sector. Such quasi-private organizations would include the United States Postal Service, regulated regional telephone monopolies, and publicly supported television and radio broadcasting. Since finding a clear-cut boundary in reality between the public and private sectors is usually problematic, one way to apply this definition might be to determine the degree to which the success of an organization or activity nominally in the private sector depends on the effective transmission of information between it and the government, covering essential aspects of its decision-making, and to that degree consider the organization a part of the governmental process. Thus, for example, a publicly supported television station may be owned privately, but its actual operations, because of either a desire to keep its tax-exempt status or because of specifications in its charter, is largely dictated by what regulating authorities consider to be in the public interest. Even a business concern that is not considered by law to be a public utility (i.e., imbued with a public interest), can become absorbed into the governmental process if it exclusively serves government or is heavily regulated, as has happened, for example, to commuter railroads.[30]

Before discussing the characteristics of the governmental process and its commonalities with the market process, let us first note two obvious and important differences between them, which I have already mentioned.

First, although several conditions are necessary to maintain the market process, the one most critical for order and coherence to emerge amid flux – the center of gravity of the market process if you will – is the price system, which enables agents to utilize their entrepreneurial talents to discover profitable instances of inefficiency and error owing to the dispersed and incomplete nature of relevant information. This observation is not meant to diminish the indispensable roles that private property, contract, rules of conduct, etc. play in the market process, but to emphasize that the signals generated within a well-functioning price system (in the context of non-equilibrium prices) are what enable entrepreneurial discovery to achieve a level of plan coordination among individual actors which, though likely to fall short of perfect dovetailing, has been described quite appropriately as a "marvel" (Hayek 1948: 87). Some political institutions play somewhat analogous coordinative roles in the governmental process, such as voting rules and vote-seeking behavior.

A second important difference between markets and politics is that the governmental process takes place within an organizational framework that can be guided, at least in principle, by articulable and consciously chosen objectives, giving the process as a whole a dimension of purposiveness utterly alien and, beyond a certain point, inimical to the market process. Although the defining feature of government organization[31] is the principle of conscious central direction, it would be wrong to conclude from this that government has no need for some device, analogous to the price system, that would facilitate spontaneous adjustments to changing conditions by public agents, who are at least partially ignorant of facts relevant to their decision-making. While the original structure of a given government organization may have been largely the result of deliberate constitutional design, the eventual need for public agents to respond to novel and unforeseen circumstances, which tends to conflict with that design, parallels how individuals adjust to unanticipated change and error in the market process. A changing social and economic environment can pressure the structure of government organization, as specified in its constitutional framework, to adjust. The main difference in the significance given to error and unanticipated change in the market compared to government, however, is that these are the *sine qua non* of the former, while the latter must attempt to operate *in spite of* them.[32] Nevertheless, given the nature of the informational environment within which public agents work, the governmental process will take on some of the characteristics of a Hayekian "order"[33] (though one guided largely by non-price forces), rather than a consciously directed "organization" in the Hayekian sense. Our concern is with the nature of these responses that, taken as a whole, form the governmental process, the conditions under which they take place, and their consequences.

The problem of coordination in government

Despite the need for the state apparatus to adjust to novel circumstances, government organization is still based on the model of deliberate central planning. Indeed, the problem of coordinating the plans of public agents is in principle the same one that afflicts collectivist central planning, but to a lesser degree. It is the problem of how to cope with dispersed information and radical ignorance in the absence of private-property rights and objective indicators of relative values. How, then, does the "governmental knowledge problem" manifest itself?

The knowledge problem in government

While it is conceivable in theory that government might be capable of speaking with one voice, government in practice speaks with many voices at the same time. Indeed, one might ask who or what is "the government"? The difficulty here is different from the one addressed in the previous part regarding the fluidity of the locus of power in a collectivist democracy (although clearly that is a problem that would also confront a democratic mixed economy). In this case, the problem emanates from the sheer scope and magnitude of government organization.

For example, currently, under the jurisdiction of the executive branch of the United States government, besides the councils, special committees, and commissions within the office of the executive itself, reside the myriad of agencies and programs that constitute the federal bureaucracy. There is a bureau or agency to cover virtually every aspect of social and economic life in the United States, from the Administration for Children, Youth, and Families to the Bureau of the Public Debt, as well as agencies such as the EPA, OSHA, IRS, SSA, FDA, AFDC, BLS, DEA, FCC, NASA, BATF, PBS, TVA, USDA, and VISTA to name some of those whose acronyms may be more familiar. In all, there are over three hundred.[34] Under current legislation, most are answerable to at least one of the dozens of congressional committees and subcommittees in the legislative branch of government that oversee the activities of the executive branch. Any regulation or order that one of these agencies issues can be and frequently is challenged in either a federal district court or one of the federal government's many administrative-law courts, while the resolution of a dispute concerning a particular congressional legislative act usually takes place in federal district and appellate courts. This, of course, is in addition to the fifty separate state systems, each with its own hierarchy of courts, and federal courts with special jurisdictions, such as the National Labor Relations Board, that regularly address issues similar to those argued at the federal level. Moreover, individual states have legislatures, executive agencies, and departments that issue their own statutes, orders, and regulations, which interact in complex ways with their national counterparts (Wagman 1991).

This glance at the components of American government should lend plausibility to the proposition that knowledge relevant in one part of the government is likely to be dispersed among anonymous public agents in its other branches, departments, agencies, committees, courts, etc. This governmental knowledge problem then hampers the coordination of diverse and often contradictory plans within government.[35] Thus, Mises observed that

> under government interference with business the unity of government policies has long since disintegrated into badly coordinated parts. Gone are the days when it was still possible to speak of a government's policy. Today in most countries each department follows its own course, working against the endeavors of the other departments.
>
> (Mises 1969: 85)

Several factors, of course, may each be partly responsible for the increasing complexity and progressive difficulty of central planning in the governmental process as the scope of government grows (including those to which "public choice" draws our attention). In keeping with the aim of developing an Austrian political economy, in this book I emphasize those that relate to the governmental knowledge problem. Again, the main test facing the governmental process from this viewpoint is to coordinate the various parts of the state control apparatus without the benefit of endogenously and spontaneously established relative prices.[36]

Given the collectivist nature of government organization, however, in what sense is it meaningful even to speak of a governmental process in which public agents spontaneously adjust to changing circumstances? That is, if in a maximal collectivist state, the scope for entrepreneurial discovery is too limited even to begin to harmonize effectively the independent plans of every actor, and thus too limited to generate a spontaneous coordinating process, what is the basis for expecting to see such a process in a less-than-maximal state? While the next chapter addresses this question more completely, it will suffice to say here that the answer lies, I believe, in the relation between the relative sizes of the state and the catallaxy, because the success of government or bureaucratic organization depends to a high degree on the information-generating capacity of the remaining market process. That is, the public sector is like a small collectivist state that exists within a larger international catallaxy, which is able to allocate scarce resources based on the relative prices of goods exchanged in foreign markets. While government institutions by themselves are highly imperfect mechanisms (as we will see later in this chapter) for removing plan inconsistencies and achieving successful coordination, nevertheless, in conjunction with the relative prices of commodities in the private sector that government authorities can use as referents and guides in their own planning, they may fulfill their objectives satisfactorily enough from the perspective of public choosers to avoid for a time what Claus Offe has termed a "legitimation crisis" (Offe 1984: 35–64). This suggests that as the market process's effectiveness in creating knowledge becomes compromised, the governmental knowledge problem grows correspondingly less tractable, and the prospect for crisis grows more likely.

The more immediate goal, however, is to scrutinize the actual coordinating forces and mechanisms of the governmental process. But not before first examining one of the most important institutions in modern mixed economies; one that is both an organizational tool for achieving governmental coordination and is itself a source of coordination problems.

The nature of bureaucratic management

Bureaucracy is the institutional form of the modern interventionist state.[37] Whether democratic or authoritarian, a modern state typically governs through a hierarchical network of offices in which the primary activity is rule-following, rather than profit-seeking behavior. Yet these offices are subject to forces and conditions that shape their tasks and objectives into something different from, or even inconsistent with, those with which they were originally charged.[38] Thus, the knowledge-type problems of a state-run entity are also those that confront a bureaucracy.[39] Administering a nationalized concern, for example, entails bureaucratic management, either because the state runs it directly or because the regulations imposed on it are extensive enough to make it bureaucratic in the present sense.

Specifically, "bureaucratic management" is "the method applied in the conduct of administrative affairs the result of which has no cash value on the market" (Mises 1969: 47), and that therefore "cannot be checked by economic calculation" (ibid.: 48). One is a "bureaucrat" when rule-following is the principal guide in one's job. That is, "The first virtue of an administrator is to abide by the codes and decrees," and when he does so, "He becomes a bureaucrat" (ibid.: 41). This is in stark contrast to "profit management," under which a manager's ultimate objective is to seek to make profits by serving the interests of consumers, bound by no official codes or decrees in their conduct, save that of respecting property rights and abstaining from fraud. Thus,

> The only directive that the general management of the various sections, departments, and branches is: Make as much profit as possible. And an examination of the accounts shows him how successful or unsuccessful they were in executing the directive.
>
> (ibid.: 33)

To the extent that a firm competes purely within the catallaxy, the goal of profit-making permeates the entire enterprise, whether it's a small company or a giant corporation, from the chief executive officer to the "frontline operators" in direct contact with consumers.

According to Mises, the price system, along with double-entry bookkeeping, enables managers to record the cash value of all costs and revenues connected with every transaction between production and final sale, which greatly simplifies the task of avoiding losses and pursuing profits (ibid.: 32). Because bureaucratic management must operate, in effect, without either of these aids, it suffers from a severe, yet unavoidable, disadvantage when compared with profit management in the private sector.

Unavoidable, that is, assuming that the state must substitute for the private sector in the production of certain goods and services for reasons of political or especially economic necessity (as is said to be the case with pure public goods). If this necessity extends to all or nearly all important spheres of social cooperation, as the proponents of various forms of collectivism would argue, then the indispensable assistance that the price system and double-entry bookkeeping lend to economic calculation would be entirely absent. This would, of course, make it practically impossible for the private firm to coordinate its plans with those of its current suppliers and customers. But it would also greatly hinder bureaucratic managers in their efforts to discover instances of plan discoordination in government, since they could no longer rely on market prices that reflect the expected value of resources employed within the bureaucracy and of closely related outputs as an indirect way of determining, in a non-arbitrary fashion, whether or not bureaucratic undertakings were value-enhancing. If, on the other hand, the level of substitution of public for private provision of services in the mixed economy is fairly low, this problem would occur at a much more modest and perhaps manageable scale.

Additional factors handicap the performance of bureaucratic management. According to some students of bureaucracy, bureaucratic agencies work under political constraints and pursue objectives that are largely alien to profit-driven organizations. One authority on bureaucracy, James Q. Wilson, observes that bureaucratic organization determines not only whether a government agency performs according to expectations, but also – if its original goals are ill-defined or its stated objectives vague – largely what those expectations will be. Moreover, bureaucratic organization and performance are highly sensitive to the internal culture of an agency, the type and intensity of external interest-group pressures, the observability of day-to-day procedures and final outcomes, and the vagaries of the political environment. And public administration faces a greater diversity of constraints or "red tape" than does private administration (Wilson 1989: 35, 120–2, 315–20). These consist of considerations far removed from profit-seeking, but relate more to, for example, "political accountability," "equity" of hiring and firing practices based on political rather than economic concerns, and "fiscal integrity" to avoid the appearance of graft and political corruption (ibid.: 316, 323–5, 362–3). These considerations of internal political culture and constraints have led many to conclude that bureaucratic management is inherently inefficient.

This suggests that the usual standards by which economists gauge the economic efficiency of production and organization are irrelevant when it comes to bureaucratic management. If bureaucratic management is limited to a few areas of social activity, the impact on the market process will be relatively minor. As its importance in the mixed economy grows, however, the irrelevance of the efficiency concept and the other information-related difficulties already mentioned can generate enormous coordination problems for the politico-economic system as a whole. (This aspect of bureaucracy is taken up again in Chapter 6.)

Finally, Mises and Wilson have both observed that when citizens complain about bureaucracy, because there may be no workable alternatives to public administration in many cases, their criticisms are often misplaced. Yet they also argue that these complaints could reflect a more reasonable apprehension about the pervasiveness of bureaucracy rather than with its performance, so that the problems of which they complain concern not bureaucracy itself, but the size of government. Wilson, for instance, cautions that "the greatest mistake citizens can make when they complain of 'the bureaucracy' is to suppose that their frustrations arise simply out of management problems; they do not – they arise out of governance problems" (Wilson 1989: 376). The governance problems relate to the size of the state in the sense that "you can have less bureaucracy only if you have less government" (ibid.). This echoes Mises's caution of over forty years earlier that "those who criticize bureaucracy make the mistake of directing their attacks against a symptom only. . . . What people resent is not bureaucratism as such, but the intrusion of bureaucracy into all spheres of human life and activity" (Mises 1969: 7, 18).

Even if Mises and Wilson are right that the problem is ultimately not bureaucracy but "big government," understanding and appreciating the connection between the size of the state and the relative performance of bureaucratic organization is still of great importance. So long as interventionism is, as it appears to be, the guiding doctrine of all really existing mixed economies today, bureaucracy will remain an abiding and pertinent scientific and practical problem.

Coordinating mechanisms in government

In the following, I have grouped the various forces and mechanisms within government that assist political plan coordination under three broad categories. The first is "political entrepreneurship," which concerns the applicability of the concept of entrepreneurship, developed as part of the Austrian theory of the market process, to the governmental process. The next category pertains to the effectiveness of public-interest behavior alone, in coping with the governmental knowledge problem. Finally, there are the various institutional devices that to one degree or another lend cohesion to the plans of public agents (including vote-seeking, log-rolling, and budget maximization), although one can only do this, for reasons given below, by assuming narrowly self-interested motives.

Political entrepreneurship

The earlier discussion of collectivist planning argued that the absence of explicit relative prices in the governmental process would not by itself preclude the possibility that alert actors could to a limited extent discover instances of plan discoordination. It does, however, raise the dual questions of whether these instances could be *systematically* discovered and what *incentives* exist for political agents to do so. There are two possibilities with respect to the question of incentives. The first is that most public agents act in the public interest most of the time (i.e., that they are public-spirited), where the rewards of such public-spiritedness may be intangible. The second possibility is that agents are motivated by narrowly self-interested concerns such as (re)appointment to political office, increasing prestige or political power, pure monetary bribery,[40] or (re)election. Whatever the motives of public agents, however, the presence of dispersed knowledge and radical ignorance in government is the fundamental obstacle of achieving plan coordination therein. Moreover, in the absence of an effective self-correcting mechanism, governmental responses to changes in political preferences, expectations, and external conditions would be slow and cumbersome. While the price system of the catallaxy helps to guide decision-making in the public sector, unless government contracts out or privatizes the lion's share its functions (which is likely to be at odds with the standard reasons for state provision in the first place), its usefulness will be limited when government is large relative to the catallaxy. Therefore, the absence of a price mechanism relevant to the entire governmental process necessitates other methods of information conveyance.

Before going further, let us pause for a moment to reflect on what it means for the governmental process to be coordinated. This is important because the normative evaluation of "slow and cumbersome" governmental adjustment depends on the nature of the plans public choosers, or groups of public choosers working together, seek to fulfill. For instance, if an absolute majority of voters strongly and persistently prefered a chief executive whose agenda was weighted more heavily toward domestic issues and away from foreign policy, an informational conveyance mechanism that failed to respond to this preference would be considered flawed. On the other hand, if a majority of public choosers in the heat of passion voted to execute the remaining minority, we would in a more thoughtful moment probably applaud the constitutional restraints that would hinder this effort. An informational mechanism that reacted swiftly to the slightest change in the political climate could very well make planning more difficult by destabilizing governmental institutions and creating unnecessary uncertainty.[41]

Although the smooth functioning of the market process depends on a well-coordinated public sector, the desirability of complete dovetailing of governmental plans can still be highly problematic. For example, in the context of democratic government, consider log-rolling (i.e., vote-trading) and vote-seeking among elected officials. Not surprisingly, in some cases these behaviors are a net benefit to the particular constituency represented and sometimes not; or they provide a net benefit to that constituency at the expense of citizens elsewhere. Thus, Senator A votes for a bill of which her constituents disapprove in order to gain the crucial vote of Senator B for a bill that she favors. Or Senator C runs on the promise to bring new jobs to his district and to acquire the funds through a general tax on all citizens, indirectly harming the constituents of Senator D.

One solution to this analytical problem might be to extend the assumption of benevolence or public-spiritedness beyond public agents to the citizenry itself. This means that citizens would cast their vote only for those representatives who propose measures that would benefit everyone (or harm no one), rather than their own narrowly selfish interests. There would be neither rent-seeking nor involuntary redistribution in any aspect of the political process, and all plans of public agents, to the degree that they are consistent with the public interest, would either directly or indirectly benefit the entire citizenry, or at least not harm anyone. Under this assumption, governmental plan coordination, and the political entrepreneurship[42] that brings it about, would be favorable or neutral toward voluntary social cooperation.

Public-spirited behavior

Whether a well-functioning democracy or dictatorship, the assumption of benevolence or public-spirited behavior on the part of citizens and public authorities means that the state uses political power only to pursue ends that tend to promote the general welfare.[43] The state might be, to use Olson's (1982) term once again, a benevolent "encompassing organization."[44] What, if any, are the limits of benevolence insofar as public policy is concerned?

There is an adage in economics that says that the market economy is the most effective system for economizing on all scarce resources, including virtues such as benevolence. In the context of market-process theory, however, the limits of benevolence extend beyond the obvious fact of its relative scarcity, for there are things that benevolence alone cannot do. Even a benevolent public agent (i.e., dictator, bureaucrat, politician) is typically radically ignorant of plan discoordination in distant parts of the public sector. Unless the local knowledge of the inconsistency in plans is effectively communicated, public agents will be unable even to begin to formulate effective solutions. One might argue that a truly benevolent public agent would "put himself in the shoes" of the public, so that their problems and disappointments would also be his. Besides the high transactions costs of attempting to monitor closely the activities of a great number of citizens (not to mention the intrusion into privacy), the more significant fact remains that compared with the individual private agents affected, with their strong self-interest and unique contextual knowledge, the ability of even benevolent public agents to discover plan inconsistencies is weak indeed. Unless we are willing to assume that public choosers are also omniscient, it is hard to see how benevolence by itself could be as effective in solving the governmental knowledge problem as the price system is in solving the knowledge problem in the market.

The most obvious analog to the price system of the market process is the voting mechanism of the governmental process. This mechanism, in conjunction with the desire of public agents to get (re)elected to political office,[45] provides both a means of transmitting information about political preferences and an incentive for public choosers to discover this information. Thus, some form of voting could in principle bring the preferences of citizens (private agents) to the attention of benevolent public agents, who could perhaps then act on those instances of plan inconsistency that they discover. If, for example, different departments of government pursue policies at odds with one another (e.g., the Department of Health and Human Services mounts a campaign to reduce the demand for cigarettes while the Department of Agriculture subsidizes the supply of tobacco), the election of an executive with strong and well-known views on the subject in question might be able (through pressure and judicious appointment of department heads) to remove these discrepancies. Or if a majority of voters favor cigarette-smoke-free public spaces, they might be successful in passing a referendum to that effect.[46]

Of course, even if the voting mechanism functioned perfectly in reflecting the actual preferences of voters, not all branches of government are directly linked to the voting mechanism. In the United States, for example, the president appoints the chairman of the Federal Reserve Board, judges in the federal judicial system including the Supreme Court, and the heads of the bureaucracy under executive jurisdiction. Civil servants who are not political appointees are hired and promoted by the bureaucracy itself. Congress appoints members of its own staffs and offices. Here, the efficacy of formal mechanisms that enable or charge elected office-holders to monitor and review the behavior of non-elected arms of the state apparatus, such as congressional review of presidential appointees and federal agencies, are not the issue. What is important is whether the voting mechanism is still effective in harnessing contextual knowledge for governmental elements one or more stages removed from the democratic voting procedure.[47] If it is not, then some other, possibly informal, institutions are needed to guide the non-elected parts of government in a way that would tend to bring the expectations and plans of individual public agents into better coordination. According to Wilson (1989: 59–65), for example, among the important attributes public agents often bring with them to their bureaucratic duties are professional norms, which can under certain circumstances overcome the proclivity toward narrow self-interest.

Political self-interest

A representative democracy provides several levels on which coordination through the voting mechanism or related institutions might operate. At the most basic level of political action in democratic systems, as we have seen, voting behavior on the part of the public and vote-seeking on the part of candidates for elected office might serve to summarize dispersed information in a meaningful and immediately recognizable form. At the level of legislatures, log-rolling is the political analog to voluntary exchange in the market. It is the result of discovering "double coincidences of wants" among public agents. Of course, it is only when we admit narrow self-interest back into the analysis that log-rolling becomes feasible, since if all public choosers were benevolent they would not knowingly engage in trades that harmed others.

The existence of narrow self-interest makes available all varieties of rent-seeking and redistributive activities as potential sources of information. Money bribes,[48] especially, which attach a cash value to specific governmental services, can facilitate the comparison among different governmental lower-order goods by providing an objective indicator of political preferences that balloting and referenda alone, for reasons already given, are incapable of reflecting. To the extent that money bribes are the result of voluntary choices *within* the governmental process (even though political means must ultimately be used to supply the services provided), they will coordinate plans within that process.

Unfortunately, as has already been noted, the presence of narrow political interest deprives plan coordination of significance as a *normative* criterion for the governmental process, since the coordination of plans that employ political means may not promote the general welfare. Nevertheless, with respect to the *positive* analysis of the governmental process, political self-interest can serve to promote plan coordination.[49] If, however, there is more than one way to harmonize public-sector plans, this raises the question of how the governmental process might select the most "effective" or "preferred" alternative. I will continue this line of argument in a moment.

Limitations of non-price coordinating devices

The voting mechanism may be the most effective information conveyance device in the governmental process. It comes closest to the price system in its ability to generate meaningful and easily recognizable signals to guide political action. Although there is a certain superficial similarity between the number of votes cast for a candidate or proposal and the money prices paid for commodities in the catallaxy, crucial differences exist between these two institutions, which political economists, particularly those in the tradition of public choice, have long identified.

Votes are not prices in several senses, most of which follow from the fact that, with the exception of proportional voting systems, no more than one person can fill a given opening in the so-called "political market." That is, while many can run for an office, there can only be one winner. This follows from the nature of political power.

Under a majority or plurality rule, the political market makes an "all-or-nothing" choice between political alternatives, while in the private market there can be, and typically is, more than one "winner" at a given time. This feature of most voting rules means that only those votes cast for the sole winner matter, while in the private market every dollar spent has some impact on the outcome at any given time. Despite tremendous advances in telecommunication and information processing, the perceived cost of voting (particularly its information-gathering aspect) for a given individual tends to be high relative to the perceived cost of shopping for ordinary commodities. Thus, at the national level in the United States for example, elections for president take place only every four years, for the Senate every six years, and the House of Representatives no less than every two years. This means that the voting mechanism is glacially slow in adjusting to changing political preferences and conditions when compared to the price mechanism, which updates the entire system of relative prices continuously (though not perfectly) with every dollar spent on the private market. This sluggishness affects even proportional voting systems, which do remove some of the all-or-nothing character of majority and plurality rules. The number of political alternatives (referenda, political candidates, bond measures, etc.) competing for votes that crowd the typical ballot are nevertheless extremely limited when compared to the number of substitutes that crowd the shelves of the local supermarket and shopping mall.

To reiterate, under all voting rules, but especially under majority voting, only those who voted for the winning candidate can be said to have had their preferences satisfied. But even this is saying too much, for only if a voter is in the position of casting the *deciding* vote (i.e. if his vote is the tie-breaker), will he be certain that his vote had a significant impact on the outcome. Moreover, only under this highly unusual circumstance will the voter be certain that voting according to his genuine preferences is rational. For if he still votes knowing full well that it will have practically no effect on the outcome, then his vote must be based on something other than his preference for the alternatives, so long as the cost of voting is for him even only slightly greater than zero.

The implications of this fact on the nature of really existing democracy are disturbing. The principal implication, on which several others are based, is that the voting public may choose to remain "rationally ignorant" of important aspects of the political process, after weighing the minuscule expected benefits of voting against the relatively much higher expected costs. From this phenomenon, which we might also call the high costs of monitoring the political process, follows such phenomena as voter abstention, suboptimal production of information in a campaign, and the intentional (and rational) misrepresentation by candidates of their true positions (Mueller 1989: 205–6).

More fundamentally, however, the very meaning of democracy becomes highly obscure under these circumstances. Brennan (1986), for example, argues that if the electorate do not cast their votes based primarily on their preferences over the alternatives on the ballot, as the above argument suggests, but on other considerations (e.g., a sense of civic duty, a desire for social acceptance), this compromises what we ordinarily mean by democracy. For then the voting mechanism fails accurately to reflect the true political preferences of a voter, but instead expresses their valuation of a bundle of complementary goods. This is quite apart from large-numbers problems in voting – i.e., problems that arise from strategic voting and the like – which, if they are also considered, muddy the waters even more.

In the absence of the voting mechanism, or to the extent that it either fails to reflect the "underlying data" or is too remote from significant areas of government, the entrepreneurial discoveries and political exchanges that drive the governmental process must take place through the political equivalent of *barter*, with the increased likelihood of undetected plan discoordination that that system of exchange entails.[50] But even if somehow all plans within government were perfectly coordinated, even assuming public-spiritedness and benevolence, on what basis could this outcome be compared with other possible ways in which public-sector plans could be coordinated? In the market process, plan coordination combined with the agreement of all the subjective perceptions of each actor with the objective data (which includes the perceptions of other actors), means that the least-cost outcome would obtain after all opportunities for entrepreneurial gain had been exploited. For if a different pattern of plan coordination could do the job with less expenditure of resources, for example, an entrepreneurial incentive would exist for individuals, who may be unaware of their role in the process, to adjust the system toward that alternative pattern, if of course the perceived costs of making the transition are low enough. But in the absence of an objective indicator of relative values, such as money prices, how could political entrepreneurs compare alternative patterns of governmental plan coordination, should they exist? Under barter, the value of resources and services is difficult to evaluate in part because there is no standard unit of account or medium of exchange. Under the money-price system there is an objective accounting basis for calculating profit or loss, even though actors attach different significance to the monetary unit.[51]

To summarize this last line of argument, governmental plan coordination in the absence of a price-like mechanism is highly problematic. First, the very notion of plan coordination becomes normatively questionable in the presence of narrow self-interest. Second, the voting mechanism, the closest analog to the price system in government, itself suffers in comparison with the effectiveness of the price system in overcoming the knowledge problem. Finally, in the absence of a good indicator of political preferences as well as a standard unit of account for governmental services and a medium of exchange, the governmental process must essentially rely on barter arrangements to bring inconsistent plans into harmony. This makes it even more difficult to ensure that the governmental process even tends toward what in some sense is the best method of public-sector plan coordination.

Is the governmental process a spontaneous order?

The process by which government operates falls short of qualifying as a spontaneous order. Even if self-correcting tendencies do tend to bring inconsistent public plans into better coordination, an important property of spontaneous orders is that of self-sustainability; that is, once in motion the order is able to organize and renew itself indefinitely. What Hayek in the following passage says about the nature of "complex phenomena," applies also to spontaneous orders:

> Whether it will be useful to elaborate and study a pattern of a particular kind will depend on whether the structure it describes is persistent or merely accidental. The coherent structures in which we are mainly interested are those in which a complex pattern has produced properties which make self-maintaining the structure showing it.
>
> (Hayek 1967a: 27)

Governmental processes *per se* are not spontaneous orders because they depend on wealth created in and appropriated from the catallaxy. (This does not rule out the possibility, however, that the interventionist process – which includes the non-equilibrium interaction between the public and private sectors – is a genuine spontaneous order.)

CONCLUDING REMARKS

The market process and governmental process each face the knowledge problem and have specific institutional mechanisms to cope with it. The coordinating force in the market process, however, consists of the independent decisions of a myriad of entrepreneurially alert actors who are guided by a complex and spontaneously generated system of relative prices. Despite the need for government to adjust to novel circumstances, central planning is the defining principle upon which all states – from the minimal to the maximal state – are based. While most believe that only government can perform certain social functions, the methods of information conveyance within the governmental process work clumsily at best. In the minimal state, this problem is offset to the extent that the government can rely on the information-generating properties of the market process. More generally, if government is necessary but odious (owing to the intrinsic difficulties of even limited central planning), catallactic competition is an indispensable condition for maintaining both order within it and its legitimacy in the eyes of the public. But there are limits to the degree to which the market process can supply the informational needs of the governmental process. Indeed, the inherent difficulties of central planning, particularly in the limited central planning undertaken in mixed economies, are exacerbated by the spontaneous and unforeseen interactions between the market and governmental processes, which increase with the size of government in relation to the catallaxy. Not only do government and catallaxy each then have to cope with coordinating their operations in the face of their respective knowledge problems, but the government's efforts to control catallactic forces generate feedback from the market process that vastly increases the scope and magnitude of the overall knowledge problem. Let us now turn to these issues.

4

TOWARD A THEORY OF INTERVENTIONISM I:
The framework

This chapter and the next address two of the principal aims of this book. One is to contemplate particular instances of intervention within the context of an overall interventionist *process*. In that process the myriad and often conflicting plans of the mixed economy constitute vital elements of a general social dynamic in which government and catallaxy are both in flux. The other aim is to construct a single coherent framework that integrates two ideal types of interventionism: the welfare state and the regulatory state. Toward these ends, the present chapter seeks to identify and analyze the main factors underlying the dynamics of the interventionist process in general, while the next chapter compares, contrasts, and examines the interaction between the distinctive dynamics of the welfare and regulatory states.

The first section of this chapter isolates those insights from the collectivist calculation debate that are germane to the analysis of interventionism. The next section presents important details regarding the knowledge problem in the mixed economy. The following two sections, which constitute the bulk of the chapter, investigate the nature of the expansionary and contractionary phases of the interventionist process, respectively. After this is a brief discussion of whether or not, taken as a whole, this process is a spontaneous order in the sense of Hayek. Finally, by relaxing the assumption of public interest, the last section addresses whether and in what way political self-interest affects the analysis.

LESSONS FOR INTERVENTIONISM FROM THE CALCULATION DEBATE

The previous chapter addressed the question of whether and to what extent the calculation debate is applicable to the analysis of operations within the governmental process in a mixed economy. Let us now consider the propriety of taking an argument originally designed to critique pure collectivism and extending it to capitalist systems with limited government intervention – i.e., activities that exceed those of the minimal state.

We have seen that devastating consequences for social cooperation accompany the total abolition of private control over the means of production. Those consequences stem from the destruction of the very system of relative prices that enables profit-seeking entrepreneurs to detect plan inconsistencies and bring individual plans back into harmony. The loss of private control over the means of production on a system-wide scale completely severs the link between nominal relative prices that guide individual decisions on the one hand, and contextual knowledge and expectations on the other, thus rendering the "signals" these prices transmit catallactically meaningless.

Recall that *de facto* state control over a resource through intervention is consistent with *de jure* private ownership. Complete government control of resources held nominally in private hands (i.e., a *Zwangswirtschaft*) has the same consequences for the price system as outright collectivization, since resources in each case are allocated according to the decisions of state authorities rather than the spontaneous forces of the unhampered market. This suggests, however, that somewhere along each of the alternative "roads" of progressive intervention between the minimal state and complete *de facto* central planning – e.g., increasing regulation, expanding nationalization and monopolization of industries, the growing welfare state, or some combination of these – the effectiveness of the price system as a means of utilizing contextual knowledge and revealing error begins to breakdown. Thus I infer that to the degree that the mixed economy embodies the properties identified in this study as essential to collectivism, the lessons from the Austrian critique of collectivist central planning *mutatis mutandis* apply to the interventionist process as well.[1]

According to Lavoie, one of Mises's most significant contributions to the study of comparative economic systems was his placing of interventionism "in a wider context by relating it to the alternative economic systems of capitalism and socialism" (Lavoie 1982: 170). Although the framework Mises developed to critique interventionism was somewhat wanting in exhaustiveness and consistency,[2] a theme that appears to unify his comparative-systems analysis as a whole is the relative success with which any system – whether capitalism, interventionism, or collectivism – solves the problem of rational economic calculation. For Mises, the main obstacle to calculation under collectivism was the absence of profit and loss signals, generated within a system of market prices, which guide individual planning and promote social cooperation. Later, Hayek focused more closely on the extensive division of knowledge that the price system makes possible, which led him to emphasize the price system's capacity to harness dispersed local knowledge (i.e., contextual knowledge of time and place) and to coordinate diverse plans (Hayek 1948: 33–56, 77–91; 1978: 179–90). Thus, the theory of interventionism can derive a salient lesson from the calculation debate – i.e. to focus on the fundamental question of how well the mixed economy copes with the knowledge problem, where the capacity to cope is tightly bound to the efficacy of relative prices, the guideposts of profit and loss, in reflecting the contextual knowledge of the underlying technology, resources, tastes, and expectations of anonymous actors.

The freer actors are entrepreneurially to adjust relative prices to perceived changes in these underlying data, and in turn to adjust to them, the better will the price system serve its coordinative function. Since that freedom is directly related to the *degree* of private control over resources and meaningful price flexibility, this once again suggests that the lessons of the calculation debate are robust in the sense that complete state (*de facto* or *de jure*) control over all means of production is not necessary for the knowledge-based problems that plague complete collectivism to begin to manifest themselves in the mixed economy. The less freedom actors have to adjust to new (political, catallactic, or cultural) circumstances, the less effectively the price system will promote plan coordination; and the worse the price system performs this crucial function, the more likely and extensive will be the negative repercussions of intervention. Thus, although Mises did not himself frame the issue in this way, the dynamics of central planning (limited or unlimited) in the context of the knowledge problem tend to undermine both collectivism and interventionism. We should expect to find, therefore, that the knowledge problem is the chief source of the unforeseen difficulties that attend particular interventions and is responsible for the "self-defeating" nature of both particular interventions as well as interventionism as a system. I will soon have an opportunity to justify this claim.

THE NATURE AND SIGNIFICANCE OF THE KNOWLEDGE PROBLEM IN MIXED ECONOMIES

In the governmental process considered in isolation, the scope of the knowledge problem is limited to radical ignorance and contextual knowledge among the various agents who work within the confines of the government sector. Intervention in a mixed economy, however, must cope with the consequences of the knowledge problem in the catallaxy, as well. The interaction between the market and governmental processes when both are in flux significantly increases the size of the *overall* knowledge problem in society.

Spill-overs

When radical ignorance and discoordination prevail in government and market at the same time (i.e., when governmental and market processes interact), errors committed in one sector tend to generate errors in the other, the repercussions of which typically spill back into the first sector, and so on. If, for example, in order to cover an unanticipated budget deficit the state attempts to increase tax revenues by significantly raising marginal tax rates, wealth-producing actors in the catallaxy have an incentive to reduce their taxable incomes (with due regard to the possibility of partially offsetting income effects). If they do so by producing less marketable output, this is likely to have serious negative effects for resource owners in input markets and the producers of complementary goods in output markets.[3] Entrepreneur-producers in other parts of the catallaxy as well as owners of labor and other inputs in widely scattered factor markets would be forced to alter their plans in ways they probably had not anticipated, and some time is likely to pass before they discover a course of action that better harmonizes with the plans of others. In any event, if entrepreneurs in the private sector produce less output and less taxable income, this will also frustrate the original aim of the intervention, which was to increase tax revenue. In short, the intervention exacerbates the very problem the state originally intended to correct. It could also lead in this instance to further intervention to address the under-production and unemployment that would be among the unanticipated side-effects of the tax. In general, then, the expanded knowledge problem in the interventionist process means that an intervention by any given government agency, in the absence of knowledge of all relevant facts in the private *and* public sectors, results in unexpected responses in the market process. These have implications for the agency in question as well as unknown repercussions for other parts of both the market and governmental processes.[4] To the extent that these contradict the goal and directives of the state apparatus, they provide justifications for further intervention, given the existence among sufficient numbers of public choosers of a "statist mentality" – that is, an attitude favorably disposed to an active and expansive role for the state in the market. (I examine the role of ideology in greater detail later in this chapter.)

Entrepreneurial discovery versus incentives

Israel Kirzner's concepts of *stifled entrepreneurial discovery* and *superfluous entrepreneurial discovery* (1985: 119–49) are indispensable aids in a thorough analysis of the interventionist process. The standard economic treatment of taxes, regulations, and other legal restrictions on trade tend to focus on their effects on the *incentives* of agents to engage in activities in which the marginal costs and benefits (i.e., the components of the conventional choice framework) are known, and on the *equilibrium* values of price, quantity, and quality. In contrast, the analysis of stifled and superfluous discovery focuses on the impact of intervention on the *discovery* of new knowledge (i.e., on the capacity to perceive the choice framework itself) and on competitive rivalry in the *market process*.

To gain a sense of the difference between incentives-based and knowledge-based approaches to interventionist dynamics, I will briefly relate it to microeconomic regulation and macroeconomic fiscal and monetary policy. Suppose the state issues and strictly enforces a prohibition against commercial vehicles driving over 200-miles per hour.[5] In standard economic analysis this would represent a non-binding constraint under the reasonable assumption that, with current technology, commercial vehicles ordinarily would never even approach the prohibited speed. Market-process analysis, however, must also consider the effects of the speed limit on entrepreneurial discovery. Under the circumstances presented in the example, actors will now not notice potentially profitable production processes that require transport faster than this speed limit, and they would also be more likely to pass over technical advances that could make this happen.[6] In addition, too much investment will take place over time in technologies that depend on lower-speed travel. As in standard analysis, the current costs of commercial transport remain unaffected, yet a subtle though very real impediment to economic development now exists because of the regulation.

Similarly, in order to raise revenue the state might try to impose a direct tax on entrepreneurial profit (considering it merely residual income), perhaps in the form of a "windfall-profits" tax, in the belief that such a tax would be neutral with respect to economic activity. This, of course, is not the case. As with an extraordinarily high speed-limit, an entrepreneurial-profit tax might have no immediate incentive effects, yet it would discourage the entrepreneurship vital to the functioning of the market process (Kirzner 1985: 93–118). It could also encourage bribery and graft among political entrepreneurs. Should the state instead decide to resort to credit expansion in order to finance its expenditures, the Mises–Hayek trade-cycle theory (Mises 1966: 538–86; Hayek 1967b; 1975a; 1975b) suggests that entrepreneurs would be more likely to overlook, at the margin, otherwise profitable investments that involve relatively less time-intensive production (i.e., stifled discovery) in favor of more time-intensive production processes (i.e., superfluous discovery), owing to the distortions in the structure of intertemporal relative prices and interest rates that a policy of credit expansion tends to bring about. Since money is on at least one side of every exchange in a modern catallaxy, of the various kinds of limited intervention, deliberate monetary manipulation (credit expansion and contraction) has potentially the profoundest and most widespread impact on the system of relative prices.[7] The consequences of monetary policy for entrepreneurial discovery and intertemporal plan coordination are therefore potentially quite severe. (Later I show how the boom and bust cycle that accompanies unwise monetary policy embodies many of the features that define the interventionist process as a whole.)

Class-one and class-two errors

Kirzner (1963) has also offered an interesting and, for the present study, extremely valuable two-fold taxonomy of entrepreneurial learning, which I present in the following example. Suppose you need to sell your car on a given day and someone offers $5,000 for it. Suppose further that you deliberately refuse the offer, thinking that someone else is willing to pay substantially more. If you are right you earn an entrepreneurial profit, if wrong, you suffer an entrepreneurial loss. Note, however, that if you erred in your *judgment* and *deliberately* passed up an opportunity to make a small profit with the hope of making a larger one, your error will *inevitably* come to your attention. That is, unless you are a complete dullard with no alertness whatsoever, you will realize your error when at the end of the day your car remains unsold. It takes very little entrepreneurial alertness to feel genuine disappointment in this situation.

Now let us imagine a different scenario. Suppose you pass up the opportunity to sell your car for $5,000, not because you are overly optimistic (or overly pessimistic),[8] but because you are utterly *unaware* of the offer. Here you have erred because of sheer *ignorance* rather than poor judgment. But more significantly it is not at all inevitable that this kind of error[9] will come to your attention; indeed the error may go unnoticed indefinitely. Someone (you or someone else) may eventually be entrepreneurially alert enough to notice it, but being entrepreneurially alert in this case is no more inevitable than achieving a market equilibrium, and for the same reason. To realize this kind of error, therefore, requires an act of what might be called *dynamic* learning.

For convenience, I will term the first kind of error (an error in judgment) a *class-one error* and the associated learning process (inevitable learning) *class-one learning*, and the second kind of error (an error owing to radical ignorance) a *class-two error* and the associated learning process (dynamic learning) *class-two learning*.[10] While the significance of this classification will become clearer later in this chapter, note for now that although both kinds of learning involve entrepreneurship, *ceteris paribus*, class-one errors are easier to discover than class-two errors, and the more errors committed and the larger the proportion of class-two errors in a system relative to class-one errors the greater the challenge to entrepreneurship to coordinate conflicting plans.

Finally, stifled discovery and superfluous discovery can be either class-one or class-two errors, depending on the circumstances that give rise to them. In the Mises–Hayek business-cycle theory, for example, the intertemporal errors that entrepreneur-producers commit are largely class-one, since according to the theory the malinvestments that take place during the boom inevitably fail when consumer preferences reassert themselves and produce shortages in less time-intensive lines of production. On the other hand, the 200-mile-per-hour speed limit stifles discovery in a way that no one will necessarily realize. Static inefficiency or deadweight losses, however, are more often, though not exclusively, the result of class-two errors, and their removal is not in any sense inevitable but rather depends heavily on entrepreneurial alertness (spurred on perhaps by competitive rivalry). Class-one errors typically produce the more familiar non-equilibrium phenomena of surpluses and shortages, which are central to the Misesian critique of interventionism. (Indeed, Mises's failure to emphasize the importance of class-two errors and learning constitutes a serious gap in his analysis of the mixed economy.) In fact, it is because their existence is more easily discerned than class-two errors that class-one errors play a central role in fueling the interventionist process. Recall from the price-control example of Chapter 2 that it was the appearance of shortages that brought the negative consequence of a price ceiling (though perhaps not its source) to the attention of public choosers. Class-two error contributes a dynamic element into the interventionist process in the sense that it is responsible for injecting most of the radical ignorance that creates high levels of uncertainty and discoordination within the system.

While errors of both kinds are the *sine qua non* of entrepreneurial discovery in the market process, the difference between discoordination in the catallaxy and, let us imagine, the same level of discoordination caused by interventionism is that additional factors accompany the latter that render entrepreneurial discovery relatively more problematic, as we shall now see.

Learning outside of equilibrium

In equilibrium, learning is pointless. Far away from equilibrium, learning is futile.

Outside of equilibrium, if relative prices are to enable actors to learn how to coordinate their diverse and partially conflicting plans, those prices need sufficiently (though not necessarily perfectly) to reflect actual underlying scarcities and the expectations of market participants,[11] otherwise decisions guided by them will "compound rather than correct, previous mistakes" (Rizzo 1990: 21). Thus, being near equilibrium "seems to be a *necessary* condition for the spread of correct foresight about what others will do and for the homogenization of opinion about the external data" (ibid.: 19; emphasis original). The price system is like a compass that, owing to some geological quirk, works better as you near your destination.

It is of course conceivable that the market process might on its own accord propel itself so far from equilibrium that even the tendency to equilibrate becomes highly uncertain. In this chapter, however, I attempt to show how progressive interventionism compromises the very capacity of non-equilibrium relative prices to adjust in an equilibrating manner. This simultaneously drives the mixed economy away from equilibrium and jeopardizes its ability to find its way back. It thus increases the likelihood of being far away from equilibrium and decreases the likelihood of getting back. Here, to continue the analogy, fiddling with your compass gets you lost in the first place and, because of the combination of natural magnetic forces and your fiddling, you find yourself very far from home with a broken compass. This does not mean, I hasten to add, especially in light of the discussion in Chapter 3 of the nature of the market process, that under laissez-faire capitalism the price system functions perfectly and the system achieves a competitive equilibrium.

THE EXPANSIONARY PHASE OF THE INTERVENTIONIST PROCESS

The interaction between governmental and market processes in the context of the knowledge problem, combined with ideological change (which also serves to sustain the interventionist process but is separate from the knowledge problem, *per se*), produces a series of market-level and less severe system-wide crises. The cumulative outcome of these minor crises is a major system-wide crisis that forces public choosers to decide between thorough-going collectivization, on the one hand, or a radical reorientation toward laissez-faire capitalism, on the other. Moreover, the timing of the crisis depends on the obstacles to learning in the form of

Simoneon bounded rationality, Kirznerian radical ignorance, and the ability of the market process to replenish what Mises termed the "reserve fund" out of which interventionist policies are ultimately financed.

This section, by far the longest of the chapter, first explores how and why state intervention in the context of the knowledge problem tends to generate patterns of negative unintended consequences. It next examines the role of exogenous and endogenous ideological change in sustaining the interventionist process, and then inquires into the causes and consequences of the economic crisis that interventionism brings on. Finally, it suggests how the underlying analysis of these largely macroeconomic patterns might relate to and impinge on the level of individual markets and vice versa.

Why are the consequences of intervention perverse?

At the heart of Mises's critique of interventionism was his contention that a policy of limited government intervention into the market process leads to unintended consequences that even its sponsors deem undesirable. These consequences can appear as direct or indirect results of an intervention; that is, either as unwanted effects that emanate directly from the intervention or as effects of later interventions that were believed necessary to alleviate the problems that the initial intervention caused. Mises himself did not deal in his critique with calculational or knowledge-based considerations adequately enough to address the question of why public authorities would so doggedly pursue an inherently flawed policy to the point of bringing on a major politico-economic crisis. I have proposed that the answer has to do not only with ideology, as Mises seemed to suggest, or with structural or personal incentives, as public choice has emphasized, but also with the knowledge problem in government and catallaxy. In constructing an argument in support of this proposal, it will be helpful first to isolate what might be called the internal and external responses to an intervention.

Internal and external responses

The *internal response* takes place within the area of the catallaxy, or the aspect of catallactic activity that is the principal target of an intervention. It refers to the most immediate attempts to circumvent or adjust to a given intervention. Thus, for example, the internal response to an increase in marginal tax rates is for the income earners immediately affected to divert their energies from the creation of taxable to non-taxable income. Similarly, the regulation of rates of return on investment in certain industries (e.g., cable television) could create an incentive for these industries to enlarge their capital stock beyond optimal levels (i.e., the so-called "Averch–Johnson effect"); or unemployed persons who receive transfer payments might in response extend their period of unemployment; or credit expansion by a central state bank that initially diverts investment toward more time-intensive production processes could also stimulate (vertical and horizontal) mergers within the catallaxy that violate antitrust prohibitions. Thus, the internal response consists of unintended consequences that are internal to the area or aspect of the catallaxy at which the state directs an intervention.

In contrast, the *external response* is an unintended consequence that takes place outside the target of an intervention.[12] This response consists of entrepreneurial adjustments in the governmental and market processes, outside the area or aspect of market activity immediately affected. For example, entrepreneurs who produce goods complementary to those whose production is now curtailed because of higher taxes may decrease their own production and also lay off workers, which will further shrink the state's tax base. Marginal investors who would have invested in the more highly taxed industry now invest elsewhere. Public agents working with governmental programs that were supposed to have been funded out of higher taxes will either have to adjust somehow to lower-than-expected revenues or find alternative sources of funding. Government tax writers may be induced to rewrite the tax code in order to close the loopholes that the previous rules created (recall Charles Schultz's description of this process from Chapter 1[13]). And so on.

One of the benefits of isolating these two responses is that it permits us to distinguish "unintended consequences," from the more familiar concept of economic externalities. While it is true that unintended consequences, as the term is used in this study, necessarily includes effects on so-called third parties (i.e., agents whose well-being a decision affects but whose preferences do not inform that decision), it also encompasses effects that occur within the immediate target area of given interventions. If the state forces a factory to install scrubbers to reduce its smokestack emissions, not only might the resulting acid rain damage the property of third parties, but this regulation might also place the factory at an unexpected competitive disadvantage *vis-à-vis* factories that already use newer, low-emission equipment and processes or factories located in countries with less stringent environmental regulations.

A further difference between externalities and unintended consequences (including external responses) is that measuring externalities entails the calculation of (suboptimal) equilibrium values (e.g., the value of the deadweight losses generated by negative externalities), while this is not the case with negative unintended consequences, since in the analysis of the interventionist process the focus is on the *discoordination* resulting from the actions of entrepreneurs that frustrate the intentions of public authorities.[14] That is, although I have argued in Chapter 3 that measuring the degree of discoordination is inherently impossible since it entails the measurement of a counterfactual (namely, the extent of the departure of actual events from events that would have taken place had actors known what they do not know), it is still possible to determine whether the consequences of an intervention, or a policy of interventionism, is desirable *from the viewpoint of its supporters*.[15] This orientation is radically different from that of the standard analysis of externalities, in which those responsible for an externality might *know* they exist, but lack the *incentive* to incorporate it into their calculations. By contrast, the very concept of *unintended* consequences would seem to rule this out. Owing to radical ignorance and (as I argue later in this chapter) bounded rationality, most of the ramifications from any action will be far beyond an actor's capacity to observe. In the standard analysis, for example, the deadweight loss from excessive production under negative externalities need not ultimately redound to the party responsible for them; whereas I intend to show that the negative unintended consequences of an intervention impinge on or are noticed by its supporters frequently enough to render that intervention, and indeed the whole policy of interventionism, undesirable to them.[16]

Incentive and discovery effects

Internal and external responses stem from the distorting influence of an intervention on the structure of relative prices. There are, however, two distinct effects that follow from such distortions. One effect results from changing the constraints actors already perceive, and might be described as a change in the structure of incentives. I will call this the *incentive effect*. This is the effect standard analysis normally takes into account such as when, for example, highly taxed producers choose to reduce or disguise their taxable incomes. The other effect arises owing to the tendency of an intervention to create either barriers to discovery or superfluous opportunities for discovery. I call this the *discovery effect*. Thus, a higher marginal tax rate not only alters the relative value of known alternatives – say, work and leisure – it also reduces the likelihood that entrepreneurs will notice new, currently undiscovered ways to produce wealth in areas in which income is relatively difficult to disguise (stifled discovery). On the other hand, it may also open profit opportunities that would not have existed in the absence of the higher taxes (superfluous discovery), such as when new tax legislation creates legal loopholes that clever accountants can then profitably exploit or when legal barriers to competition prompt the discovery of new methods to produce competing products and services, either legally or illegally.[17]

Both effects need to be taken into account to appreciate fully the nature of interventionist dynamics in the mixed economy, but the second effect deserves special emphasis. This is because the radical ignorance that underlies the discovery effect[18] is the seed of a radically unpredictable consequence (although the incentive effect can also give rise to unanticipated outcomes), and unintended consequences are in turn what fuel the interventionist process. In the standard analysis of regulation, for example, the attempt to reduce taxable income is a response to an artificially lowered relative value of work (i.e., a higher marginal tax on income) that is predictable in principle. The timing and manner in which actors respond, of course, as well as the spontaneous external responses that occur in the market and governmental processes later on, are not predictable except in the very general sense of a "pattern prediction."[19] Nevertheless, both effects should be included in the analysis of mixed economies, not least because acting upon changed incentives (the incentive effect) can itself cause discovery effects.

In summary, the public sector initiates and sustains the interventionist process, where this process is driven by the consequences, particularly the unintended ones (in both government and catallaxy) of intervention. Looking more closely at these unintended consequences, one can further identify internal and external responses to the primary target area of an intervention, both of which, however, reflect distortions in the network of relative prices and values. Moreover, both kinds of responses have incentive-based and discovery-based aspects, the latter of which is particularly important for an explanation of the nature of the interventionist process because it enables this process to manifest its characteristic unpredictability and spontaneity. These are important, incidentally, for understanding why even public-spirited public choosers would be reluctant to abandon an inherently unworkable policy of interventionism.

The sources of negative unintended consequences

To begin to see this, recall that all interventions involve implicit or explicit income transfers of some kind, since any intervention produces both "winners" and "losers" (i.e., subsidized and taxed actors, respectively). This is useful in explaining more precisely how and why interventions generate negative unintended consequences through their impact on the entrepreneurial-competitive process. While still retaining the assumption of benevolence among public choosers, I first examine how and in what sense purposeful action in the market, in the face of new profit (subsidy) and loss (tax) situations resulting from changes in the network of relative values, tends to contradict the intent of the advocates of an intervention.

As a first approximation, it might be helpful, though not entirely accurate, to think of an intervention as the state's attempt to bring a particular area of the catallaxy under its "control." Because state control entails the restriction of private action, it tends to lower the value of targeted productive resources. And because the value of productive resources will then be correspondingly higher (at least from the viewpoint of private resource owners) in uncontrolled areas compared to the controlled area, resources will tend to flow from the latter to the former. While some of these flows can be anticipated, spontaneous entrepreneurial discoveries within the disruptions created by an intervention ensure that at least some will be novel and highly relevant to its success.

This first approximation will actually serve as the basis for the discussion in Chapter 5 of the impact of nationalization and non-price regulation on the market process. Its inaccuracy as a general description of the consequences of an intervention, however, has to do with the ambiguity of the term "control," which fails to convey the idea that intervention produces both winners and losers, at least some of whose identities are impossible to predict. For example, as mentioned earlier, a regulation mandating a reduction in smokestack emissions tends to favor owners of newer factories at the expense of owners of older ones that emit more smoke per unit of output owing to the vintage of their technology. Thus, because a given control benefits and harms different actors, inside and outside the target area, the pattern of the flow of resources into and out of a controlled area can become quite complex. I will therefore treat these two consequences of a given intervention separately.

To the extent that intervention constitutes an implicit or explicit tax, owners of productive resources will tend to shift their investment at the margin from the taxed to the untaxed areas of the market (including ones that might exist within the target area itself). This has two aspects, which correspond to the earlier characterization of the unintended consequences of an intervention as either incentive- or discovery-based. Specifically, not only does the lower relative return on investment in the taxed area give profit maximizers an incentive to invest elsewhere among *already known* alternatives (incentive-based aspect), but the intervention that changes the relative valuation will also cause *discoordination* by masking profitable investment opportunities that would otherwise have been discovered (discovery-based aspect). When or whether actors will eventually notice these opportunities depends on what class error it is. I will be arguing, however, that as the expansionary phase progresses, the absolute and relative incidence of class-two errors will increase. The masking of such opportunities along with the creation of superfluous ones, in government as well as catallaxy, constitutes perhaps the most important part of the negative unintended consequences of intervention that feed the interventionist process.

Furthermore, the growing multiplicity, diversity, interdependence, and remoteness of the consequences of a given intervention, resulting from both incentive and discovery considerations, generates ever higher levels of *complexity* in the interventionist process. The combination of growing complexity and the continual commission of errors renders it increasingly difficult for public choosers accurately to identify and comprehend, or even to become aware of, all of the outcomes of a given intervention that are relevant to its success. Consequently, it also becomes increasingly difficult for them rationally to evaluate the totality of both the contents and the important ramifications of the individual policies that comprise the general policy of interventionism. This then helps to explain why benevolent public authorities might continue to embrace interventionism even in the face of impending systemic failure, since complexity and discoordination within the mixed economy obscure the link between policy actions and experienced outcomes. (In a moment I will show how ideology complements these other two factors in obfuscating this link.)

Similarly, to the extent that intervention constitutes an implicit or explicit subsidy, it induces resource owners to undertake added investment at the margin in activities that from the perspective of plan coordination may be considered wholly superfluous. Once again, an intervention alters the relative value of investments, this time, however, by artificially raising the returns to the target area. As resources flow from the now sub-marginal to the supra-marginal investments (again, both inside and outside the target area), this not only reduces or altogether eliminates production in the unsubsidized areas that are already known (incentive-based aspect of the subsidy), but it also masks potentially profitable investments in areas that might otherwise have been discovered and exploited but now will not be (discovery-based aspect). If, for example, the state provides zero-price health care to the unemployed, this will tend to discourage both known and yet-to-be-discovered methods of delivering health care, some of which might possibly have turned out to provide the same service at a lower cost (or better service at the same cost). As already noted, it is important to realize that the effects of taxes and subsidies from a particular intervention take place concurrently, which further compounds the difficulty for public choosers of precisely predicting its ramifications. I take up the issue of learning delays again later in this part.

Why are the consequences undesirable overall?

But even if one grants that an intervention gives rise to unintended consequences that increase and obscure discoordination and heighten complexity, I have yet to explain why it should cause unforeseen problems that are serious enough to have the *net* effect of contradicting the intent of its sponsors, or (more weakly) of producing a state of affairs less satisfactory to them than the conditions the intervention was intended to remove. A critic of interventionism should be able to substantiate a statement such as the following:

> The imposition of regulatory constraints necessarily results, therefore, in a pattern of consequences different from and, *most plausibly, distinctly less desirable* than what would have occurred in the unregulated market.
>
> (Kirzner 1985: 145; emphasis added)

What makes the pattern of consequences from regulation not only different from but "most plausibly" less desirable than otherwise would have been the case, and how does this follow from the unpredictable nature of the process of discovery in the market? One could argue, for example, that the positive "spin-offs" from heavily subsidized government efforts – the United States space program is a favorite example – more than compensate for any lost production or technical progress that might have occurred otherwise.[20]

But consider the position of the advocates of interventionism more closely. Would all supporters of the space program condone the uses to which the technology derived from it have been put, for example, in improving the performance of intercontinental ballistic missiles? Or, perhaps more problematically, would they applaud the absence of discoveries that were not made because the state spent tax revenues on the space program? That is, would it matter to them that discoveries in medicine, literature, recreation, alternatives to rocket-powered space flight, and so on, might have occurred but did not because of government spending decisions and because taxes and government borrowing crowded out private investment? In fact, of course, it is impossible to conduct a complete cost–benefit analysis of the space program, even putting to one side the intractable problems of measuring costs outside of equilibrium (Buchanan 1969: 38–50), owing to the very nature of the "undiscovered costs" (or for that matter the "undiscovered benefits").

This line of reasoning appears to prove too much, however, for then how would it be possible to pass any kind of scientific judgment, favorable or not, on the space program or any other intervention? There is a firmer, though perhaps empirically modest, foundation from which to evaluate the normative impact of an intervention that does not rely on standard cost–benefit analysis. It is based instead on an appreciation of the fundamental tension between the principles of spontaneous order and conscious design, discussed in the previous chapter.

While in the catallaxy every action taken under uncertainty and ignorance does to some degree disturb current plans in unforeseen ways, incentives exist for entrepreneurs systematically to adjust to these disturbances so that, on the whole, the market process remains orderly. In contrast, the principle of organization around which the governmental process operates does not easily accommodate the spontaneous responses of entrepreneurs in both the public and private sectors. Of course, the principle of organization also plays an integral role in purely market institutions (e.g., the hierarchical structure of the firm), and, as such, it is a factor that can promote or retard the effectiveness of the market process. In the catallaxy, however, balancing the benefits of central planning against the benefits of entrepreneurial discovery is the responsibility of imperfect but profit-seeking actors. Meanwhile, the benevolent though non-profit-seeking agents of the state who impose various forms of central planning on the catallaxy are considerably less likely to achieve the proper balance between organization and order that will promote social cooperation, owing to the relatively clumsy learning procedures available to them.[21] Thus, extending the principle of organization, a "blunt instrument" in the hands of government, to the market process through government intervention interferes with and constrains the tendency of private-sector entrepreneurs to make necessary adjustments to unexpected changes. While there may be winners (unintended and intended) who benefit from expanding intervention, the added rigidity that it imposes degrades the effectiveness of the market process as a whole, which in the longer term tends to harm all.

Furthermore, an intervention incites losers to try to find ways to re-establish their pre-intervention preferences and levels of well-being, while at the same time it gives winners an incentive to employ both economic and political means to secure their superfluous gains (although here narrow self-interest may be re-entering the discussion). Both kinds of responses have repercussions that tend to thwart the intentions of public authorities. If, for example, the government tries to ban the domestic sale of cocaine, this will set off a torrent of entrepreneurial activity by consumers and producers who will aim to satisfy consumer preferences by circumventing the ban legally or illegally. As these transactions continue to "slip through the fingers" of the authorities, any further intervention will have to struggle against mounting problems of detection and enforcement.[22]

Finally, the growing complexity and discoordination that accompany intervention also compromise the ability of public-sector entrepreneurs in the governmental process to respond in ways that are necessary to complement the actions taken by other agencies in the government. Consequently, any given agency will have a poor idea of how complementary or conflicting are the programs of other agencies (if it is even aware of them). In this regard, Charles Wolf has noted that determining the aggregate external effects of public policy "*ex ante* may be even harder for nonmarket 'derived' externalities because of the bluntness of nonmarket instruments and the frequent remoteness of their effects both in time and in place" (1990: 97, n35). I would go even further and argue that this observation holds in the *ex post* sense as well. Thus, for example, an extension of welfare benefits to cover all persons in a country regardless of legal status may be unintentionally at odds with immigration policy by encouraging illegal entry into that country.[23]

It is quite possible, however, that some interventions produce outcomes that its supporters applaud. Rent controls in New York City have lowered the real rents of many, though not all, New Yorkers. Credit expansion can sometimes stimulate investment. Medicare and medicaid often provide health care to those who seem to need it (as well, of course, to many who do not). While I have been assuming benevolence on the part of public choosers so that there is no difference between announced and intended goals, in the world of public choice (and the real world of politics), however, narrow political interest raises the possibility of opportunistic behavior. In that case, determining whether a given negative consequence is actually an unintended one becomes problematic. Thus, some have contended that the higher unemployment among, and the reduced competition from, low-skilled minority youth that accompany an increase in the minimum wage may be precisely the reason for organized labor's consistent support for this policy.[24]

Three meanings of "frustrated intentions"

What, then, are we to understand by "net negative unintended consequences" or, more simply, "frustrated intentions"? We know that Austrian political economy evaluates the success of an intervention from the perspective of its supporters. The rest has been largely implicit in the Austrian analysis of interventionism. Thus, I offer the following three interpretations:

The first is the *strong version*, which states that a particular intervention will not only fail to achieve the end sought after, but will in fact produce the opposite, or nearly the opposite, result. Rent controls (and, later, rent stabilization) in New York City, for example, which were intended to counteract the effects of wartime inflation and make housing more accessible and affordable,[25] in a matter of a few years produced housing shortages and skyrocketing rental rates that have grown only more chronic with the passage of time. And minimum-wage legislation, which is supposed to raise the living standards of low-skilled labor, is actually a significant cause of unemployment among individuals in this category when it raises wages above levels that would have been established on the unhampered market.[26]

Yet, as we have seen, it is possible to identify interventions that have been, at least on the face of it, reasonably successful. A case in point is the Old-Age Assistance program of the Social Security Administration. Despite recurrent fiscal problems over the years, the SSA has largely managed to achieve its goal of sending out the appropriate "social-security checks" on time to eligible citizens (Wilson 1989: 160; Goodsell 1985: 137). Another example often given is the measures taken by city, state, and national governments during the 1970s and 1980s to eliminate "smog" that are purported to have improved the visual appearance of the skies above most major American cities.[27] Thus, there may be exceptions to the strong version – sometimes supporters of an intervention are its long-term net beneficiaries.

But the analysis of interventionism in this book, as well as the Misesian critique of interventionism on which it is based, does not rest exclusively or even primarily on the strong version. Rather, I maintain that Austrian political economy relies chiefly on two other interpretations of negative unintended consequences. The first of these, the *weak version* has two aspects. According to one aspect of the weak version, supporters of intervention might get what they want, but they also get what they do not want. For instance, while some of those who advocate rent control in New York City may pay real rents that are lower than market rates, the long-term consequences for the average apartment dweller have been artificially high real rental rates, a stagnant housing stock, and low vacancy and turnover rates. Moreover, according to one estimate, up to half of all "homelessness" in major American cities such as New York can be traced to rent regulations and related zoning ordinances (Tucker 1990: 34–67). After five decades of rent control, chronic housing shortages have in this way become a problem even for those New Yorkers privileged to have a rent-controlled or rent-stabilized apartment.[28] Today they encounter the problems of homelessness in many ways. The sight or even the thought of open destitution is aesthetically or morally repugnant to them, or the impact on municipal budgets for shelters and related public services now impinge on them through higher municipal taxes. Compounding these negative consequences is what some authorities claim is the record number of homeless in major cities, New York City in particular, drawn there no doubt by, among other things,[29] the relatively generous services available to the homeless. Thus, this aspect of the weak version states that supporters of an intervention will themselves find the conditions after the intervention on balance less desirable than the original state of affairs that the intervention was intended to improve.

The other aspect of the weak version is suggested by the concept of class-two error. Specifically, when public choosers get what they want from an intervention, other, potentially more valuable, alternatives from within the catallaxy are obscured. For example, if a large coalition of public choosers were to petition the state for and receive guaranteed lifetime employment, this could hamper catallactic development to such a degree that future positions that they would have considered on the whole more desirable will now never arise. And because the obscured alternatives are counterfac-tual, mere potentialities rather than concretes (i.e., the alternative positions never appear), their discovery may be highly problematic. Now, one might argue that the purely voluntary choices actors make within the catallaxy suppress development and the emergence of potential alternatives in the same way. As the earlier example of the 200-mile-per-hour speed limit illustrated, however, the state employs methods of competitive exclusion (i.e., political means) vastly more effective in suppressing entrepreneurial discovery than anything found in the unhampered catallaxy. This means that the discovery of excluded alternatives is even more difficult and uncertain in the case of state intervention. In short, getting what you want from the government often means not knowing what you could have had.[30]

The third interpretation of negative unintended consequences takes a broader perspective than even the long-term consequences of a given intervention or set of interventions. Rather, it looks at the repercussions on interventionism as a whole – i.e., the negative unintended consequences of interventionism as a doctrine or policy on the long-term vitality of the overall politico-economic order. This more *general version* argues, like the strong version, that proponents of interventionism – at least its benevolent proponents – in fact fail to get what they want. (In this sense it is simply an extension of the strong version.) That is, instead of a stable middle way that manages to generate the material prosperity of capitalism while reaping the benefits of deliberate state control, interventionism as a policy inevitably results in instability, delegitimation and crisis, and a return to either a purer form of capitalism or thorough-going collectivism. (I attempt to substantiate the last claim later in this chapter.)

Thus, while the strong version frequently holds for the reasons I have given in this section, the arguments developed in this book pertain primarily to the weaker and, especially, the general versions.

The role of ideology in the interventionist process

Reinforcing the distorting effects of intervention on the relative prices and values that guide action in the mixed economy is its influence, direct and indirect, on the ideology of public choosers. While theoretical analysis (or public choosers themselves) cannot predict precisely how an intervention will affect the prevailing ideology, it can still reveal aspects of the incentive and discovery characteristics that underlie ideological change and thereby tell us something about how and why such changes might take place. I describe these aspects and patterns here in a general way, and present in Chapter 5 a more detailed exposition, which I also use to explain in Chapter 6 why it would be reasonable to expect instability in the minimal state. This section outlines how discoordination and ideological change interact to generate the interventionist process.

Directing the interventionist process

For the purposes of this study, *ideology* will refer somewhat narrowly to a public chooser's attitude toward state expansion. If the negative unintended consequences of interventionism and the entrepreneurial responses to them in government and catallaxy are what drive the interventionist process, then the prevailing ideology determines the general direction, toward either more or less government, that that process will take. Thus, *ceteris paribus*, the more strongly averse to state expansion public choosers are in general, the less likely it is that it will happen. Or as Robert Higgs comments, "ideologies constrain as well as propel political action" (1987: 47). Moreover, the likelihood that public choosers will actually repeal previous interventions increases with this aversion, as well as when a set of conditions (which I outline in subsequent sections of this chapter) is in place. I maintain this claim with the understanding that the locus of choice (i.e., those who ultimately determine the course of public policy) naturally depends on the political system and institutions (e.g., direct democracy, constitutional monarchy, or dictatorship) through which political preferences can be expressed.

Despite the negative manner in which I have framed it, this formulation, *mutatis mutandis*, applies also to citizens who strongly prefer state over private provision of goods at the margin. Also, not every instance of intervention need result in a marked or even a perceptible change in ideology, since the impact of intervention on ideology is also cumulative in nature. Thus, what follows in this section pertains mostly, though not exclusively, to the interventionist process as a whole, rather than to particular instances of intervention.

Recall Mises's classic example of a price ceiling (see Chapter 2, above). There, the imposition of controls causes a shortage, yet the response of public choosers, *given* a general ideological propensity toward interventionism on their part, is to implement a new set

113

of controls (subsidies and more price ceilings) to deal with the shortage. Of course, public choosers may not at first even be aware of the full extent of the problems that an intervention has caused. For reasons that should by now be familiar to the reader (but that Mises did not himself emphasize) their ability to perceive a shortage, or similar kinds of error, tends to diminish as the level of intervention in the mixed economy increases. Although an intervention tends to produce disappointment and dissatisfaction, which are the manifestations of class-one learning, the pursuit of an interventionist policy might continue either because of the way in which an interventionist ideology *interprets* a given set of facts, or because something hampers the *perception* of the negative consequences of an intervention.[31] Let us assume that a person's ideology does not significantly affect his ability to perceive a class-one error resulting from an intervention, although this is certainly possible. (I discuss the issue of perception later in the chapter.) Under this assumption, a statist would be just as likely or unlikely as a libertarian to perceive the shortage that follows the implementation of a price ceiling. His ideology, however, would make a difference in the interpretation of that problem. In an ideological climate in which benevolent public choosers are reluctant to use political means, were the same fact (a shortage) to become known, it would be more likely to be interpreted as a failure of the initial policy than of some aspect of the market process.

Thus, given a strong ideological preference for additional intervention among sufficient numbers of public choosers, an internal logic – consisting of negative unintended consequences with the entrepreneurial and ideological responses to them – will sustain the interventionist process. With a predisposition on the part of public choosers (which all need not share with equal intensity) to view favorably (or at least not oppose) interventionist solutions to perceived socio-economic problems, the negative consequences of intervention and the accompanying entrepreneurial adjustments, in both the market and governmental processes, foster a tendency toward state expansion that encounters little resistance even among those whom it will ultimately harm. Moreover, the discoordination that follows state expansion prompts changes in ideological preferences (in a manner that I will describe in a moment) that support further state expansion through intervention as a remedy.[32] Should ideological conditions and entrepreneurial alertness eventually enable public choosers to realize that the source of the discrepancy between outcomes and intent stems directly from interventionism itself, two responses are possible, both of which entail the rejection of interventionism in favor of some more coherent doctrine. One is to embrace a more comprehensive form of collectivism, and the other is to reject collectivistic solutions in favor of a purer form of capitalism. However it finally manifests itself, the *denouement* of the entire interventionist process will generally take some time to happen (for reasons that I explain in the three sections that follow the next subsection).

The logic of ideological change

If ideology is essentially a matter of personal preference, then from the standpoint of standard economic methodology, which takes preferences as a given, a *completely* endogenous economic explanation of ideological change may be an unreachable goal. On the other hand, a completely exogenous account of ideological change would hardly be an explanation at all. The process of ideological change that I outline here departs somewhat from standard methodology in that it makes ideological change partly endogenous. Only partly so, however, because it also includes a crucial role for the indeterminacy of (exogenous) genuine choice, especially at what I will in a later section term the "nodal points" of the interventionist process. The factors that influence the ideological preferences governing individual choices are therefore both endogenous and exogenous in nature. Although these choices reflect exogenous and indeterminate factors, the politico-economic circumstances surrounding them influence ideological preferences among public choosers in broadly predictable ways. How, then, does the present analysis combine endogenous and exogenous elements to explain ideological change?

A given citizen's utility depends, of course, on his experience of a myriad of different things. For the purposes of the present analysis, let us focus on only one of the factors that relate to the political life of a given citizen in his capacity as a public chooser. This is his *moral aversion to the use of political means at the margin* (moral aversion) to redistribute or acquire wealth.

Assume that each citizen is a purposeful, goal-directed actor who seeks to improve his perceived condition in the context of partial ignorance. A *marginal change* in ideological preference is a response to changes in the constraints that a citizen faces in trying

115

to achieve the socio-economic conditions consistent with his ideology, while at the same time his underlying ideological preference remains constant. That is, while the subjective trade-off between public and private provision of services at different levels of utility for a given citizen remains unchanged, changes in the perceived relative cost[33] of public versus private provision can alter the margin of analysis. For the present analysis, the most important source of such changes in the relative cost of provision will be errors on the part of government in the calculation of the quantity, quality, or price of the service in question, which in turn lead to an increase in the level of participation in the political process. Thus, the two factors I focus on here that could cause a reduction in moral aversion are *errors in public policy* and the *number of other citizens perceived to use political means.*[34]

According to standard economic theory, what keeps small-scale interpersonal social relations from succumbing to the perverse incentives of the "prisoners' dilemma" (i.e., the temptation to cheat opportunistically on an agreement) is the tendency for most of these relations to be on-going and repetitive. Placing the prisoners' dilemma in such a "supergame" setting, in which players find themselves in a similar set of circumstances again and again, they might realize that following certain social rules and conventions (such as, for example, those upon which Glazer's "fine structure of society" is based) will lead all players to choose the socially optimal strategy (Axelrod 1984). In the context of the present discussion, should the cost of observing social taboos against gaining personally from intervention (i.e., moral aversion) exceed the benefits of observing them, the constraints of the supergame will begin to weaken.

When a public-policy error takes place, whether costly or beneficial to a given public chooser, such as when the taxes imposed on him to finance a public good are set either too high or too low, the relative cost of political action falls and/or the relative benefit rises. This is because, *ceteris paribus*, the public chooser will have an incentive to engage in political action either to correct an error that harms him or to retain an intervention that works in his favor. In this way his resistance to taking such action will be lowered. Should he actually enter the political process, this will have the important side-effect of increasing the number of actors whom others might perceive to be using political means. This secondary effect represents an added force that further

116

increases the likelihood that others will become participants in the political process. Thus, an intervention, insofar as it disrupts the relative values that actors with only partial knowledge rely on to carry out their independently formulated plans, causes errors in public policy. Such errors increase the likelihood that private actors will engage in or, at the least, not resist, political action.

The incentive that public choosers have to increase their political participation because of public-policy errors result in marginal changes in ideological preference. The secondary effect operating externally through the number of participants in the political process represents an *endogenous shift* in ideological preference. Thus, for example, because changes in the tax law make it less worthwhile for private individuals to donate to a private college, its administrators and board decide to trade-off some independence for financial security and accept a government subsidy (reflecting a marginal change in ideological preference). This not only increases its own participation in the political process – e.g., by actively seeking a government subsidy – but it also reduces the aversion of other private (perhaps non-academic) institutions to accepting government funding, even though the tax-law change may not even affect the latter directly (reflecting a total change in ideological preference). Moreover, the college's own resistance to the use of political means is doubly reduced: first, directly because of its acceptance of the subsidy (marginal change), and, second, because its administrators and board perceive that others are now also accepting government funding (total change).[35]

While I may have given the impression that ideological change plays something of a supporting rather than an initiating role in the interventionist process, once in motion an ideology favorable at the margin to further intervention sustains that process. Without the added impetus provided by shifts in ideological preference, the motive force of the ideological dynamic would probably, but not necessarily, be expended long before the system had moved far enough along the politico-economic spectrum to reach a major system-wide crisis. But a shift in ideological preference can be either an exogenous or an endogenous occurrence. A wholly *exogenous* shift can take place at any time. The interventionist process, however, is particularly prone to exogenous shifts at what I call the "nodal points" of the interventionist process – the occasions in which circumstances compel public choosers to decide whether to continue or repeal interventionist policies. The attributes of these nodal points is the topic of the next section.

Crisis and change in the interventionist process[36]

Aside from the two world wars, from the perspective of political economy perhaps the principal watershed events of the twentieth century are the Bolshevik revolution in 1917, the world-wide depression of the 1930s, and the fall of "communism" in the late 1980s and early 1990s. In the United States, the Great Depression and the governmental response to it, Johnson's "war on poverty" of the 1960s, and the stagflation of the late 1970s, represent some of the watersheds in the history of American political economy. (Perhaps the "Reagan revolution" of the 1980s might someday in retrospect also be seen as an historical turning point.) These events are watersheds in the sense that each seemed to define anew the role of government and the uses of state power. Usually, though not always, these new definitions brought an increase either in the power and extent of the state, or in the scope and intensity of government activity. That is, these events resulted either in greater and often novel governmental activity and intervention into the sphere of private exchange and action, which was most often the case, or, less often, a dramatic reduction in that power. While no single theory can presume fully and satisfactorily to explain episodes in human history that are the outcome of a complex conjunction of forces, it is reasonable to expect of a particular theoretical framework that it be able to detect the presence of a common thread that not only unites these events in some non-trivial fashion, but also accounts for at least some of their more salient features.

One implication of the discussion in this book so far is that the combination of government direction and market forces in the mixed economy tends to produce instability in the politico-economic system.[37] This instability, consisting as it does of coordination problems and dwindling financial reserves, breeds crises of varying scope and severity. These crises, in turn, represent *nodal points* in the development of public policy – i.e., important opportunities for rethinking policy that could lead either to further state expansion or to a reversal of that trend. The existence of significant plan discoordination creates the conditions for a crisis, which involves the failure of policies to achieve their specific objectives (strong version), or the policy-induced creation of highly undesirable outcomes (weak version), or the general breakdown of the politico-economic system as a whole (general version). A crisis occurs when a critical proportion of public choosers actually perceive one or more of these conditions to prevail with respect to a policy or social institution they deem of fundamental social importance.[38] Over time the mixed economy may be subject to many such episodes of crisis followed by relative calm, because the full recognition of the ultimate source of these episodes in the inner contradictions of interventionism, both as doctrine and actual policy, tends to entail a rather slow learning procedure (for reasons I examine, below). The remainder of this section will argue that, although a crisis, particularly a major one, could serve to stimulate this learning procedure and make more apparent the origin of the local and systemic problems in question through a shift in ideological preference, certain obstacles hinder public choosers" perception of that origin especially as crises spread and intensify. Moreover, if they do perceive it, this might not be enough to overcome the prevailing statist ideology, or it might be too late for them to take effective action to preserve the existing politico-economic order.

The decision public choosers confront during each of these critical episodes or nodal points in the interventionist process is whether to continue to endorse the overall policy of interventionism in some form, which would lead to a debate over what kind of interventionist response would be appropriate to cope with the effects of the crisis; or to reject interventionism, in whole or in part, which would lead to a debate over the best way to decontrol the politico-economic system, or at least that part of it in most need of reform. In short, the relevant alternatives are the familiar ones of more economic freedom and less intervention, on the one hand, or more intervention and an extension of collectivistic methods, on the other. Once again, however there must come a point on the road to collectivism, if that is in fact the road chosen, when incremental changes in public policy will be insufficient to improve social, political, and economic conditions, and more radical measures will be needed.[39]

Delays in learning owing to complexity and ignorance

That point, however, will tend to occur quite late in the expansionary phase, i.e., as the system approaches collectivism. There are several factors that determine the timing.

Contrary outcomes, internal contradictions, and ideology

First of all, two conditions are necessary (though not sufficient) for the emergence of a crisis. The first is what I will term the *perception of contrary outcomes*: the relevant public choosers (i.e., those whose decisions largely determine the content of a policy) find the outcomes of intervention in some way and to some extent contrary to those that they intended (i.e., a form of class-one learning). Drug-enforcement officials, for example, might find that stricter enforcement of narcotics laws and greater expenditure of resources toward that end appear to be counter-productive or less effective than expected in stemming the growth of the illicit-drug trade. The second condition (also a form of class-one learning) I will term the *perception of internal contradictions*: the relevant public choosers realize that these, and perhaps other contrary outcomes that they may have noticed elsewhere in the system, are the consequences of the very policies they are trying to implement, so that those policies, or the set of complementary policies of which they are a part, contain inherent flaws that compromise their success in some important way.

Even if both of these conditions are met, however, the resulting crisis does not mean that public choosers will necessarily reject the policy in favor of more radical alternatives. For example, were drug-enforcement officials to realize that prohibiting the consumption of certain narcotics, by driving up the benefits of the illicit-drug trade relative to the costs, was itself responsible for higher crime rates and other social maladies (Thornton 1991), they and their supporters might nevertheless conclude that tougher sanctions should instead be placed on the sellers of the drugs, or that they could better control drug consumption by spending more on the enforcement of existing sanctions. They might not yet be ready to embrace either making consumption of those narcotics a capital offense or complete decriminalization.

In a crisis, public choosers will thus have to decide how and to what extent they should challenge existing policies. As we have seen, this decision will have much to do with their ideological preferences, which color the interpretation of the information they perceive.[40] Movements in the relative cost of government intervention cause marginal changes in ideological preference that, along with changes in the structure of these preference themselves, will determine the future direction of the interventionist process. It is important to keep in mind that the speed and direction of endogenous ideological changes are largely a function of how public choosers perceive the costs and benefits of further intervention, and that this in turn depends on how clearly they see the link between intervention and the problems it creates. It is entirely possible then that, as the market process and public policy begin seriously to conflict, public choosers' perceptions will be too blurred to allow them to select the proper solution.

Complexity and discoordination

This implies that whether the environment is ripe for radical change also depends on the discernment of public choosers. In addition then to frustrated intentions and appropriate changes in the ideological milieu, another necessary condition for the significant discontinuities in the demand for intervention that take place at nodal points in the interventionist process is a high degree of entrepreneurial alertness on the part of public choosers. Unfortunately, the circumstances generated within the interventionist process hinder exactly the kind of entrepreneurial discovery that would lead to the recognition of contrary outcomes, internal contradictions, and the shortcomings of interventionist doctrine. While intuition might lead us to expect that public choosers' enthusiasm for interventionism should cool as they become aware of failures in government policy – i.e., the persistent errors and disruptions that accompany attempts to address alleged market failure – two factors tend to cloud their perception of its inner contradictions.

First, the interventionist order grows in *complexity* as government activity grows in scope. Growing complexity in turn runs up against the "bounded rationality"[41] of decision-making public choosers. Every intervention, by further complicating the environment within which they operate, increases the computational complexity of the problem-situations which public choosers must solve. In this environment, given the cognitive limitations of the human mind, keeping track of even those consequences of past interventions that are predictable in principle, in order to intervene effectively in the future, becomes increasingly difficult. Taken as a whole, the depth and scope of the computational problems in an expanding interventionist order make the planning and implementation of public policy an enormously complex affair (Wolf 1990: 77). Thus, as the process evolves, computational complexity significantly raises the *cost of information* to public choosers regarding the full depth and magnitude of the problems that surround interventionism, and this (combined with the ideological factors already mentioned) reduces the likelihood that they will push for the appropriate radical solutions.

Second, expanding government control will increasingly compromise the capacity of the price system to signal opportunities for the entrepreneurial discovery of error, especially class-two errors – i.e., errors of sheer ignorance of inefficiencies and opportunities lost that require dynamic learning to remove – that intervention has been creating. Recall that interventionism both increases the level of *discoordination* within the system (throwing you farther from your destination) and makes it more difficult to eliminate this discoordination (by damaging your compass). As the expansionary phase of the interventionist process develops, the incidence of plan inconsistencies and class-two errors will thus grow apace. And because the radical ignorance and inefficiencies contained in these class-two errors represent a greater challenge for entrepreneurs to discover even under a well-functioning price system, intervention-generated relative-price distortions will severely hamper the entrepreneurial discovery process. As discoordination worsens, prices will eventually become more obstacles than aids to discovery, making it ever more difficult for entrepreneurs in government and catallaxy to notice opportunities to improve voluntary social cooperation in general. It will also make it more difficult for public choosers to perceive the fundamental source of the systemic problems until the mixed economy has become fairly "mature," which will likely, but not necessarily, occur closer to the collectivist than to the laissez-faire-capitalist end of the politico-economic spectrum.

Complexity and the knowledge problem impinge on the interventionist process in yet another way. They do so in this case with respect to the analysis of the timing of crises at two levels – one having to do with the timing of *crises within* the mixed economy the other with the timing of *crisis of* the mixed economy, itself.

The first refers to particular areas or aspects of the catallaxy in which intervention has been relatively heavy, as, for example, in the case of airline or financial-services regulation (Morrison and Winston 1986; England and Huertas 1988). The term *micro-crisis* might be fitting here. Thus, public choosers (e.g., the voting public, the Civil Aeronautics Board, Congress) may not perceive regulation as the principal source of loss, inefficiency, and discoordination for a very long time because of the problems of complexity and masked radical ignorance. The second refers to the interventionist process as a whole and concerns what might be called a *macro-crisis*, a crisis of the entire mixed economy. It may be the culmination of a series of micro-crises. For example, Charles Murray traces the ominous situation facing much of urban America to a complex of policy failures that include, in addition to Great-Society anti-poverty programs, those that attempted to address public education, crime (especially illegal narcotics), unemployment, and the family (Murray 1984: 56–134). But if a micro-crisis is difficult to perceive and correct, a macro-crisis is much more so. First, the latter takes place at a higher level of abstraction – i.e., awareness of a systemic failure requires more powerful theoretical lenses than simple perception or personal experience alone can provide. Second, a macro-crisis occurs only when public choosers recognize that the systemic failure has its genesis in the inner contradictions of interventionism. Moreover, macro-crises, such as those that follow from expansionary monetary policy or reckless deficit spending, may themselves be of various levels of severity and also cumulative in nature. At some point, however, micro- and lower-level macro-crises multiply to such an extent that the recognition at some level of a systemic failure becomes *inevitable* (i.e., an instance of class-one learning). This is so especially in conjunction with the exhaustion of the "reserve fund" that I describe below.

Ideological preferences and the combined problems of complexity and price distortions throughout the system will thus tend to hamper public choosers from discovering the contradictions of interventionism until they become too extensive and severe to overlook. Of course, from the standpoint of public choosers, the best opportunity to make this discovery is when the politico-economic system has not deviated significantly from laissez-faire capitalism, since at that point the level of complexity and the magnitude of discoordination caused by interventionism would be relatively low, and the ideological commitment to keeping the state minimal would be relatively strong. On the other hand, precisely because the problems that interventionism creates at this stage are relatively small, the incentive to alter public policy is correspondingly weak. Should public choosers miss this opportunity the rapid growth in complexity and discoordination that attends the pursuit of interventionism and state expansion will likely delay their realization, possibly until quite late in (i.e., near the collectivist pole of) the interventionist process. That is, because of the time it takes for the interventionist process to reach the point at which significant numbers of public choosers begin radically to reject interventionism, the mixed economy will likely have moved a considerable distance away from laissez-faire capitalism. One would thus expect that as the mixed economy approaches a fully collectivistic and, most likely, a centrally planned system (Prychitko 1988), recognition of the untenability of interventionism (and the merits of either complete collectivism or laissez-faire capitalism) are for some time offset by masked radical ignorance/ discoordination and the enormous informational costs owing to bounded rationality/complexity.

In the market process, entrepreneurial profits come mainly from discovering gainful opportunities to improve social cooperation by removing radical ignorance and plan inconsistencies. The sort of "gainful opportunities" that appear in the interventionist process, however, can at best serve to improve coordination of the governmental process, which, as the reader will recall from Chapter 3, is normatively ambiguous. At worst they stifle the entrepreneurial-competitive process and promote the discovery of superfluous profit opportunities in the catallaxy, both of which tend to lead to further intervention, systemic complexity, and discoordination as long as the statist mentality prevails. Eventually, however, complexity and coordination problems will grow so serious and widespread that they will begin directly to affect a critical proportion of the advocates of interventionism through specific incidences as well as systemic failure. Under these circumstances, and in particular when what Mises termed the *reserve fund* – i.e., the accumulated private wealth out of which interventionist projects are financed – becomes exhausted, systemic failure and crisis become inevitable, and public choosers will no longer have the luxury of putting off making radical changes in the politico-economic system.

Summary

An expansion of intervention causes negative unintended consequences and frustrates intentions in roughly the following sequence: (1) Actors in the catallaxy respond to the resulting distortions in relative prices, internally and externally, in ways that tend to reassert their preferences. (2a) The government sector is slow to adjust to these unanticipated events owing primarily to the sluggishness of its learning procedures. (2b) Some of the responses of private entrepreneurs in the first round negatively affect other private actors, who then may support additional intervention, depending on their ideological preferences at the margin. (2c) By inducing changes in ideology (marginal and total) and compromising the price system, intervention generates class-one and a disproportionate number of class-two errors within both government and catallaxy, which represents an increase in discoordination. (3) The additional intervention, if it is forthcoming, will set the first two stages into motion again, especially as public choosers discover and misinterpret class-one errors, and further reduce the reserve fund. (4a) Continued intervention into the market process also further lowers the reliability of the price system indirectly through the erosion of property rights (see Chapter 5 for a more complete analysis). (4b) Problems relating to bounded rationality in the context of spiraling complexity will also appear. (5a) The long-term effect of gradual but continual increases in intervention is to expand the sphere of government over the catallaxy, which means that bureaucratic management will affect a larger share of the politico-economic system. (5b) This implies that prices will, in general, be driven ever farther from their equilibrium values, which further reduces the likelihood of entrepreneurial correction of class-one and especially class-two errors. (5c) Another implication of rising complexity and the market process's diminishing capacity to utilize contextual knowledge is that public choosers will have difficulty perceiving and recognizing the source of minor systemic crises until quite late in the interventionist process.

The crisis of the mixed economy: "depletion" of the reserve fund

An essential point in the social philosophy of interventionism is the existence of an inexhaustible fund which can be

squeezed forever. The whole system of interventionism col-
lapses when this fountain is drained off: The Santa Claus
principle liquidates itself.

(Mises 1966: 858)

We have observed a number of times already that all forms of
intervention – direct redistribution, regulation, and nationalization
– entail forced transfers. To reiterate, this fact of political life is
important to this study mainly because it helps us to understand
better the timing, as well as the inevitability, of the ultimate crisis[42]
toward which the interventionist process tends, rather than for its
power to reveal the interests and incentives motivating public
choosers. Hence, while it may be true that "the essence of the
interventionist policy is to take from one group and to give to
another" (ibid.: 855), to understand the political economy of mixed
economies we are not thereby obliged to assume that the primary
intent of every intervention is to redistribute income and wealth.
Monetary and fiscal policy, for example, do require redistributive
effects (e.g., "forced saving") in order to stimulate or dampen the
macroeconomy, but this does not necessarily imply that their ultimate goal is to transfer income. An analysis of public policy that
refrains from always inferring intentions from outcomes not only
remains legitimate and useful, but it is in accord with the realities
of social complexity and radical ignorance.

Nevertheless, it is important from the perspective of a theory
of interventionism that we do recognize that an "essential point"
in the doctrine of interventionism is that, in some sense, "the higher
income and wealth of the more affluent part of the population is
a fund which can be freely used for the improvement of the
conditions of the less prosperous" (ibid.: 855). What the supporters
of interventionism overlook is that if a significant proportion of
public choosers come to acquire such an attitude, it will ignite a
chain of political actions that will tend to consume the very pri-
vately-generated reserve fund out of which the state finances its
interventionist policy.[43] Moreover, as I tried to argue in the previous section, by the time public choosers finally discover and
fully appreciate the link between interventionism and the social
and economic problems that it engenders, it is likely to be too late
in the interventionist process for them to move quickly enough to
avert a systemic breakdown. The same is also true of the foresight
of public choosers with respect to the consequences of depleting

the reserve fund. That is, complexity and discoordination will again result in the same kind of bounded rationality and dulled perceptions, this time regarding public policy's too rapid consumption of the reserve fund, that combine to delay public choosers' rejection of the "Santa Claus principle" until it is too late. The size of the available reserve fund thus acts as the *ultimate* constraint on interventionism. If accumulating complexity and discoordination problems fail to produce the final crisis of the mixed economy, the depletion of the reserve fund will.

Replenishing the reserve fund

Of course, the rate at which the reserve fund is drained is only one of the two factors that determine its size at any given time. The other obviously centers on the ability of the catallaxy to continue to create wealth rapidly enough to keep the reserve fund replenished in the face of the increasingly heavy costs of interventionism. This in turn relates to the efficiency of production and to the responsiveness of the entrepreneurial-competitive process in discovering profit opportunities by both detecting and avoiding plan discoordination.

With respect first to the marginal productivity of labor, a diminution in the reserve fund closely corresponds to a reduction in the stock of capital, as both occur when the rate of net private savings falls and depreciated capital is not fully replaced. And since *ceteris paribus* a reduction in the capital stock will cause marginal, and eventually total, labor productivity to drop, taxing the reserve fund to finance intervention will have a doubly negative impact on the production of private wealth (Mises 1966: 844–5). Moreover, the negative incentive effects of government control will also reduce labor-force participation and total product. (This phenomenon is discussed in greater detail in Chapter 5.)

About the inefficiency of production in a heavily controlled economy *per se*, little needs to be said here. Complexity and discoordination problems make production inefficient while at the same time making it difficult to discover inefficiencies. Thus, wealth production will tend to remain below capacity. Indeed, progressive intervention, quite apart from its impact on the dynamic aspects of competition discussed in the next paragraph, will (to use the language of standard theory) draw the system farther away from the production possibilities frontier.

With respect to the responsiveness of the entrepreneurial-competitive process, as we have seen, a mixed economy that approaches full collectivism is subject to growing complexity and chronic discoordination owing to the near absence of a spontaneously adjusting price system that tends systematically to reflect the knowledge and expectations of a myriad of actors in society who are perforce anonymous to one another. The former Soviet Union, for example, was a highly mixed economy in which interventionism was practiced on a scale much larger than, but not fundamentally different in kind from, that of the political capitalism practiced in Western democracies.[44] The lack of sophisticated domestic markets for capital and other vital factors of production severely hampered the spontaneous operation of (largely illegal) entrepreneurial-competitive forces in the former Soviet Unions's nongovernmental sector. Economic policy-makers had to depend on prices established in domestic black markets as well as the comparatively freer markets of non-communist countries,[45] which, in the manner explained in Chapter 3, served as information supplements in a system in which official domestic prices were unreliable guides for planning. Thus, despite massive intentional and unintentional redistributions (generally from more to less productive lines of activity in the politico-economic system), its reliance on black markets and the information it was able to glean from beyond its borders helped the Soviet Union to survive. As recent events have demonstrated, however, these less hampered markets (and whatever foreign aid it received from the West) were insufficient to sustain the reserve fund against the cumulative effects of persistent discoordination and error. Thus, whereas the static efficiency effects of interventionism pull the economy away from the production possibilities frontier, these dynamic discoordination effects actually collapse the frontier itself.

Systemic breakdown and the feasibility of radical reform

Our understanding of how certain social and economic institutions promote the entrepreneurial-competitive process suggests that a relatively collectivistic system, such as the former Soviet Union, must have been, in an abstract but meaningful sense, persistently "farther away" from full plan coordination (with respect to its own set of underlying data) than is typically the case in systems such as that of the United States. If it is also true that "informational problems grow as the distance from equilibrium grows," and that "the strength of the tendency toward equilibrium decreases the farther we are from equilibrium and vice versa" (Rizzo 1990: 24), this might help to explain why a systemic breakdown often presages a radical change in public policy in the interventionist process. First, without a breakdown, even if public choosers discover the fundamental source of the intervention-induced problems, they may simply be incapable of reforming the system, since, far from equilibrium where informational problems are severe, any *piecemeal* policy action would likely only make matters worse and in unanticipated ways. Second, jettisoning the imbroglio of regulation- and transfer-related rules and programs in their entirety, as well as completely breaking up the bureaucratic and other entrenched interests that exist in the interventionist environment at the expense of the wealth-producing sector of society, may be a necessary precondition for successful radical reform. If a radical system-wide "purging" may be the only workable policy (though still extremely difficult, politically[46]), then perhaps the most favorable circumstance under which this could take place is if the entire politico-economic system has collapsed or is on the verge of doing so. Public choosers could then effect the necessary radical change when the politico-economic apparatus is re-started.[47]

Measurement and measurement problems

An empirical measure of the reserve fund available to a mixed economy (local or global) would, of course, be highly desirable. An apparently straightforward indicator, or one that at least reflects its magnitude, might be the total exploitable private wealth in a politico-economic system at a given time. One would of course be interested not only in the size of the fund at any given time, but also, as we have just seen, in the rate at which it grows relative to the growth rate of governmental spending at all levels. If the fund is being depleted at a rate faster than it is being added to, in the absence of outside support its exhaustion and the accompanying systemic breakdown is inevitable. In the absence of accurate data, or reliable statistical estimates, actually measuring the reserve fund and its rate of growth may be impracticable, although with such data in principle it might be roughly approximated.

In a highly interventionist mixed economy, however, official or reported estimates of private wealth may tell an incomplete story. First, as already mentioned, in such economies the unofficial sector often contributes a significant share to the stock of private wealth. Not only does this sector serve in this way to replenish the reserve fund, it also functions as a safety valve that attempts "to fill in the gaps created by the official system" (Boettke 1993: 65). Somewhat ironically, it is the high degree of discoordination within the governmental process as interventionism expands that is responsible for the official ineptness and moral decay that give rise to "black markets" and that for a time delay the inevitable crisis. Thus Mises observed: "But for the inefficiency of the law-givers and the laxity, carelessness, and corruption of many of the functionaries, the last vestiges of the market economy would have long since disappeared" (1966: 859).

In addition to black markets, infusions of foreign aid may give analysts an unrealistic picture of the financial viability of the system. Subsidizing the reserve fund of economic "basket cases" can delay the onset, or reduce the severity and frequency, of their various crises.[48]

Finally, in a mixed economy that is quite far from laissez-faire capitalism, owing to the discoordinating effects of heavy intervention, the system will also have reached a station perilously far from full equilibrium,[49] so that rather than promoting catallactic discovery, whatever remains of the price system will likely cause more chaos than coordination. In this situation, as we have seen, the incidence of radical ignorance is high owing to the difficulties of class-two or "dynamic" learning in a highly distorted price system. The class-two errors and complexity generated by interventionism will increasingly limit the accessibility of the theoretical total reserve fund. In the waning days of the Soviet Union, for example, it was reported that a high percentage of its agricultural harvest lay rotting in the fields while large numbers of nearby city-dwellers experienced chronic hunger, owing to the lack of coordination within distributional networks. Hence, while the reserve fund is the ultimate constraint on the interventionist process, a great deal of inaccessible wealth may still exist when the state runs out of finance. This additional limit on the reserve fund is the reason why I have modified the discussion of the exhaustion of the reserve fund with the term "accessible," and it is why the word "depletion" appears in quotation marks at the beginning of this subsection.

Example: Business-cycle policy

Because it illustrates so many of the concepts discussed thus far (save for class-two learning), the Mises–Hayek theory of the business cycle might be considered a paradigm for both micro- and macro-type crises. This theory explains that monetary authorities (the relevant public choosers in this case) who deliberately expand credit in order to generate or maintain rates of economic growth that they deem acceptable, will both create and encounter a complex and not wholly desirable chain of events.

In bare outline,[50] when monetary authorities artificially inject credit into the banking system (e.g., through open-market operations) the consequent increase in the overall supply of money and credit *ceteris paribus* lowers the market rate of interest for loanable funds below the rate that would more accurately reflect the actual time preferences of savers. One of the short-term effects of this sort of credit expansion is the tendency to stimulate investment in production processes that involve more time-intensive production at the expense of those that involve less time-intensive production. Roughly speaking, credit expansion discourages production for consumption in the relatively near future in favor of production for consumption in the relatively distant future. Because the theory assumes that credit expansion itself does not systematically influence the saving–consumption preferences of actors, it predicts at least two consequences that benevolent public choosers would not have originally intended: a general shortage of consumption goods and relatively higher prices in the near future, and a general surplus of consumption goods and relatively lower prices in the more distant future. Moreover, because at some time in the more distant future a general surplus of consumption goods will occur and time preferences will begin to reassert themselves by pushing up the interest rate, public choosers need to decide whether to cope with this condition, when it arises, through voluntary or political means – that is, whether or not to address the crisis through further intervention in the credit market or elsewhere. Here, ideology (and narrow self-interest as well, of course) is critical, and the decision contains, as we have already seen, an important element of exogenous indeterminacy. But since the cost of intervention in the minds of public choosers will have fallen owing to an increasing magnitude of error in monetary policy (resulting in a marginal change in ideological preference), and since authorities have already engaged in intervention, thus lowering the level of reluctance on the part of public choosers (resulting in a shift in ideology), endogenous ideological forces are likely to reinforce the propensity to increase rather than decrease the level of intervention and to offset whatever inclination there might be to resist further intervention. As Hayek and Mises have each remarked:

> It is probably entirely utopian to expect [central banks to contract credit] so long as general opinion still believes that it is the duty of central banks to accommodate trade and to expand credit as the increasing demands of trade require.
>
> (Hayek 1967b: 117)

> [T]he banks and monetary authorities are guided by the idea that the height of interest rates as the free loan market determines it is an evil, that it is the objective of a good economic policy to lower it, and that credit expansion is an appropriate means of achieving this end without harm to anybody but parasitic moneylenders.
>
> (Mises 1966: 573)

In addition, because their interactions are complicated and their effects unpredictable and remote, and because the resources of public choosers and their awareness are both limited, the ramifications of credit expansion (or of activist monetary policy generally) may be extremely difficult to detect and fully comprehend. If subsequent rounds of interventionist credit expansion do take place, the added intertemporal discoordination and dislocation will exacerbate the negative unintended effects that have already occurred. Because of this dislocation and discoordination, a steadfast pursuit of an interventionist monetary policy would eventually wreck the productive capacity of the catallaxy and drain the reserve fund as well. Following a progression of lower-level macro-crises, then, the interventionist process will eventually reach a point when a general crisis of the mixed economy, a major macro-crisis, will begin to threaten, at which time public choosers will have to decide the more fundamental issues of the role of government in the catallaxy and the desirable scope and magnitude of state activity (at least with respect to the vitally important aspect of monetary policy).

Micro-crises

The manipulation of money and credit in a developed mixed economy is a form of intervention fraught with such destructive potential, of course, because monetary exchange enters virtually every corner of catallactic activity. Similarly, wholesale nationalization of industry and comprehensive wage and price controls each in their own way profoundly disrupt the market process.[51] Less pervasive forms of intervention, such as drug prohibition or forced income transfers, may or may not by themselves also produce difficulties of macro-crisis proportions. We have seen how municipal housing policy (e.g., rent control, urban renewal, and zoning ordinances) can have unfortunate side-effects. Housing shortages, skyrocketing rents and real-estate prices, and homelessness are all to a significant extent the present-day fruits of failed interventionist urban policies of the past. Whether these will reach the magnitude of a macro-crisis, however, remains to be seen.[52] We can view macro-crises, crises *of* the mixed economy, as consisting of a series of lower-level crises, although the whole here is, as it were, greater than the sum of its parts.

The framework developed thus far also helps to explain how intervention leads to crises at the "micro level," the level of particular markets or lines of activity. The analysis of interventionism involves looking at the responses to an intervention in terms of the internal and external responses of various areas of the catallaxy as in the following sequence:

perceived problem in a → intervention in a → problems in a & b → intervention in b → another problem in a → another intervention in a → problems in a, b, & c → more intervention in a, b, & c → crisis in a → etc.

Our attention is drawn in this feedback process both to external responses and to the original target area of the intervention and the subsequent internal responses that occur there. What Jonathan Hughes memorably describes as the "hydralike nature" of the problem (1991: 136), comes through clearly here.

An interventionist macro-crisis occurs when so many areas of the catallaxy are brought under the policy of piecemeal control that the entire system threatens to breakdown. The period between the occurrence of new problems in a given area and the decision of whether or not to intervene further represents a nodal point.

After a certain point of persistent intervention, a crisis will occur in a given market.

Imagine how the waves that radiate from a stone dropped into a small pool, after encountering a large obstruction (such as the edge of the pool), return to their origin, and in the meantime set up patterns that reinforce or interact with the original wave. If there are no other disruptions such as another falling stone, natural forces would eventually smooth out the ripples and return the pool to calm. To complete the analogy, therefore, in addition to the interacting wave patterns that result from a single dropped stone (which might represent the purely catallactic responses to a particular intervention), in the interventionist process it is as if the ripples from the original stone were somehow to induce other stones to fall elsewhere in the pond (perhaps thrown by well-meaning but misguided people who want to stabilize the pond's surface), which sets up patterns of disruption even more complex and sustained. Or, more relevant to the interventionist process, the patterns of disruption will be sustained only so long as public choosers support interventionist solutions to the problems that previous intervention has created.

Interventionist ideological preferences and a lack of entrepreneurial alertness will support interventionist solutions until the level of discoordination becomes so high that successful planning in the area in question is no longer feasible, or the area becomes a serious bottleneck in the market process, such that it is brought to a point of crisis. The area will cease to operate effectively when the wealth of those who financially sustain it (e.g., private investment, private purchases, or public support) is dissipated because resources migrate to other areas of the mixed economy and because discoordination has curtailed wealth production in it. This is analogous to the exhaustion of the reserve fund at the macro level. Before reaching a point of crisis, however, public choosers will probably have had several opportunities to renounce their interventionist ideology (which are the nodal points of the interventionist process within this area).

The history of the American health-care industry can serve to illustrate the complex forces that early acts of intervention can set into motion. The genesis of one current problem in the health-care industry lies in the wage and price controls that the United States government imposed during World War II. Because of the controls, employers were induced to compete for scarce labor (owing to conscription) by offering tax-exempt medical benefits that were outside the domain of the wage and price control board. Congress's unsuccessful attempt to repeal the tax-exempt status of employer-provided medical benefits preserved the curious link between employment and health insurance that has, among other things, inefficiently tied workers to their jobs, raised the real cost of health insurance to part-time and self-employed workers, and engendered much of the current anxiety many workers feel over the possibility of being unable to obtain health insurance because of "pre-existing conditions" (Wasley 1992: 55–7).

But other aspects of the health-care plight spring from seemingly disparate sources that are, however, linked via the dynamics of the interventionist process. Much of the perceived need for employer-provided health-care benefits, for instance, arose from escalating medical costs, which in turn arose largely from government regulations at the local as well as the national level. The licensing of doctors has restricted the supply of health-care providers both by artificially limiting the number of those who can practice medicine and by broadly defining what in fact constitutes that practice, thereby excluding competent and effective health-care alternatives to licensed physicians. The requirement to obtain "certificates of need" in order to build new plant and equipment in the health-care industry restricts the number of hospitals and medical clinics. State health authorities continue to lengthen the list of required benefits that health insurance must carry by law, thereby increasing the cost of insurance. A somewhat less obvious factor driving up health-care costs has been the rising rate of violent crime in the United States, which has increased the cost of, among other things, emergency-room services in hospitals and drawn resources away from illness not related to violent crime.[53] Much of this violent crime can be traced to the so-called "culture of poverty." A part of this problem in turn centers on poor, young, and unwed mothers on public assistance who are burdened with having to raise their children in the absence of a legal and resident father, owing in part to the perverse incentives that characterize AFDC (Aid to Families with Dependent Children) (Murray 1984: 154–66). Some social scientists maintain that children from such homes demonstrate a greater-than-average difficulty in absorbing traditional social norms and mores, including those that promote respect for the rights of others.[54] In addition, this culture of poverty has put such pressure on government health-care provision that medicaid (the public program that channels funding for health-care to the poor) and medicare are currently the fastest growing item in the federal budget (Sharp *et al.* 1994: 240–2).

These interventions, diverse and apparently unrelated, are nevertheless linked through a logical dynamic that has generated a host of social and economic problems, only one of which we focus on here. They have combined to swell the cost of health-care provision in the United States to what many are now calling a crisis level. This has prompted a number of "solutions," most of which would involve more rather than less intervention (see Goodman and Musgrave 1992). As this sector represents a large part of the gross domestic product, 14 percent in 1994 and growing by most estimates (Sharp *et al.* 1994: 231), a crisis in the health-care industry would not *by itself* challenge the foundations of interventionism as a general policy or the system that embodies it. The next stage of the interventionist process, however, will involve either substantial deregulation or a significantly increased role for government in the provision of health care. The long-term consequences of the latter, considering its likely negative catallactic effects and given the prevailing ideological climate, could very well kindle a macro-crisis.

Overview of the exposition thus far

Let us now review the main features of the expansionary phase of the interventionist process. Beginning with a set of relative values (e.g., prices, opportunity costs, interest rates, etc.) and ideological preferences among public choosers, an act of intervention changes these initial conditions by modifying ideological preferences (marginally and totally) and disturbing relative values in unanticipated ways, thereby reducing the degree of coordination that might otherwise have existed among individual plans. Interventions produce such negative unintended consequences because (1) they exacerbate the knowledge problem by erecting barriers to entrepreneurial discovery and creating wholly superfluous lines of activity, (2) they increase social complexity and intensify bounded rationality, and (3) they produce a sequence of unintended surpluses and shortages. Emerging from the interaction of these forces is a new set of relative values and ideological preferences that serves as the context (i.e., a nodal point) in which public choosers must decide (exogenously) the next step in public policy. For reasons given earlier, there is a strong likelihood that public choosers will opt to address intervention-spawned problems with further intervention in some form. As the discoordination, error, and negative unintended consequences multiply, social cooperation through the price system, as well as the price system itself, begins seriously to breakdown on the one hand, while on the other hand the reserve fund out of which interventionist policies are financed becomes drained, either or both events heralding a general crisis of the mixed economy. At that point, interventionism having lost its legitimacy, there is no longer a middle ground. Public choosers must decide between more thorough-going variants of either capitalism or collectivism.

Finally, in the interventionist process as described in this book, vast expansion of political power and bureaucracy takes place, not necessarily because public choosers demand that result, but because the unexpected incentives and opportunities that intervention creates stimulate actions that bring it about. To explain state expansion, then, it is unnecessary to assume that individual actors are somehow purposefully striving to achieve collectivism or a particular version of the mixed economy, or even that they deliberately choose to extend political power for their own selfish ends in the sense of rent-seeking. What we do need to assume is that at least some have a strong preference for additional intervention, that they act entrepreneurially to opportunities that present themselves in the public and private sectors, and that they act in the context of social complexity and the knowledge problem. Well-intended and public-spirited intervention is entirely consistent with the interventionist process.

THE CONTRACTIONARY PHASE OF THE INTERVENTIONIST PROCESS

A theory of interventionism should address the dynamics of state contraction. These dynamics, however, are in most respects symmetrical to those found in the expansionary phase, and to the extent that the symmetry is exact or nearly so, I need not dwell on them. Thus, in very general terms, as the level of intervention into the catallaxy eases, property rights become more coherent and stable, prices become less distorted with respect to expectations and objective data, and entrepreneurial discovery is better able to perform its coordinative function amid lower levels of complexity and plan inconsistency. As I will explain in a moment, depending on how radically the system turns back toward laissez-faire, unintended consequences will again play an essential role in propelling the interventionist process. The pressure of ideological change will tend to reinforce the general movement toward laissez-faire through marginal changes and shifts in ideological preference (but with some important differences that I will address below and in the next chapter). The combined forces of relative-price adjustment and ideological change will operate on both the micro- and macro-economic levels. Meanwhile, revived intertemporal planning and production activity will rebuild the structure of production and replenish the reserve fund. But for those aspects of the contractionary phase that represent important breaks in the symmetry, it will be necessary to elaborate further.

As the reader is by now well aware, when the mixed economy reaches a major macro-crisis, public choosers must reject interventionism or else remain muddled in chaos. Since it is most likely that by that time the system will have reached a point approaching the collectivist end of the politico-economic spectrum, should public choosers and the public authorities who execute their choices decide to embrace a more thorough-going form of collectivism, this would entail a less drastic transformation than would be the case of a return to something approaching laissez-faire capitalism. Although the jump to collectivist central planning would naturally mark an important departure from interventionism both philosophically and in practice, in a certain sense it is just an acceleration of the more moderate tendency within the expansionary phase to substitute political for catallactic methods of exchange. After state expansion under an interventionist regime, should public choosers effect a revolutionary push toward some form of pure collectivism, the system would simply reach much sooner the position toward which it was already tending.[55] (Indeed, the present analysis would cast doubt on the possibility of a truly Fabian-style evolution into complete collectivism.)

Discontinuity

In the process of state expansion, government grows without anyone consciously intending for it to do so. In contrast, the decision to rein in and reverse the trend of state expansion is a deliberate one, consciously made given the ideology of and the information inevitably acquired by public choosers at the time of a macro-crisis. Because the circumstances of this decision demand radical and swift measures, the relative gradualism that generally characterizes the expansionary phase of the interventionist process (excluding war) will tend to contrast rather starkly to the contractionary phase, which is likely to involve, at least in its early stages, a considerable degree of discontinuity and unevenness. The contraction of interventionism following a macro-crisis tends not only to be more abrupt, but also to entail measures that are more sweeping. We would tend to see, for example, relative to the pace of the expansionary phase, widespread deregulation and decontrol of the catallaxy, an unprecedented reduction of income transfers, and the rapid sale of substantial portions of state-owned assets to the private sector.

Piecemeal "dis-intervention"

This does not mean, however, that the dynamics of contraction will necessarily lead to a complete return to laissez-faire capitalism. But it is especially important to note that if the *dis-intervention* (to coin an awkward but useful new word) is in this sense only partial, the same dynamics found in the expansionary phase of state activity to produce unwanted outcomes will emerge once again in the contractionary phase. Just as we can expect piecemeal intervention to create negative unintended consequences, piecemeal dis-intervention will do the same, and for similar reasons. Nodal points will again arise, at which stage public choosers must decide, based on their unfolding knowledge and ideological preferences, whether to address the unexpected problems by re-intervening or by further dis-intervention. Let us briefly consider some cases from recent experience that exemplify this phenomenon at the micro and macro levels of the interventionist process in order to identify the sources of these negative unintended consequences.

Consider the deregulation of airlines in the United States. In late 1978, Congress enacted the Airline Deregulation Act, which ended the Civil Aeronautics Board's authority over fares and flight routes as of January 1983 and transferred the Board's responsibilities for antitrust and international regulatory matters primarily to the Department of Transportation (Weiss and Klass, 1986: 45). The efforts to deregulate, however, stopped short of reducing government controls in related areas that provide complementary services, such as air-traffic control (still under FAA jurisdiction) and airports (mainly municipally owned) (ibid.: 68–9). Thus, while there have been no shortages of pilots, attendants, airplanes, fuel, and flights in the deregulated sector, serious congestion and safety problems persist in the still-regulated complementary areas. Public authorities, responding to public concern, have since periodically raised the issue of re-regulating the airlines (while proposals to deregulate these other areas appear not to be taken as seriously).

Bottlenecks appear to be one of the principal features of partial dis-intervention.[56] While decontrolled areas tend to respond vigorously to economic freedom, the complementary services needed to sustain increases in the production of wealth and income that typically accompany dis-intervention may not be forthcoming owing to the discoordination and artificial constraints hampering the still-controlled areas. With a few notable exceptions (e.g., the Czech Republic), recent efforts in Eastern Europe as well as the People's Republic of China to decentralize politico-economic power have caused serious bottlenecks in those areas of their respective economies that have not kept pace with free-market reforms made elsewhere in the system. In the case of China in particular, inflation and economic disruption were the unintended consequences of partial reform that began in the late 1970s after a serious macro-crisis, which led to the public discontent so brutally crushed in the summer of 1989.[57] In the former Soviet Union, a recent macro-crisis has produced sweeping political but very limited economic reforms. The absence of genuine radical reform, combined with a very unstable political environment, has generated a level of public unhappiness that raises the real possibility of a return to collectivism. Without further economic decentralization, however, serious social and economic dislocation and deterioration seem inevitable.

It appears that the more piecemeal and less radical the dis-intervention and reform, the more likely it will be that public choosers will elect to return to intervention. The inertia created by constraints operating in controlled areas can thwart the release of individual initiative and entrepreneurial alertness in the decontrolled areas, depending on how radical and sweeping the reforms actually are. This is because, in addition to incumbents who now have the opportunity to exercise a higher degree of initiative and alertness than they have before, outsiders possessing those qualities will also try to enter the decontrolled areas and, if successful, will add to the already mounting demands made on the suppliers of controlled complementary services. If the size of the controlled sector containing complementary services remains relatively large, discoordination will not only persist, but additional discoordination will likely appear owing to the serious bottlenecks that will tend to emerge. Under these circumstances, rapidly rising prices in the decontrolled sector are inevitable, with political pressure to reimpose price controls or some form of compulsory rationing almost irresistible. Although writing in a somewhat different context, the comments of a prominent expert on comparative economic systems is germane: "Arbitrarily selecting some targets while ignoring others can backfire and lead to the failure and discredit of the process of democratization and economic transformation" (Kornai 1990: 18). Thus, the severity of these bottlenecks appears to be directly related to the proportion of the catallaxy that is still subject to intervention – the larger the remaining public sector, the worse the problems tend to be.

Recidivism

While the dynamics of state expansion exhibit an almost inexorable quality, this appears less true of the dynamics of contraction. This is due, first, to the effect of a residual statist mentality that may yet color the ideological preferences of public choosers who will have only recently rejected interventionism. After years or decades of supporting interventionist policies, their proclivity to propose re-intervention in reaction to the problems that partial dis-intervention begets is still likely to be quite strong. Since the intensity of the ideological reversal among public choosers from a relatively statist to a more libertarian view largely determines how drastic or radical the actual movement away from collectivistic policies will be, the half-hearted commitment implicit in the piecemeal rejection of interventionism, and a correspondingly limited move toward laissez-faire, suggests that such policies are likely to be much less successful than more radical ones in achieving the long-term goals of dis-intervention. In 1990, for example, Vaclav Klaus, then finance minister of the former Czechoslovakia, remarked about efforts to "make a third way between capitalism and communism" that "we have tried this. We wanted to make a New Man, with only unselfish thoughts. I am afraid it is not possible" (Fund 1990).

Moreover, because of the wealth-creating initiative and alertness released by dis-intervention, the drain on the reserve fund will also begin to slow. As capital accumulation and net capital investment once again take place, the marginal and total productivity of labor will rise, adding to the reserve fund. Thus, as dis-intervention continues, the shrinking of the reserve fund will eventually reverse itself and even show a net gain. But this means that a financial constraint that might have kept public choosers from using political means to prevent the transition to a freer economic system from harming particular groups and individuals will begin to loosen. Given the aforementioned habits formed under state expansion, it would be especially hard for public choosers to refrain from using intervention to try to aid and protect those who might suffer during the transition. Old habits and better finances thus feed the propensity for public choosers to re-adopt interventionist policies.

If, however, the dis-intervention is sufficiently radical, a momentum will tend to build within the ideological and catallactic dynamics that strengthens the tendency of public choosers to decide in favor of less intervention (though of course this decision is still not wholly endogenous). The negative unintended consequences of partial dis-intervention will become fewer and the inclination to deal with them through the use of political means will gradually diminish, and the benefits of dis-intervention will become more apparent as higher rates of saving and capital accumulation eventually increase the supply of consumer goods. Indeed, the middle and latter stages of this phase of the interventionist process – if indeed public choosers permit the system to advance that far in the direction of laissez-faire – will therefore mirror the steady, cumulative character of the expansionary phase.

If the system does evolve into a form of minimal-state laissez-faire capitalism, however, does this spell the end of the interventionist process? For reasons that I develop in Chapter 6, this is not necessarily the case. There I argue that, while the possibility exists for a stable minimal state, there are latent forces within even the minimal state that will tend to destabilize and prod it back onto the interventionist path.

THE INTERVENTIONIST PROCESS AS A SPONTANEOUS ORDER

In Chapter 3, I characterized the market process – along with most of the customs, rules, and social institutions that combine to promote it – as a spontaneous order. (This follows the approach of Hayek (1967a), whose own investigations into the nature of social order build on the conceptual foundations laid by Carl Menger (1985).) It is likewise valid to describe the interventionist process as a spontaneous order, despite the prominent role played within it by deliberate, though not comprehensive, socio-economic planning; or by what Hayek (1978) has termed "constructivism." Interventionism gives rise to a social process that is the "result of human action but not of human design" (Hayek 1967a: 96–105).

The "spontaneity" of the interventionist process in this context refers to both its *genesis* and its *self-sustainability*. To begin with, the interventionist process does not require a deliberate act on the part of any public chooser to set it into motion. While the assumption of benevolence may or may not be sufficient to establish this fact, it is certainly the case that, given the level of complexity and the division of knowledge involved, a human mind could no more comprehensively plan the interventionist process than it could the market process. It is nevertheless possible that public choosers familiar with the consequences of distorting interferences with the market process could, with sufficient political power, intentionally initiate an interventionist process. They would, however, be unable to control or even predict what would emerge in any but the most general way. In any event, such a deliberate act is, once again, unnecessary for the genesis of that process.

Next, the interventionist process is self-sustaining in the sense that it has the capacity to organize and regenerate itself. The notion of a self-"organizing" interventionist process might at first appear to present a paradox, since the object of this book has been to study the instability of mixed economies. The organization in question here, however, refers to the underlying logic of the process, which consists, as we have seen, of entrepreneurial adjustments to distortions in the politico-economic system that take place in the context of an evolving matrix of ideological preferences. The dynamics of that logic are what drives and directs – or organizes – the interventionist process.

The self-generating property, in turn, relates to the capacity of the interventionist process (which embraces both government *and* catallaxy) to produce the wealth needed to fund interventionist policies. Since the taxation that must take place during the expansionary phase tends relentlessly to consume capital and discourage saving it may be hard at first to see how one could characterize this process as self-generating. This study views the interventionist process broadly, however, so that both state contraction and state expansion are components of it (even though the *policy* of interventionism itself is more properly associated with the latter than the former phase). And the process of state contraction, as we have seen, releases the human resources and entrepreneurial alertness that produce catallactic profits and "surplus value." (Recall that it is because the governmental process, discussed in Chapter 3, lacks this self-generating property that it falls outside the category of spontaneous order, even though it is largely self-organizing and fairly unpredictable.) Interventionist-minded public choosers might then be tempted to exploit this surplus in some subsequent return to interventionism, transforming it into a renewed reserve fund. Indeed, the observation of an empirical tendency for politico-economic systems perpetually to cycle between minimal and maximal states would lend support to the view of the interventionist process as a spontaneous order. (A necessary part of an analytical framework that would explain this cyclical behavior, the instability of the minimal state, is the topic of Chapter 6.)

Finally, do the patterns that emerge out of the dynamics of the mixed economy constitute an order in the Hayekian sense?[58] I maintain that the interventionist process is indeed an order in this sense. Although I will be unable to substantiate this claim more fully until Chapter 7, the analysis thus far has already identified certain patterns and regularities that will tend to form within any given interventionist process. First, there will be a tendency for an interventionist mixed economy to experience crises at the micro- and macro level. Second, a macro-crisis represents a potential turning point for such a system as a whole, such that we can expect at that point to observe dramatic shifts in policy in the direction of either more or less interference with the catallaxy. Third, the contractionary phase of the interventionist process, at least in its initial stages, will entail more rapid and radical change than generally takes place during the expansionary phase. Fourth, macro-crises will tend to occur closer to the maximal-state than to the minimal-state end of the politico-economic spectrum.

144

RELAXING THE ASSUMPTION OF BENEVOLENT PUBLIC INTEREST

Introducing political self-interest at all into a framework that purports to investigate the implications of benevolent state intervention may seem puzzling. Insofar as the empirical relevance of this framework is concerned, however, it is germane to question whether and to what degree injecting political self-interest, that dominant theme in discussions about real politico-economic processes, might change the analysis and its conclusions. Furthermore, recall that the reason for minimizing the role of narrow self-interest on the part of public choosers was primarily methodological – to see whether it was possible to sustain public-choice conclusions (positive and normative) about the overall effects of interventionism without having to rely on selfish political motives – and not to diminish its relevance for political economy. Indeed, narrow self-interest is a feature too important to ignore in any description of the actual practice of interventionism. By relaxing the assumption of benevolence I hope to show that public choice and Austrian political economy are complementary rather than rival approaches, and that a full account of interventionism and the interventionist process should include them both. The successful synthesis of public choice and Austrian political economy might in fact constitute the most general theory of interventionism. But that is a topic for another study.

In a sense, this book has taken an approach to public-policy analysis that is highly idealistic. That is, my task has not been to criticize the operations of mixed economies as they necessarily are (though I do intend for the implications of my analysis to be relevant to really existing systems), but to examine the forces at work in an "ideal" mixed economy inhabited by benevolent public choosers. As a result, to the extent that it has been possible to abstract from narrow or political self-interest, I believe I have shown how and why, in the presence of the knowledge problem, public choosers' good intentions are not enough to produce good public policy, even from their own viewpoint. Again, I have attempted to distinguish simple self-interested behavior (self-interest without political guile), which is an indispensable component of any analysis of human action (including the present one), from the kind of narrow self-interest that is a common feature of public choice, as, for example, in models of rent-seeking.

Yet maintaining a clear and unequivocal separation has been difficult. In the analysis of ideological change, for example, I argued that a public chooser might either engage in political activity to retain benefits he has erroneously received through flawed public policy, or at least not seek to correct the error, even though a truly public-spirited citizen would probably not act that way. (On further reflection, however, to the extent that entering the political process *at all*, even to correct an error that favors oneself, reduces the reluctance of others to use political means, guile may be less important.) The analysis of the governmental process in Chapter 3 mentioned various coordinating devices – such as log-rolling, bribery, and budget maximization – that are inconsistent with a public-interest viewpoint (although other important coordinating devices that were discussed, such as vote-seeking and benevolent entrepreneurial alertness, are consistent with it). Finally, the decision of resource owners to direct investment from more to less constrained areas of the catallaxy, or from taxed to subsidized areas, though still broadly compatible with simple self-interest, also indicates at least a willingness to exploit intervention-created opportunities that is perhaps not entirely in keeping with the idea of benevolence.

Besides being a challenge to keep them conceptually distinct, the separation between simple self-interest and narrow political interest, and indeed the assumption of benevolent public interest in general, is certainly unrealistic. It was implausible (though not impossible to imagine), for instance, that public choosers would support explicit income transfers for purely non-selfish reasons; that citizens would vote only for those measures that they were sure would benefit everyone and not just themselves; that rent-seeking coalitions and turf-conscious bureaucratic managers would be absent from the interventionist process; and that these same groups would not dominate policy formation and stand in the way of rejecting the interventionist policies that justify and support them. Indeed, state expansion itself may not only incline public choosers toward more intervention, but it will very likely also transform benevolent public choosers into narrowly selfish ones.

In the end, the difficulty of completely removing narrow self-interest from the present analysis is likely a reflection of the indispensable role that it plays in the workings of actual political processes and institutions. To reiterate, it was never the intention of this study to argue against the empirical relevance of public-choice-type approaches to political economy. To explore really existing political landscapes more fully – rather than, as I have up to this point, the politico-economic implications of conducting benevolent public policy amid ignorance – obliges me to take into account, and perhaps even to incorporate into the theory of interventionism, the explanatory power of political self-interest.

Fortunately, it appears that relaxing the assumption of benevolent public interest leaves the conclusions of the analysis of this study mostly unchanged. Indeed, those cases in which narrow self-interest modifies the analysis generally reinforce rather than contradict its conclusions.

Rent-seeking

Rent-seeking entails the expenditure of resources to secure economic rents, which include, but are not limited to, those that the state can offer through intervention (Tullock 1967; Krueger 1974). In particular, the gains that rent-seekers receive through their exploitation of the political process represent a forced transfer of income from third parties. Permitting rent-seeking into the present analysis would simply expand the set of incentives to use political means beyond those that public choosers possess under a regime of benevolence. Therefore, allowing the possibility of rent-seeking among public choosers simply reinforces already existing tendencies for the state to expand. And, like benevolent action, rent-seeking will also produce negative unintended consequences that destabilize the mixed economy.

Collective action: interest groups and bureaucratic self-interest

As was the case with rent-seeking, adding organized collective action by public choosers, in both the private and public sectors, expands the number of factors that contribute to state expansion. In this respect it will tend to hasten the arrival of a macro-crisis.

If collective action can overcome the problems of initially organizing and then policing the coalition (e.g., through "selective incentives" of some sort (Olson 1982)), it will represent a formidable obstacle to political or economic changes that threaten its interests. In this way, collective action introduces an element of political inertia into the process that is less apparent in individual rent-seeking (although individual acts of rent preservation by persons with vested interests are also a source of inertia). This inertia has an impact on both the expansionary and contractionary phases of the interventionist process. Since state expansion is generally more consistent with the interests of collective-action coalitions than is state contraction (because a growing government budget offers the possibility of Pareto-like improvements within the governmental process that shrinking or constant budgets do not), one would in general expect these coalitions to resist attempts to reduce the size of government and to favor policies that increase it. This will have the effect of delaying the rejection of interventionism at the point of macro-crisis (or at points of micro- and lower-level macro-crises, as well). Hence, the existence of special-interest groups and bureaucratic sluggishness will also tend to delay the ultimate turning point of the interventionist process, and therefore exacerbate the severity of the eventual crisis.[59]

This delay, if it sufficiently offsets the opposing tendency of collective action to hasten the macro-crisis, could either give rise to an even more radical reform when it does take place (Olson 1982), especially if it is a reform in the direction of laissez-faire capitalism, or give coalitions a chance to water-down or effectively sabotage the reforms that threaten their interests. If there is such a return to a more moderate version of the regulatory or welfare state, collective action will increase the likelihood of a reversion back to interventionism for two reasons. First, the reforms of the interventionist mixed economy will be less radical than they would have been in the absence of such coalitions, leaving a substantial amount of residual institutional discoordination and instability within the system. Second, since a moderate or piecemeal reform is more likely than a radical one to permit such coalitions to weather the reform process, those that survive could represent organized, post-reform pressure groups that might then demand the reinstatement of their former interventionist benefits and protection.

Political self-interest in the governmental process

The governmental process was defined in Chapter 3 as the order emerging from on-going adjustments by public agents to perceived changes in conditions within government. While actions in the private sector may initiate some of these changes, it is the responses to them in the public sector that constitute the governmental process.

I will refrain from repeating here the observations made in Chapter 3 regarding the problematic character of plan coordination within the governmental process. It is perhaps enough to recall that, while political self-interest can serve to better coordinate plans in the public sector – which, because of the governmental knowledge problem, tend to conflict with one another – such coordination may no longer be in the broader interests of all citizens, when narrow self-interest motivates political entrepreneurship. Strategic voting, for example, among both citizens and legislators, becomes possible with political self-interest. A well-functioning governmental "machine," driven to a greater or lesser degree by greed and personal ambition, is no less likely than a loosely coordinated one to generate the negative unintended consequences in the catallaxy that will drive the interventionist process.

Complements or substitutes?

What I have been calling "Austrian political economy," the study of the causes and consequences of public policy in the context of radical ignorance and dispersed knowledge, is, I believe, quite compatible with public choice. Although, owing to its largely neoclassical equilibrium-based method, the latter tends to place too much emphasis on the intended effects of narrowly self-interested action, while the former views the dynamics of the mixed economy as a whole as the unintended and unwanted outcome of public policy, there is no reason why these two outlooks could not in principle complement rather than contend with each other.

While I have criticized public-choice analysis for (what has seemed to me to be) this narrow perspective, augmenting it with an Austrian one might not radically alter its existing theoretical structure. For example, adopting an Austrian outlook would not entail jettisoning the theory of rent-seeking, but it would lead us to ask what its discoordinating consequences would be for other areas of the mixed economy (external responses) in the presence of radical ignorance. The same would hold true, I believe, for its basic approach to bureaucracy.[60] Its various analyses of voting rules and paradoxes, democratic institutions, and the logic of collective action would be affected even less.

It is important to realize also that the assumption of benevolent public interest, while important for this study, is not an indispensable assumption of Austrian political economy in general, which can accommodate political self-interest quite easily. At the same time, incorporating political self-interest would need not entail adopting the perspective of equilibrium analysis, and, as we have just seen, it would appear not substantively to alter the conclusions of Austrian political economy.

In a sense, then, public choice and Austrian political economy are two independent though highly complementary approaches to the study of public policy. Each does seem to fill in analytical "gaps" left by the other. In any particular instance, for example, the analyst will need to decide whether one is more appropriate than the other, or how to marry parts from each to form a construct appropriate for the problem at hand. Thus, where the focus of attention is on intended results and deliberate outcomes (e.g., explaining log-rolling or why unions might support raising the legal minimum wage), a public-choice model would be more suitable whereas an Austrian approach might be better suited to investigate cases in which unexpected outcomes appear to depend more on questions of knowledge than on motives (e.g., the unintended socio-economic effects of the policies of the Social Security Administration, which many often cite as an example of a government agency that appears to "work" (Goodsell 1985: 82–109).)

Since Austrian political economy and public choice are each capable of standing on their own, public-policy theorists might find it optimal simply to continue to pursue their research along the lines of either the former or the latter approaches. Such a strategy would perhaps be quite reasonable. Yet, if it does turn out, as I have argued, that Austrian political economy and public choice are highly complementary, an equally sensible strategy would seem to be for public-policy theorists to attempt to unite the two into a single coherent framework – a general theory of political economy.

Before this can be done, however, the important areas of difference discussed in Chapter 1 need to be resolved, perhaps the most important of which is the emphasis in Austrian theory on non-equilibrium processes versus public choice's neoclassical orientation toward equilibrium endstates. This is the source of other, though less profound, differences such as the attitude exhibited in much of the public-choice literature of "inferring intentions from outcomes" (Wagner 1989: 46–7). Thus, it may turn out that these differences are largely irreconcilable. On the other hand, scholars like Mancur Olson, whose work in many respects can be seen as a middle ground between the two approaches, perhaps give us reason to remain hopeful.

CONCLUDING REMARKS

The interventionist process is a spontaneous order, sustained and set in motion by the unforeseen adjustments of entrepreneurs and public choosers, in the market and governmental processes, that are the destabilizing and unwanted responses to public policy implemented in the presence of dispersed knowledge and radical ignorance. The expansionary phase of this process brings about a series of micro-crises and lower-level macro-crises in the catallaxy that culminate in a major macro-crisis that de-legitimizes the interventionist mixed economy, at which point public choosers must decide whether to follow the path of collectivism or capitalism. The contractionary phase follows immediately upon a deliberate selection of the latter (and as we shall see in Chapter 7, according to Mises's critique of socialism, it is also the inevitable outcome of a move to pure collectivism). In general, changes take place more rapidly in this phase than in the expansionary phase, especially in its initial stages, owing both to the magnitude of the discoordination confronting public choosers and to the premeditated nature of their choice of freer markets. The mixed economy in transition will, like the expansionary phase, manifest negative unintended consequences to the extent that the rejection of interventionism is only partial. These consequences could derail the reform process and send the system back onto an expansionary path. Relaxing the assumption of benevolent public interest on the part of public choosers only slightly modifies these conclusions, opening the possibility of a unified Austrian–public choice framework that could represent a general theory of interventionism.

In this chapter I made no distinction among the varieties of intervention that exist often, side-by-side, during the expansionary phase. Yet important differences in the manner in which this process unfolds originate in the distinctive dynamics of each of the ideal types of intervention. The next chapter identifies and analyzes these dynamics.

5

TOWARD A THEORY OF INTERVENTIONISM II:
Roads to collectivism

Modern mixed economies combine elements of regulation, redistribution, and nationalization in a variety of ways.[1] Identifying and isolating the categories of intervention that shape these systems and then analyzing the resulting "pure" forms can reveal important differences among them (though still perhaps at a fairly high level of abstraction) that will enrich our understanding of interventionism. Thus, while the dynamics of both the welfare state and the regulatory state are variants of the interventionist process and therefore share a common inner logic (which it was the burden of Chapter 4 to adumbrate), there do exist between them interesting and significant differences in the way in which that logic unfolds.[2] In this chapter I attempt to tease out these differences in order to add important details to the picture of the dynamics of the mixed economy presented so far.

At least two other major issues remain unresolved owing to the generality of the previous analysis. The first concerns the relation between direct regulation of prices and what might be called non-price regulation. The second has to do with integrating the nationalization of industries within the overall theoretical framework of this study. I also address these issues in the present chapter.

Much of Chapter 4 could be read as a general description of regulatory dynamics, insofar as it may have given (explicit) relative-price changes the central role, and a somewhat secondary, though still highly important, role to endogenous changes in marginal and total ideological preference. This asymmetry between the forces of relative prices on the one hand and ideology on the other is a distinct feature of regulatory dynamics. Apart from integrating non-price regulation and adding a few details, that description needs little modification to make it applicable specifically to the regulatory state.

Regarding the transfer dynamics of the welfare state, however, the picture is far less complete. In part, this is because the importance of changes in ideology are at least on a par with (implicit) relative price changes. Consequently, while Chapter 4 examined at some length the kinds of ideological change and their role in the interventionist process, the present chapter concentrates more closely on the nature and causes of endogenous changes in ideological preferences. In addition, because redistribution distorts relative prices somewhat more subtly than does regulation, it will be necessary to examine carefully how this takes place. Much of the present chapter is thus devoted to adapting the theory of interventionism to the distinctive features of the welfare state.

Among the advantages of distinguishing between the dynamics of the regulatory state and the welfare state are the following. Doing so, first of all, serves to identify any significant features that are uniquely associated with the particular path toward collectivism that a mixed economy might follow. Second, as discussed in Chapter 2, because any intervention, regardless of the intent behind it, redistributes income (Rothbard 1977; Posner 1971), even pure regulation will to some degree produce the effects of a pure transfer. Likewise, insofar as explicit income transfers distort relative prices they will also produce patterns typical of regulatory dynamics. Thus, the interventions within one pure form of the mixed economy will exhibit some of the properties of the other, which the approach taken in this chapter should help to untangle. Finally, this method of analysis might be helpful in better conceptualizing how regulation and transfers interact to produce the complex patterns found in really existing mixed economies, even though it might not yet allow us to predict precisely what will emerge from such an interaction.

REGULATORY DYNAMICS

As defined in chapter 2, under *regulatory-state capitalism* public choosers support intervention to improve the level of economic efficiency beyond what they think the catallaxy alone is able to attain. Thus, rather than attempting principally to effect what they deem is a more just or fair distribution of resources (as is the case in the pure welfare state), in the regulatory state public choosers favor interventions into markets in order to engineer what is from their perspective a more optimal allocation of resources. The related concept of *regulatory dynamics* refers to the spontaneous and on-going adjustments within a politico-economic system to government regulation. It is the particular form that the dynamics of the interventionist process takes in the regulatory state.

Examples of regulation in this sense would include product-quality and worker-safety rules, limits on production and market entry, directives concerning environmental protection and personal health, Pigouvian taxes and subsidies (i.e., directed primarily at enhancing efficiency rather than redistribution), and restrictions on alleged monopolistic or anti-competitive business practices that are thought to reduce social welfare. One might also include market-specific price controls and profit ceilings, although the effects of these (as well as anti-discrimination and employee-hiring mandates, worker-safety regulations, and import and export restrictions) are frequently redistributive in nature, so that it might be more accurate to regard them as income transfers. Finally, monetary, fiscal, and incomes policies, to the extent that they address supposed macroeconomic market failures – such as chronic unemployment, inflation, and the business cycle – could also be included here.

The role of price distortions in regulatory dynamics

Price distortions are the dominant and driving force behind regulatory dynamics. (Approaches, such as those of Peltzman (1976), Wagner (1989), and others in the "new political economy" discussed in Chapter 1 that treat regulation exclusively as income transfers tend to obscure this important detail.) The internal and external responses to regulatory price distortions generate excessive complexity and plan discoordination, the latter of which consists of surpluses and shortages in various lines of activity and the barriers to discovery that tend to obscure them. In time, complexity and discoordination become both the cause and the consequence of the spontaneous and destabilizing responses of actors in government and catallaxy who act under partial ignorance. In this way, distortions in relative prices drive the interventionist process, while directing that process, broadly speaking, toward either more or less intervention is the role of ideology.

As explained in Chapter 4, in the private sector a regulation-induced shortage or surplus creates "losers" and "winners." The associated disappointment gives entrepreneurs the incentive to bid prices up in a shortage or down in a surplus, the effects of which can impinge on related lines of activity in unanticipated and typically undesirable ways. In addition, this could also induce entrepreneurs to discover previously unthought-of (and, from the point of view of a pre-intervention world, superfluous) methods of doing the same or similar things; or it could reduce their alertness to the possibility of plan adjustments that would better align subjective perceptions with objective facts.[3] Such superfluous and stifled entrepreneurial discoveries, both of which owe their existence to radical ignorance, introduce the elements of radical uncertainty and unpredictability that give the interventionist process its truly dynamic character. These "incentive" and "discovery" effects create negative unintended consequences that pressure public choosers either to support the repeal of the regulation or to favor further intervention,[4] depending on the prevailing ideology and the reliability of their perceptions. If they choose further intervention, it may consist of more regulation aimed at the same target area to cope with an internal response, or a different sort of intervention altogether directed toward a newly perceived problem that has arisen in a more distant region of the catallaxy owing to an external response to the initial regulation. (I have more to say about the nature of this choice at the end of the present chapter.)

As determined in Chapter 3, the discovery effect in the governmental process could cause public authorities to err either by being *utterly unaware* of opportunities to coordinate the multitude of separate public policies and to anticipate the interaction between these policies and the market process (i.e., a class-two error), or by *deliberately passing up* such opportunities (i.e., a class-one error). An example of the latter would be the case in which, even though it is clear that the passage and enforcement of municipal rent control has created a shortage of affordable housing, a benevolent city government is still unwilling to repeal the controls and instead chooses to raise taxes to subsidize particular tenants. These kinds of errors, of course, also beset entrepreneurs in the private sector, who base their choices on incomplete or faulty information – but with a difference.

Within any politico-economic system, nearly every action an individual might take, whether in government or catallaxy, has both negative as well as positive unintended consequences.

Whether it is a private firm marketing a new form of medical service, such as so-called "managed-care," or the state legislating a new national health-care program, each to some degree will have repercussions that were not foreseen or aimed at. The private introduction of a cheaper and more powerful compact computer could reduce the time needed to apply, say, a new medical technique sufficiently to lower the cost to a wider range of patients; on the other hand, this same computer innovation might also lower the cost of breaking into and stealing private databases. Likewise, a national health program might make it possible to insure a larger number of currently uninsured citizens, but it might also seriously lower the quality as well as the quantity of current medical services or discourage future cost-saving and quality-enhancing breakthroughs in medical science (Goodman and Musgrave 1992).

Whether and to what extent negative unintended consequences are discovered and eliminated and positive unintended consequences are discovered and promoted will obviously depend on how well the adjustment process within a politico-economic system performs. The explanation presented in Chapter 4 of why intervention produces unintended consequences that even its sponsors would consider on net undesirable is obviously relevant here, as is also the analysis of Chapter 3 on the effectiveness of governmental versus market-process coordination. The former argued that as intervention increases, market signals (especially relative prices) become distorted, hampering entrepreneurial alertness in detecting certain errors and at the same time redirecting it toward other "superfluous" areas. The latter argued that, compared to the market process, the necessarily blunt and relatively clumsy knowledge-conveyance mechanisms of the governmental process adjust more sluggishly and ineptly to unexpected situations. To the extent that the government's activities dominate those of the catallaxy (i.e., to the extent that the state intervenes into the market process), negative unintended consequences will tend to dominate the positive ones.

Although the principal paradigm on which the present study is based is Mises's account of the unintended consequences that arise from price controls, the next section extends that paradigm to encompass non-price regulations as well.

How non-price regulation distorts relative prices

The present analysis is not limited to direct price controls. If it were, it would exclude from its scope a great many of the kinds of regulation practiced in modern mixed economies. Because the theory of regulatory dynamics is centered on relative-price distortions, how to integrate non-price regulations into it is a reasonable concern that needs to be addressed. To begin to do so, let us first examine what is behind this concern.

The standard economic theory of regulation makes a distinction between a regulation such as a price floor that distorts the equilibrium market price of a commodity by directly controlling that price, and one such as a work-safety rule that increases the costs of selling (or, equivalently in equilibrium, lowers the benefits from purchasing) a commodity. A minimum-wage law under otherwise perfectly competitive conditions in the labor market will produce an excess supply of labor, which is the sort of contrary outcome that may prompt further intervention. In the case of the safety rule, however, one might argue that the now-higher price of the output in question is simply a reflection of the now-higher cost of selling. In the first case, that is, a regulation obviously *distorts* the relative market price of a good by artificially raising it relative to the prices of other goods; in the second case, while a regulation also artificially raises a relative price, this simply *reflects* higher selling costs. (This same observation could be made *mutatis mutandis* regarding a price ceiling on the one hand, and a business subsidy on the other, the first producing a distorted lower-than-market price and the second resulting in artificially lower costs for the firm.) Hence, it might appear that the analysis of regulatory dynamics applies only to the rather limited area of price controls. Happily, this is not the case.

There are at least two possible ways to link these apparently dissimilar kinds of regulation. The first takes the point of view of strict neoclassical equilibrium analysis,[5] while the second takes that of market-process theory. Regarding the first, observe that while output prices are undoubtedly distorted under a price floor, a work-safety rule distorts output prices because such a rule introduces an artificial cost that does not in fact accurately reflect perceptions of agents *within the market process*. The higher equilibrium price of these products now does a poorer job of reflecting underlying scarcities, which reduces the flow of resources into this line of production below the optimal level and creates a deadweight loss to society.

For our purposes, regrettably, this line of reasoning is fruitless. It perforce includes only the perceptions of agents within the market process and must explicitly exclude those of actors who are engaged in the political process. To include the latter would effectively rule out the possibility of anything but the most transitory state of excess demand or supply. This is so within a strict neoclassical, perfect information context because, should the expected cost of engaging in the political process to remove a work-safety rule be greater than the expected benefit, there would be no incentive to adjust plans nor, from a normative standpoint, should there be. The situation would essentially be an equilibrium, and an optimal one at that, because from a strict neoclassical perspective *known* costs can never be an obstacle to optimality. Or as Kirzner has argued: "If we can assume that what is known to one is known to all, then ... it seems difficult to imagine the possibility of any social allocation of resources that might be pronounced socially *in*efficient" (Kirzner 1992: 186; emphasis original). Disequilibrium, the essential condition for regulatory dynamics, could not exist in such a world. And since excluding the perceptions of political actors is wholly arbitrary in an analysis of political economy, a strict neoclassical perspective is of little help in explaining regulatory *dynamics*. Within that approach there is no way usefully to bring non-price regulation into the framework of regulatory dynamics.

The second way of linking price with non-price regulation is to recognize that *before* the markets in question have reached their new equilibria, both kinds of regulation will indeed generate a disequilibrium – or, more realistically, the regulation will exacerbate an existing non-equilibrium situation – which will be fodder for further regulation. From this perspective, the negative unintended consequences of explicit price controls and of cost-altering regulations flow from the disequilibrating nature of their "short-term" effects. Persistent non-equilibrium conditions, however, characterize actual markets. And even under reasonably stable real-world circumstances, non-equilibrium prices will not perfectly reflect underlying scarcities (although of course the discovery of price discrepancies is central to the coordinating function of entrepreneurship within the catallaxy). Introducing regulatory distortions into this process, then, exacerbates the "short-term" disequilibriating effects, making class-one errors even more evident to policy-makers, and lengthens it (if this is even necessary) enough to allow them to intervene again if they so choose. The additional intervention, especially in this non-equilibrium environment, would only rarely promote coordination. More likely it would have the opposite effect.

In addition, because non-price regulation distorts relative prices in this second way, it will create barriers to discovery by diminishing the effectiveness of entrepreneurial alertness, which will lead actors to overlook otherwise profitable opportunities for plan coordination and pursue catallactically unnecessary ones (Kirzner 1985: 119–49). The discussion of transfer dynamics later in this chapter further argues that intervention in general also tends to hinder the entrepreneurial discovery process by eroding private ownership rights – one of the foundations of the market process.

An outline of regulatory dynamics

Suppose that the ideological climate within a regulatory state is such that, in addition to the current level of regulatory intervention, public choosers are willing to support (or at least not object to) an additional act of regulation in response to a problem perceived to issue from the operation of the unhampered market process. This regulation distorts the network of relative prices in a ripple effect that emanates from the area targeted by the regulation and spreads outward to the rest of the catallaxy, leading to disappointment (as revealed in surpluses or shortages) in activities both close to and remote from the targeted area. Confronted with these new and unexpected conditions, entrepreneurs manifest internal responses and external responses. The object of interest here is not with admittedly important deadweight losses from a price distortion, but rather how intervention by artificially altering rates of return on investment via price distortions generates further unanticipated discoordination elsewhere in the system.

These unintended consequences are what induce the endogenous and exogenous ideological changes described in Chapter 4 that tend to reinforce the perception that more rather than less regulation is the appropriate response to the deteriorating state of affairs. This happens when the number of public choosers, and their level of disappointment with the *status quo*, becomes significant enough that there is a fall in the perceived relative cost of maintaining personal and social constraints against the use of political means. This, combined with a state of affairs in which the concatenation of politico-economic interactions are too complex (Simon) or obscure (Kirzner) to be easily comprehended or perceived, might be sufficient to induce public choosers to call for further regulation to deal with the perceived causes of their disappointment. A network of newly distorted relative prices along with a modified set of appropriate ideological propensities thus invites the benevolent state to intervene further, which brings on a new round of relative-price distortions, ideological shift, and negative unintended consequences.

Regulation, insecurity, and ideological change

Another feature of regulatory dynamics that warrants further discussion has to do with the impact of regulations on ideological change. We have already examined the relation between intervention and ideological change in Chapter 4. There, the number of actors who enter the political process plays a prominent role in shifting ideological preferences. Here, in addition to this numbers effect, the emphasis is on the way the regulation of competition promotes the demand for further intervention by increasing the feelings of insecurity on the part of those engaged in the competitive process.

Success under capitalism necessitates rapid adjustments on the part of competitors. Generally speaking, those who are better able to recognize and adjust to changing circumstances will prosper while those with less adaptability will do relatively (though not necessarily absolutely) worse. We have seen that regulation tends (among other things) to hinder the capacity of competitors to perceive and adjust to changing conditions. This impairs their ability to act entrepreneurially – i.e., to discover and attempt to satisfy the demands of prospective customers – which in turn tends to lower their return on investment, where "lower" returns could mean hardships ranging from reduced profit to unemployment and poverty. In the face of these regulation-induced difficulties, these competitors must at least attempt to revise or alter plans in ways that they did not originally foresee. The upshot of these additional unexpected changes is to increase the uncertainty and reduce the level of security that actors experience under capitalism, which, given the dynamism of that system, may already be perceived to be quite high relative to a more conservative and static politico-economic order.⁶ Moreover, if a regulation applies unequally and in an unpredictable manner among competitors (thus violating the rule of law), this uncertainty, added to the aforementioned hardship and unexpected plan revisions, further increases the level of felt insecurity. Thus, capitalism *per se* may not be solely or even primarily responsible for the severe insecurity many associate with it (granting that unexpected changes in general are undoubtedly more characteristic of modern capitalism than, say, feudalism), but rather regulations that hinder the adjustment process. In any case, this insecurity will tend to encourage public choosers to demand more intervention in the hopes of trading some individual freedom for more personal security. In general, however, the additional regulation will tend to heighten rather than ease this sense of insecurity for reasons already outlined.⁷ Unchecked, this trade-off between freedom and security will cause profound social and economic instability.

Categories of regulatory intervention and their effects

Chapter 3 examined the role of the price system in coordinating the plans of anonymous individuals who act under partial radical ignorance. Clearly, a complex network of spontaneously adjusting relative prices is indispensable to the market process. Based on its importance in promoting coordination and social cooperation (i.e., by providing signals to guide individual action), it may be possible roughly to rank each of the broad categories of regulatory intervention according to its power to disrupt the price system and thus generate the frustrated intentions and discoordination that fuel the interventionist process. The following is an attempt to provide such a ranking.⁸

Monetary manipulation

Unlike other commodities that the state may regulate, money is on at least one side of nearly every exchange in a mature catallaxy. Thus, compared to other forms of regulatory interventions, those that are meant to manipulate the purchasing power of money have potentially the greatest impact on relative prices and the market process. First and foremost among the devices modern governments have used to alter the purchasing power of their currency is credit expansion. Indeed, recall from Chapter 4 that the unfolding of the business cycle, according to the Mises–Hayek theory, is a paradigm for the interventionist process. Its unintended consequences (shortages of consumer goods) provoke a spiral of further interventions (accelerating credit expansion) until a crisis is reached (hyperinflation and the stagnation of production), at which point public choosers must decide, usually too late, how to reform their policy. No other act of intervention is so capable of disrupting the flow of the market process as deliberate monetary expansion or contraction.

Price control

After monetary manipulation, regulations that impinge directly on entrepreneurs' ability to adjust prices to new conditions are the most disruptive and the most likely to produce severe negative unintended consequences. Because relative prices are the principal, though not the only, social coordinating "device" in the market process, the consequences of interfering with its operation are far-reaching indeed. Wage and price controls at the macroeconomic level are the prime examples of this sort of direct distortion of the price system.

It is reasonable to expect that price controls applied to a subset of the catallaxy (what one might think of as "microeconomic" price control) will be less disruptive in the short run. If, however, the particular activity regulated is a large enough subset, the consequences could approach macroeconomic proportions. Stringent state control of the prices of such activities (e.g., price controls on oil and gas in the United States during the 1970s) might not only have a short-term impact on the market process that is quite severe because of the regulated industry's position in the structure of production. Interventionist reactions to these effects could also spread rapidly through the catallaxy because there is a greater likelihood that more drastic state actions would be needed to cope with the negative unintended consequences that are on a large scale both initially and, as the interventionist process unfolds, in the longer term, as well.

Production restriction

Production restrictions – which include outright prohibitions and Pigouvian taxation and (in an indirect way) subsidies – are the next most disruptive kind of intervention. This is so largely because such restrictions, through the interaction of supply and demand, have a direct and often immediate impact on the relative price of the output whose production has been restricted. And while restrictions in production can also affect other aspects of production – such as the quality of output, choice of inputs, level of technology – these influence the market process primarily through their effect on relative prices. Furthermore, compared to the kinds of regulation mentioned thus far, the state may be better able to enforce production restrictions because their violation is somewhat easier to detect. (But as the performance of the United States government respecting the importing of illegal substances (e.g., cocaine) demonstrates, this does not mean that production restrictions and prohibitions are always or even often successful.)

In addition to direct prohibitions, production restrictions can take the form of rules aimed at regulating some aspect of the production process. One example of this is the regulation of smokestack emissions, which the government hopes will help to reduce what it perceives as damage to the environment. The higher marginal costs of production from such regulation, in conjunction with demand, tend to increase the relative price of the output, which, as I argued earlier in the present chapter, represents a genuine price distortion.

Finally, one can view taxation as a form of production restriction. All taxation, whether intended to or not, will discourage production to a greater or lesser degree. Another consequence of taxation that is separate from those of production restriction occurs if the state aims to tax entrepreneurial profits. Such a tax would serve to discourage entrepreneurship directly, and therefore degrade the market process, without necessarily disturbing relative prices in the first instance (Kirzner 1985: 93–118). (In addition to the previous discussion of this phenomenon in Chapter 4, see the next part of the present chapter under the heading "The unintended consequences of taxation and expenditure.")

Quality control

When the state attempts to regulate the quality of a product or service, it also raises marginal production costs. This, in turn, like taxation, raises the relative price of the output, and therefore has the same impact on the market process as any other kind of production restriction or non-price regulation. Like taxation, however, there is a consequence of quality control separate from its effect on production and relative prices alone, which stems from the efforts of public authorities to modify or control some or all aspects of a production process. In particular, to the extent that these efforts interfere with the ability of actors engaged in production (including labor, management, etc.) to discover a new demand or new ways of doing things, they will have a negative impact on the market process (via the discovery effect), even though they may not appear to restrict output immediately. If, for example, the state mandates that insurance companies cover a minimum of two days of post-partum care for women who give birth in hospitals, this will not only have the tendency, among other things, to reduce the number of women covered by insurance (by the law of demand), it will also tend to discourage researchers from investigating new medicines and procedures that could in fact safely speed up the in-hospital post-partum recovery process.

TRANSFER DYNAMICS

In Chapter 2, I defined "transfer dynamics," the driving force of the interventionist process within welfare-state capitalism, as the spontaneous and on-going adjustment of the politico-economic order to the use of political means to transfer income. In elaborating on transfer dynamics here, I will begin by examining the consequences of the deliberate redistribution of income through explicit taxation and subsidies. Although such transfers are often intended to effect egalitarian outcomes, and they are the principal tool of the welfare state whose primary concern I have defined as fairness in some sense, for our purposes it is unimportant whether specifically egalitarian goals in fact motivate a deliberate transfer. What is important is that the principal effect of this kind of intervention is to redistribute income.

While deliberate and explicit transfers may seem to be an overly narrow choice of subject-matter, it is, as a first approximation, an effective way to draw the contrast between the welfare and regulatory states as sharply as possible. To reiterate what was said in the introduction to this chapter, this will enable us better (1) to identify and explore any unique repercussions that interventionistic transfers and regulations may have, (2) to trace the consequences of "hybrid" forms of intervention that attempt to achieve the goals of both the welfare and regulatory states (such as minimum-wage laws), and (3) to investigate the manner in which regulations and transfers interact within mixed economies. The analytical separation made in this study between the welfare state and the regulatory state turns not so much on the (benevolent) intentions that lie behind the policies of public choosers, as on the extent to which an intervention actually regulates behavior or transfers income. This distinction is broadly consistent with the standard literature on the economic analysis of the welfare state.[9]

Degradation of price signals in the pure welfare state

Following the general outline of the interventionist process presented in Chapter 4, one can separate the forces underlying transfer dynamics into two parts – "price distortions" and "ideological change." Pure income transfers impinge on each of these forces in ways that are somewhat different from pure regulation. This section focuses mainly, though not exclusively, on the impact of income transfers on the signaling function of prices within the market process. The next section examines more extensively the causes of endogenous ideological change within the transfer dynamics.

While the impact of forced transfers on the relative price of income-earning versus leisure is well known, market-process analysis can reveal some less-appreciated aspects of the problem, especially as it concerns the relation between property rights and the knowledge-conveyance function of the price system. I will discuss these aspects, however, only after first reviewing the better known labor–leisure analysis and then examining why a redistributional policy involving taxes and subsidies that is meant to promote greater income equality will tend to have the opposite results.

165

An outline of transfer dynamics

To begin with, "relative price" in this context refers chiefly to the opportunity costs of leisure – defined as the value of time spent in non-labor activities – confronting various individual actors. The concern here is with the effects of distortions in the relations between the opportunity costs of leisure and the prices of other endeavors – specifically, labor and labor-related activities – created by forced transfers. The principal catallactic consequences of such transfers are, as with regulations, adjustments to disequilibria that in this instance take place chiefly in the labor market but which ultimately spread to the rest of the catallaxy. Transfers also affect production (i.e., the creation of value), since in most cases the quality and availability of labor, especially skilled labor, will greatly influence value productivity. There will also be long-term consequences from the substitution by entrepreneurs of capital for labor in response to either higher real labor costs or a decline in the quality of labor that results from forced transfers.

Beginning with a set of *fixed* ideological preferences, suppose the relations between opportunity costs and explicit prices initially produce a state of affairs in which public choosers are willing to support (or at least not object to) the use of political means to compel an income transfer in response to an undesirable condition that they perceive to originate from within the market process. This transfer will have two distorting influences that are not linked in the first instance with explicit relative prices.

The first influence centers on the lowered opportunity costs of leisure, both for those receiving the transfer and for those paying for it. How actors adjust to transfer-induced changes in the relative price of labor is one determinant of whether there is a reduction in total labor-force participation, labor quality (i.e., value-productivity), or both. By lowering the opportunity costs of leisure for the recipients, a transfer might encourage in them a level of leisure-taking that is higher than the coordinating forces of the market process would have warranted. At the same time, those forced to pay for the transfer experience a lower marginal value of labor income than the market process would have determined, which is likely to lower the relative opportunity cost of leisure to them, as well.[10] The end result is that both parties to the forced exchange will be less productive.

The second influence concerns the consequences on the attitude of public choosers toward state expansion (i.e., their ideology). As ideology is crucial to the dynamics of the general interventionist process, it is also a critical factor in actors' responses to redistribution. More specifically, the behavior of these actors will depend in large measure on the ideological preferences that serve as informal constraints on what might be considered "anti-social behavior" in a very broad sense – that is, behavior that tends ultimately to hamper the division of labor and social cooperation.

The aftermath of opportunity-cost distortions on the market process, in the context of a given ideology (i.e., on *marginal* changes in ideology), is two-fold. First there is the tendency to create shortages of labor in those areas of the catallaxy in which the transfer lowers the relative returns to labor and drives down the relative opportunity costs of leisure, and surpluses in those lines of production in which the transfer has the opposite effect. For example, an increase in state-sponsored unemployment subsidy may reduce labor-force participation (more will be said about supply elasticities shortly), while state-mandated improvements in working conditions in some areas may encourage an oversupply of labor. If income redistribution tends normally to flow from those who produce relatively more value to those who produce relatively less – a criticism often leveled at the welfare state – serious deadweight losses will arise, which contribute to what I termed in Chapter 4 as the "crisis of the mixed economy." With the passage of time, these internal responses within the target area of a transfer will induce external responses in industries and lines of activity in ever more remote areas of the catallaxy. The negative unintended consequences of the transfer – labor shortages and surpluses – will eventually spread through the market process. Dislocation in the labor market thus affects other input markets, such as the market for capital goods. If labor shortages were to dominate labor surpluses, for example, the net effect of forced transfers would be to raise the relative cost of labor to producers, which would tend to cause them to shift over to methods of production that are more capital-intensive than, from the perspective of the unhampered market process, they would have been.

The catallactic consequences of a forced transfer, however, are not limited to a shortage of labor (i.e., the incentive effect). There is also a tendency to overlook opportunities for improved plan coordination in production activities because of a reduction in entrepreneurial presence in those areas, or to engage in activities that would otherwise have been unnecessary (i.e., the discovery effect). This is the second part of a distortion in opportunity costs; it allows errors to continue disrupting production plans and further retards productivity.

The foregoing examined the implications of a forced transfer on the opportunity costs of leisure given a fixed set of ideological preferences. In addition, however, there are the direct effects of redistribution on the ideological preferences themselves (i.e., *shifts in the ideological preferences*) of those affected at both ends on the transfer. Likewise, it is possible to reflect on the implications of a change in ideology on the significance that actors attach to a given opportunity-cost distortion.

A reduction in the opportunity-cost of leisure *per se* may be insufficient for large numbers of actors to withdraw much of their labor. An increase or extension in unemployment benefits, for example, might do more to prolong the unemployment of those already receiving benefits than to attract new beneficiaries. But a deterioration in the belief in the virtues of personal responsibility, private property, and individual freedom (the last in contrast to a sense of personal security) might very well represent a sufficient loosening of informal social constraints to cause a significant number to work less and seek transfer benefits. Moreover, commitment to these beliefs is likely to be no less diminished in the minds of those who are forced to finance the transfer, making them less willing to undertake the effort (which includes not only ordinary labor but also overcoming the inner inertia) that would enable them to contribute at all. In other words, the phenomenon of interest here is not the inefficiencies and deadweight losses that an intervention creates (although they are important), but its impact on the propensity to shirk.[11]

Although they are analytically distinct, opportunity-cost distortions and the weakening of the moral aversion against state expansion combine to produce a complex of unintended consequences, which can further lower the resistance of public choosers to redistribution and induce further ideological change. As in the case of regulatory dynamics, the newly distorted relative prices and their unintended consequences, together with the transformed ideological preferences among public choosers, produce conditions – a new set of initial conditions – conducive to further intervention.

The unintended consequences of taxation and expenditure[12]

Of particular interest to policy analysis are the relative-price effects, under a stable set of ideological preferences, that are created by income taxation and governmental expenditure. A favorite egalitarian argument, for example, is that the progressive income tax, when combined with carefully targeted social spending, can be an effective tool for achieving greater income equality in society. Yet, from the perspective of the pre-tax distribution of income, the unintended consequence of attempts to redistribute income is to produce less rather than more equality.

Let us begin by addressing the problem of the wage elasticity of total labor supply, to which I earlier alluded. That is, since income depends on both the wage rate and the total labor supplied at that rate, the question immediately arises of whether introducing a new or higher income tax, by lowering the effective wage rate, will on net induce laborers to work more in order to make up their lost income (the "income effect") or work less owing to the lower return to labor (the "substitution effect").[13] Here I will follow Wagner (1989) and hold total labor supply constant. Holding total labor supply constant does more than merely sidestep the elasticity issue, it also helps to isolate the serious repercussions of an income tax on the *composition* of labor.

Higher income-tax rates would leave the composition of labor unchanged only if labor mobility among occupations were completely absent (i.e., if the supply of labor in specific occupations were perfectly inelastic), which is very unlikely to obtain in any but the shortest of time periods. If, for example, there are only two kinds of jobs, one involving little risk and the other involving much higher risk, and if the taste for risk is the same for all workers, we should expect the earnings from the second kind of job to be relatively higher than the first as compensation for the difference in risk. That is, this earnings differential exists because the supply of workers in the riskier-job market would be relatively smaller than in the safer-job market as a result of workers at the margin migrating from the former to the latter until the subjective marginal returns to both jobs are equalized. (If it were impossible for workers to change jobs, this migration would not take place.)

An income tax, by lowering the relative earnings from riskier jobs, will tend to induce workers to shift from higher-paying to lower-paying jobs. To see this, suppose that all income derives from labor and that differences in risk result in riskier jobs paying a 20 percent premium over safer jobs. Say then that the initial income distribution for safer and riskier jobs is L = $25,000 and H = $30,000, respectively. A progressive income tax[14] of, for example, 10 percent on L and 15 percent on H will yield post-tax incomes of $22,500 and $25,500, respectively. This means that the income tax has reduced the income differential from 20 to 13 percent, which, if preferences of workers are stable, represents a market disequilibrium – high-risk-bearing workers will now be earning too little to cover their opportunity costs. Workers will therefore tend to migrate from riskier to safer jobs, causing supply to decrease in the former (with a corresponding rise in wages and per capita income) and to increase in the latter (with a corresponding fall in wages and per capita income). In order to preserve workers' preferred 20 percent income differential, their migration might tend, for example, to push the pre-tax salaries of safer jobs toward $24,200 and the pre-tax salaries of riskier jobs toward $30,750.[15]

Determining the precise equilibrium salaries in this example would of course depend on the elasticity of supply in specific occupations. But so long as it is non-zero in a sufficient number of them – so that changes in relative wage rates cause migration – the basic conclusion would not change and the pre-tax distribution of income resulting from the redistributive-tax policy will tend to be worse from an egalitarian viewpoint. Thus, in the present example, as a result of the income tax the percentage difference in pre-tax incomes has increased from 20 to 27 percent.

The analysis of the effect of government expenditure or a subsidy on labor composition and income distribution is very similar to that of taxation. A subsidy is essentially a forced transfer of income from those earning H to those earning L.[16] Assuming that actors seek to better their conditions as they see it, we should therefore expect to see labor tending once again to migrate from H-jobs to L-jobs. The resulting fall in supply in the H-job market and rise in supply in the L-job market, will once again tend to drive pre-subsidy incomes higher in the former and depress them in the latter. As in the analysis of taxation, subsidies will have perverse outcomes owing to the incentives that intervention presents to actors in the market process.

A rich source of useful insights into the causes and unintended consequences of redistributive policies, especially as they relate to subsidies, is Charles Murray's investigation into what he alleges has been the failure of 1960s-initiated social-welfare programs in the United States (Murray 1984). Murray has formulated what he has called "laws of social programs," which distill much from the findings of his study that is of particular relevance. The following are two of these laws that are the most germane for us, both of which are simply straightforward extensions of elementary economic principles.

1. **"The Law of Unintended Rewards.** Any social transfer increases the net value of being in the condition that prompted the transfer" (ibid.: 212).

This follows from the most fundamental of all relations in economic theory, in which, *ceteris paribus*, the lower the relative price of a good, the more of that good a self-interested individual will want to consume. This relation holds for all goods. For example, while drivers may not enjoy having auto accidents, if the cost of "driving recklessly," the relevant good in this case, were lowered – perhaps owing to safety devices or being fully insured – the net value of taking care would be lowered and drivers would tend to engage in more reckless behavior. (This is the familiar problem of moral hazard.) Likewise, since a subsidy to the unemployed tends to lower the relative value or opportunity cost of being or becoming unemployed, no matter how odious people may find this condition to be, it will then tend to increase the net value of being or becoming unemployed (or, equivalently, to reduce the net value of working). The expected result is then more rather than less unemployment (or poverty, or ill health, or drug addiction, or whatever) as a direct consequence of the subsidy.

2. **"The Law of Net Harm.** The less likely it is that the unwanted behavior will change voluntarily, the more likely it is that a program to induce change will cause net harm" (ibid.: 216).

This law involves the relative responsiveness of those who currently engage in an unwanted activity versus those who do not. The less responsive persons of the first kind are to a change in incentives relative to persons of the second kind, the more net harm there will be from a program that is aimed at changing the behavior of the first.

To give a highly simplified example of this phenomenon, suppose the state wishes to reduce its citizens' consumption of cocaine. According to this second law, the more highly addicted to cocaine users are (i.e., the less likely they are to change their behavior voluntarily), the more likely it will be that a program that, for example, pays persons (of the first kind) to give up cocaine will actually attract more persons (of the second kind) to the drug who would otherwise have stayed away, so that they can later collect the rewards from quitting, than it will induce current users (of the first kind) to quit. In the same way, the more obdurate are the poor, the less likely that programs that reward them for finding their way out of poverty will actually succeed in helping them to do so, and the more likely it will be that those who just miss qualifying for the program will, through diminished caution and care, before long find themselves poor. In the language of our previous example, H-job workers are induced to migrate to L-jobs, where an L-"job" is being unemployed and poor.

Moreover, if this is true of programs, such as job training, that are at least designed to help the unemployed and poor find their own way out of a condition that authorities find undesirable, it will be even more true of programs, such as food stamps and unemployment insurance, that are even less effective in achieving that goal. Thus, without having to postulate a shift in the ideological preferences of public choosers or a fundamental change in the underlying moral values of the citizens affected by forced redistribution (both of which will be dealt with later in this part), it is possible to see how this policy can create a kind of dependency on transfers for which the welfare state is often criticized.[17]

The consequences of taxation discussed so far are examples of the "incentive effect." The "discovery effect" of taxation, however, is at least as significant for the production of unintended consequences in the interventionist process. The discovery effect encompasses both class-two and class-one errors and learning, unlike those discussed above which entail more exclusively class-one errors and learning. We already encountered the discovery effect of taxation in Chapter 4 in the analysis of a tax on pure entrepreneurial profits (i.e., a so-called "windfall-profits tax"). Recall that such a tax is, contrary to standard analysis, generally not neutral with respect to economic activity because of the way it masks potential profit opportunities. To see this, note that according to Kirzner: "It is the entrepreneur's awareness of the *open-endedness* of the decision context that appears to stimulate the qualities of self-reliance, initiative, and discovery" (1985: 109; emphasis original). Kirzner then goes on to conclude: "To announce in advance to potential entrepreneurs that 'lucky' profits will be taxed away is to convert open-ended situations into situations more and more approximating those of a given, closed character" (ibid.: 111; emphasis omitted). Such a tax would generate class-two errors – there is nothing in the nature of its consequences that would, unlike the relative-price effects that openly frustrate the intent of income equalization, *inevitably* bring them to the attention of public choosers. Hence, even if an income tax could somehow avoid creating perverse outcomes through the incentive effects of relative-price distortions, this does not mean it will be free of such outcomes. And while those negative consequences are not "perverse" in quite the same way as those that issue from incentive effects, the resulting narrowing of possibilities is something that public choosers, were they to become aware of it, would probably find undesirable.[18]

Before leaving this analysis of the unintended consequences of taxation and subsidies, let us recall that we have been operating under the assumption that the underlying ideological preferences of public choosers are fixed. The only kind of change in ideological preference permitted is what in Chapter 4 were termed "marginal" changes – i.e., the response to a change in relative prices under given ideological preferences. Later in this chapter I examine the forces and dynamics that cause shifts in ideological preferences themselves. It is important to realize, however, that even under fixed ideological preferences intervention can *initiate* a series of repercussions that may result in a full-fledged interventionist dynamic (i.e., specifically, a transfer dynamic), provided that *subsequent* shifts in ideological preference reinforce those initial tendencies. That is, the response of public choosers to negative unintended consequences, under a particular distribution of ideological preferences combined with bounded rationality and radical ignorance, may very well be to intervene further in a way that simply exacerbates the original problem. The egalitarian-minded authorities, for instance, seeing the growing levels of inequality – an example might be the higher degree of income inequality said to have occurred during the 1980s in the United States – might, without appreciating the complexity of the problem or perceiving the fundamental source of the inequality, simply pursue income redistribution more vigorously, and thereby generate what are from their point of view even less desirable results. If the additional intervention causes reinforcing shifts in ideological preferences, it will set a transfer dynamic into motion.

The impact of income transfers on property rights and prices

One of the less-appreciated economic consequences of governmental income transfers is how they indirectly influence relative prices via their impact on the integrity of the underlying property relations. In short, forced income transfers erode property rights, and this in turn reduces the dependability of prices as both guides to and reflections of expectations about the relative scarcity of resources. Moreover, for any given asset, the larger the share of its total value that the state controls, the more attenuated the private property rights to it will be. Thus, what one social theorist has said with respect to forced transfers in the case of land value also applies here: "to appropriate 10 percent of the value of land is the same thing economically as appropriating 10 percent of the land itself" (Sowell 1980: 191).

The claims to ownership that constitute private property may be taken away all at once or piecemeal. Nationalization of private income and wealth is an example of the former, while what I am calling income transfers embody the latter. Let us first examine the case of income transfers, leaving nationalization for later discussion.

In Chapter 3 I explained how private ownership of property constitutes the foundation of entrepreneurship in the market process as well as of social coordination and cooperation. To appreciate the connection between income transfers and the level of entrepreneurial activity, one has only to consider what would happen were the state to confiscate all private income for the purpose of drastic redistribution. Clearly in this instance no further scope for market-based entrepreneurial activity would remain, and the right to use and dispose of one's own property, as well as all private claims of ownership, would have become empty and practically meaningless. Thus, the myriad of private exchanges among uniquely positioned individuals, who by exploiting their contextual knowledge of time and place help to generate the price signals that reflect and guide the decisions of myriads of anonymous actors, would not occur. Under complete nationalization of resources, coordination and social cooperation within a spontaneous social order would cease to exist.

This situation is in all relevant respects identical to that of a *Zwangswirtschaft*, in which private ownership has also been effectively abolished through thorough-going regulation. Under these conditions the rights to the acquisition, use, and disposition of property, though nominally in private hands, is in reality in the exclusive control of public authorities. A situation in which the state has completely appropriated the value of the property through income transfers but retains the trappings of a catallaxy is also a form of *Zwangswirtschaft*. He who pays the piper (or controls the flute) calls the tune.

Just as one can draw on the analysis of knowledge problems under complete collectivism to analyze intermediate cases that arise within a mixed economy, so one can also apply insights from the above argument, which involves an extreme form of property-rights confiscation, to the intermediate case of less-than-comprehensive transfers of income (including nationalization). That is, if under laissez-faire there is a great deal of freedom for entrepreneurs to adjust to endogenous and exogenous changes so that the price system operates as market-process theory describes; and if under the complete collectivization of property the freedom of entrepreneurial adjustment in the market process is at a minimum and the price system is eradicated; then one can conjecture, without specifying the exact nature of the trade-off, that as the state progressively confiscates private property through income transfers, the effectiveness of the price system in helping to coordinate individual plans within the catallaxy progressively diminishes. That is, the erosion of private property, whether gradual or sudden, will not only generate errors and discoordination among individual planners in the catallaxy, but will itself act as a barrier to the discovery of these errors. Errors will tend to persist over a longer period of time, and more errors will remain undetected, because such erosion ultimately compromises the price system itself, the principal means by which agents discover and correct plan discoordination in the market process.

Having thus far analyzed the impact of redistribution in distorting relative prices and the role of those distortions in shaping transfer dynamics, under the assumption of stable ideological preferences, it is now time to investigate the causes of changes in ideological preferences themselves, as well as the consequences of those changes for the overall transfer process within the welfare state. This is the purpose of the next section.

Ideological change in the pure welfare state

Recall the three theses introduced in Chapter 1 – the gradual-acceptance, self-fulfillment, and dynamic trade-off theses – each of which, I claimed, embodies ideological change more or less endogenously. Each of these arguments relates in different ways and to varying degrees to the theory of interventionism. Indeed, of the three, the dynamic trade-off thesis may turn out to address what is in fact the dominant force driving the transfer process within the pure welfare state, with the forces described in the other two theses playing important but ultimately supporting roles. (Note that we have already seen that, in the pure regulatory state, distortions in explicit relative prices tend there to play a more central role than does ideological change.) Indeed, elements of the other two ideological forces may be seen as special cases of the more general trade-off between freedom and security, broadly conceived. With this in mind, let us first review the gradual-acceptance and self-fulfillment theses, and then focus on the dynamic trade-off thesis and its overall significance to the welfare state.

The gradual-acceptance thesis

According to this thesis, the very act of intervention *unintentionally weakens the moral aversion or psychological resistance* citizens might have to intervention, and by so doing stimulates the demand for additional intervention. The repeated use of coercion and compulsion to address social and economic problems can thus habituate citizens to the idea and practice of interventionism, and thereby increase the expected net benefit to them of employing political means. The latter phenomenon is particularly relevant to the discussion of ideological change from the previous chapter, which suggested that the number of actors who are perceived to become political agents will tend to increase the tolerance of citizens toward interventionism (i.e., that it will cause a shift in ideological preference). This, indeed, is the kind of ideological change that is closely associated with regulatory dynamics.

Nathan Glazer offers a promising alternative explanation for the phenomenon of diminished moral aversion in his suggestion that intervention gradually breaks down what he calls the "fine structure of society."[19] According to Glazer, there are limits to effective public policy that are inherent in the very nature of state intervention. In particular, public policy tends to undermine the position of "traditional agents" of social coordination and "further encourages needy people to depend on the government for help rather than on the traditional structures" (Glazer 1988: 7). This dependency begins to take place when public policy substitutes relatively formal, impersonal, and uniform state controls for the more informal, community-based, and personalized social controls of traditional community networks, thus contributing "to the undermining of confidence in and acceptance of informal social controls" that constitute the fine structure of society (ibid.: 148). Indeed, Glazer argues that "this is the basic force behind the ever growing demand for more social programs and their frequent failure to satisfy our hopes" (ibid.). This is so because those who are considered to be among the "needy" are typically identified by how far they appear to deviate from some ideal of equality. But there has also been, according to Glazer, a parallel social development in the form of a "revolution of rising expectations," in which "we become ever more sensitive to smaller and smaller degrees of inequality" (ibid.: 4).[20] The dynamics of these expectations would imply that the welfare state would continue to grow even if the degree of social inequality were shrinking. (In fact, of course, we have already seen how the very process of forcibly transferring income from one group to another could actually increase rather than decrease inequality.)

This idea of a "revolution of rising expectations" is very similar to the problem of whether to include or exclude "hard cases" from governmental assistance. It is of some interest to note that Murray claims that a fundamental change in this basic assumption took place in the United States during the 1960s. According to Murray (1984: 212), "social welfare policy in earlier times tended to deal with this problem by erring in the direction of exclusion – better to deny help to some truly needy persons than to let a few slackers slip through." Weakening or discarding that assumption "leads to programs with constantly broadening target populations" (ibid.), which is what has indeed happened in the United States since the 1960s.[21]

The impact of the change in the fine structure on the behavior of both beneficiaries and benefactors of forced redistribution is quite separate from the pure incentive effects and marginal changes in ideology that arise from changes in relative prices, which were discussed earlier in this chapter. For example, turning our attention for a moment toward the benefactors of a forced transfer, we should expect to see less voluntary charitable giving to the poor on their part, not only because a higher tax makes the relative price of giving higher than before, but also because the moral attitude of the benefactor toward the act of charity itself will have changed. According to Mises: "The discretion of bureaucrats is substituted for the discretion of people whom an inner voice drives to acts of charity" (1966: 840). Forced transfers thus weaken the social pressures that in the past would have reinforced the giver's "moral sense" (Wilson 1993) with respect to giving voluntarily to support others, even strangers, in their time of need, just as it weakens the moral sense on the part of beneficiaries that living off the charity of others is shameful.[22] "It is a system that corrupts both givers and receivers" (Mises 1966: 838).[23]

It is interesting to note in passing that in addition to this line of analysis, Glazer describes another logic of increasing intervention that is strikingly similar to the one described in this study, in which "any policy has dynamic aspects such that it also expands the problem, changes the problem, generates further problems" (ibid.: 5). The basis for this process is "simply a lack of knowledge" about the nature and significance of the fine structure of society (ibid.: 6) that brings about a state of affairs in which "whatever great actions we undertake today involve such an increase in complexity that we act generally with less knowledge than we would like to have, even if with more than we once had" (ibid.: 7). For the purposes of explaining the dynamics of the welfare state, however, Glazer appears to attach greater significance to intervention's corrosive impact on the fine structure of society and the perverse incentives that this creates. He writes,

> But aside from all these problems of . . . limitations of knowl-
> edge, there is the simple reality that every piece of social
> policy substitutes for some traditional arrangement. . . . In
> doing so, social policy weakens the position of these tra-
> ditional agents and further encourages needy people to
> depend on the government for help rather then on traditional
> structures.
>
> (Glazer 1988: 140–55)

As already noted, Glazer regards the substitution of public policy for private action as the source of the escalating demand for government intervention as well as its "frequent failure to satisfy our hopes."

The self-fulfillment thesis

According to this thesis, an unintended consequence of an intervention that is based on a spurious rationale could be to render that rationale conceptually coherent, and in so doing provide a more solid basis or a stronger justification for further intervention than was the case prior to the initial intervention.

The spurious rationale that is relevant here is so-called social or redistributive justice: the idea that the unhampered market process inevitably generates serious and unacceptable inequalities in outcomes, and that the state is in the best position to rectify such outcomes. It is spurious, not so much because of what some might object to as its misrepresentation of the nature of capitalism, but because it rests in large measure on the mistaken belief that it is possible in practice to separate the process of production from the process of distribution – a clear case of misplaced concreteness. Standard economic theory has exposed the error of this argument by showing that in the market process the entrepreneur-producers decide to produce only when they anticipate a specific pattern of demand for their product.[24] In a minimal-state catallaxy, production is inseparable from distribution, and any attempt to alter distribution must inevitably affect the incentives to produce and alter the actual patterns of production.

In fact, however, production and distribution become operationally distinct and meaningful only outside of a laissez-faire capitalist context, as when the state actually begins to collectivize factors of production. The state itself, by its very act of redistribution, reifies the formerly purely analytic and imaginary separation of production and distribution. More generally, according to Hayek (1976: 69),

> in ... a system in which each is allowed to choose his occupation and therefore nobody can have the power and the duty to see that the results correspond to our wishes ... the concept of "social justice" is necessarily empty and meaningless, because in it nobody's will can determine the relative outcomes of the different people, or prevent that they be partly dependent on accident.

The meaning of social justice becomes the most coherent in a collectivist "command" economy, since such an economy "presupposes that people are guided by specific directions and not by rules of just individual conduct" (ibid.). In this way, governmental redistribution tends to reify a distinction between production and distribution that in an unhampered market process is purely abstract and non-operational.

More importantly, the belief that the distinction between production and distribution is operationalizable opens a significant avenue for further state intervention. That is, a program of redistribution that operationalizes this distinction produces its own justification, and this can in turn prompt further intervention, through what Hayek refers to as a "peculiar self-accelerating tendency." To wit,

> the more dependent the position of the individuals or groups is seen to become on the actions of government, the more they will insist that the [sic] governments aim at some recognizable scheme of redistributive justice; and the more governments try to realize some preconceived pattern of desirable distribution, the more they must subject the position of the different individuals and groups to their control. So long as the belief in "social justice" governs political action, this process must progressively approach nearer to a totalitarian system.
>
> (ibid.: 68)

Since the expansion of intervention tends to reinforce public choosers' belief in social justice, an empirical tendency for actual welfare states to become ever more collectivistic under these circumstances may become evident. Reinforcing this tendency, as we have already seen, is the phenomenon that redistributional policies, through their relative-price and incentive effects, typically aggravate the distributional problems that benevolent and egalitarian-minded public choosers initially sought to address – e.g., by making base incomes even more unequal – thereby providing even greater justification for more intervention.

It is true that, in a very special sense, the critics of capitalism are correct when they claim that "unfair outcomes" are an inevitable feature of the market process, if by unfair they mean that individuals from time to time and to a greater or lesser degree are subject to forces over which they have little or no control. For example, the development of computer technology may have tipped the balance of comparative advantage in the United States away from the production of ferrous metals, and as an unintended result threatened the livelihood, at least temporarily, of a generation of iron and steel workers. But to the extent that public choosers recognize that these outcomes are neither directed at them or their group personally nor the intended result of deliberate actions on the part of anyone in particular – as in the pure market process they are not – the demand for intervention, while not entirely eliminated, may be contained. But, as Hayek argues,

> Once it becomes increasingly true, and generally recognized, that the position of the individual is determined not by impersonal forces, not as a result of the competitive effort of many, but the deliberate decision of authority, the attitude of people toward their position in the social order necessarily changes.
>
> (Hayek 1972: 106)

The power and authority to make such deliberate decisions originates in the state and those public choosers who serve or support its far-reaching policies. In this circumstance, the individual will have stronger grounds for feeling that he is the victim of deliberate and systematic injustice. This is the beginning, not of a "revolution of rising expectations" as in the gradual-acceptance thesis, but of public choosers' growing discontent with the *status quo* as they see it.[25]

The dynamic trade-off thesis

Among the three kinds of ideological change examined here, this thesis perhaps most effectively endogenizes ideological shifts by ingeniously integrating economic and sociological forces. It is thus for our purposes a very powerful tool for understanding the dynamics of the pure welfare state.

Recall that the "dynamic trade-off thesis" states that intervention *produces socio-economic consequences* – in particular, greater personal insecurity on the part of some or all public choosers – that are, from the perspective of the public choosers themselves, worse than the conditions that the intervention was intended to eliminate, which in turn stimulates a further demand for intervention (with an attendant loss of personal freedom) in order to reduce the added insecurity. At each successive stage of the process, therefore, the preferences of public choosers tend to shift in favor of more "security" and less personal freedom, although the tendency of the resulting intervention is, perversely, to generate even greater insecurity than had existed before.

We saw earlier in this chapter how a similar process contributes to the instability of regulatory-state capitalism, although other forces are more central to that story. Recall that in the regulatory state, regulation tends (among other things) to hinder the capacity of actors to perceive and adjust to changing conditions, which in turn reduces their ability to compete, lowers the return on private investment, and induces unintended plan revisions and redirections of social resources. The result is that they experience an increase in the level of insecurity. Their now-higher-levels of insecurity then encourage them to increase their demand for further intervention.

Forced transfers also produce insecurity and instability in a related but distinct way. To begin with, let us once again recognize that two of the hallmarks of capitalism are the rivalrous nature of its competition and the spontaneity of its emergent patterns, which over time produce unpredictable and unprecedented change. Entrepreneurial responses to such changes in environment, many of which are themselves the result of entrepreneurial actions elsewhere, produce their own unintended consequences, which, when combined with further entrepreneurial discovery in the catallaxy, generate coordinating tendencies. The order that emerges from this process is one that embodies incessant evolutionary change. As Schumpeter (1950: 82) expressed it: "The essential point to grasp is that in dealing with capitalism we are dealing with an evolutionary process.... Capitalism, then, is by nature a form or method of economic change and not only never is but never can be stationary."

Consequently, unlike life in static pre-capitalistic societies in which relative job security and fixity of status or position was the norm, life under capitalism entails not only manifestly higher (and usually increasing) average material well-being (Rosenberg and Birdzell 1986), but perhaps also the *perception* of much greater risk and uncertainty. Or, as Edward Berkowitz, in his history of the American welfare state, describes this "social democratic" viewpoint: "as nations industrialize, productivity increases, but so does insecurity" (Berkowitz 1991: xv). At this point, Glazer's "revolution of rising expectations" enters the picture. Under capitalism, that is, those who are persistently slow to adjust to ever-changing circumstances may feel they are more likely to experience *comparative* deprivation, if only for a short period of time. The perceived level of relative insecurity of persons so situated may be such that it induces those among them whose marginal preferences for intervention are relatively high to press for protection through intervention.[26] They may do so for themselves or benevolently for others whom they regard as suffering from even greater insecurity. If in response to this demand the state grants such persons or groups special protection from the distress and anxiety they associate with capitalism, the forced transfers needed to accomplish this task would necessarily reduce the wealth, property rights, and the incentives to act entrepreneurially of those who must finance it. Whether the protection is paid for directly through taxation or indirectly through barriers to competition, the consequence is the same – greater insecurity for the rest of those in society who are now left relatively unprotected. Or, as Hayek has put it:

> the more we try to provide full security by interfering with the market system, the greater the insecurity becomes; and, what is worse, the greater becomes the contrast between the security of those to whom it is granted as a privilege and the ever increasing insecurity of the underprivileged. And the more security becomes a privilege, and the greater the danger to those excluded from it, the higher will security be prized.
>
> (Hayek 1972: 130)

This, again, may well feed into "rising expectations." What Jonathan Hughes has called the "search for stability" (1991: 138) thus tends to foster policies that produce mounting instability.

The choice between freedom and security at the margin is not a *perfectly* informed one, in the sense that public choosers make it in contemplation of *all* relevant facts (or their probable occurrence). The point of the "200-mile-per-hour speed limit" example in Chapter 4, if the reader will recall, was to illustrate the "fertility of freedom" (to use Kirzner's happy phrase). That is, "freedom is fertile in creating actual (perceived) opportunities. A potential opportunity not yet noticed, may, through the addition of an increment of freedom, become an actual one" (Kirzner 1979: 233). The complication this poses for choice is that we can never be sure, although we might speculate, what those opportunities will be at the moment when we are making marginal choices

between freedom and security. The nature of what security promises, on the contrary, is typically much more concrete, articulable,
or even tangible: e.g., a steady job, a place to live, and food on
the table. Faced with a choice between, on the one hand, the
potential to realize ends that at present are only vaguely and
partially articulable, and on the other hand, a steady job, etc., is it
any wonder that public choosers opt much more readily for the
latter, especially in uncertain times? Once public choosers pay
the price for added security, however, it is not inevitable that they
will learn about the opportunities that were thereby foregone –
i.e., it is not a matter of class-one learning. While the repercussions
for the system are, as we have seen, of the type that is subject to
class-one learning (i.e., ultimately greater perceived insecurity), the
chooser need never know what he gave up even though he may
temporarily get what he wants.[27]

The other ideological dynamics *may* come into play in conjunction with the dynamic trade-off. In particular, as public choosers
observe increasing numbers of individuals using political means to
reduce insecurity, this might lessen their moral aversion à la the
"gradual acceptance thesis." Or, since individuals may feel, with
some justification, that their circumstances now are less the result
of their own efforts combined with the impersonal forces of
market demand and supply than of the arbitrary decrees of public
authorities, they may find that the previously empty notion of
"social justice" now has a more coherent meaning to them à la the
"self-fulfillment thesis." Either of these forces by themselves can
produce the shift in ideological preferences needed to bring about
an increase in the demand for a further round of intervention.

Indeed, the gradual-acceptance and self-fulfillment phenomena,
while displaying certain unique qualities, may simply be offshoots
or perhaps even special cases of the dynamic trade-off itself. That
is, in the case of the gradual-acceptance phenomenon, one of the
important elements of the set of rules, customs, and institutions
that constitute the fine structure of society is the idea that self-
reliance and individual effort are important for maintaining social
cooperation and a strong, self-regulating community.[28] I need then
only note that this idea is closely tied to personal freedom, which
is sacrificed for personal security in the dynamic trade-off. And
in the case of the self-fulfillment phenomenon, the attempt to
achieve redress for the perceived injustices of capitalism through
forced redistribution perpetuates and exacerbates the very out-

comes that benevolent public authorities sought to remove by lending greater substance to individuals' feelings of insecurity under capitalism.

Although it is likely that in actual interventionist processes these other two forces do enter the picture, they need not do so for the next stage of the dynamic trade-off to take place. The very increase in insecurity that the remainder of society now experiences will tend to induce some portion of these public choosers to increase their demand for intervention – once again, either to help "guarantee" their own security or that of others. From the standpoint of the dynamic trade-off thesis, it does not matter that their greater demand for intervention is the direct result of an increased dependence on arbitrary public authority (self-fulfillment thesis), or of the ever larger numbers of persons employing coercion and compulsion to protect their position (gradual-acceptance thesis). No doubt, however, that the presence of these other forces of ideological change would augment the demand for intervention beyond the level associated strictly with growing insecurity and thereby increase the severity of the negative unintended consequences of redistribution.

If our goal were to forge even stronger links among these forces, however, we could note that in the dynamic trade-off the *value* public choosers attach to freedom and security undergoes a fundamental transformation. According to Hayek:

> As the number of the privileged increases and the difference between their security and the insecurity of the others increases, a completely new set of social values generally arises. It is no longer independence but security which gives the rank of status ...
>
> (Hayek 1972: 130)

With this transformation comes a steady erosion of the fine structure of society and of the general moral aversion toward the use of intervention, associated with numbers of political agents, as well as the continuing reification of phenomena, such as institutionalized exploitation, under an interventionist regime. Together with the dynamic trade-off, these become the basis of an ever-growing demand for further intervention in the transfer dynamic.

Summary

The previous section discussed marginal changes in ideology, which refer both to the migration of actors among differently remunerated occupations (including unemployment) resulting from a change in the relative price of leisure, and to the policy response of public choosers to the ensuing increase in income inequality. This section dealt with the causes and implications for the transfer process (and of the interventionist process in general) of shifts in ideological preferences themselves. These shifts substantially reinforce the relative-price incentive effects that occur in both the regulatory and the transfer processes. While marginal changes may be insufficient to produce a full-fledged interventionist dynamic, the addition of ideological shifts substantially increases the likelihood of this taking place.

Once again, however, embarking on a path to collectivism is not inevitable. We have only been analyzing the endogenous element of ideological change, because the exogenous and indeterminate aspect of ideological change is, almost by definition, not subject to analysis – at least the kind of analysis that would be useful in making pattern predictions. (But an appreciation of this fact may be relevant for setting limits to what can be predicted.) As explained in Chapter 4, at each node within the interventionist process, public choosers have a genuine, though by no means easy, option of taking steps to reverse the process.

Finally, ideological change is plainly a very important part of transfer dynamics. Whether it plays a more important role here than in regulatory dynamics is a question explored in the last part of this chapter.

Nationalization

Nationalization is a species of income transfer, and so possesses essentially the same dynamic properties. For example, we have already considered one aspect of the catallactic consequences of nationalization in the earlier discussion of how income transfers distort relative prices, which guide individual decision-making and promote economic coordination, by weakening the underlying structure of property rights. There is, however, another way in which nationalization can disrupt economic coordination that we have yet to consider.

Nationalization, state monopoly, and bureaucracy

As a practical matter, nationalization entails state monopoly (i.e., a single seller protected from competitive entry by political means). In principle, of course, they are separable. The state, for example, in appropriating the assets of, say, a school might refrain from meddling directly with the assets and decisions of the remaining private schools in the market for education. It would be naive, however, to believe that those competitors would not sooner or later find themselves at a considerable competitive disadvantage with respect to the government school, which not only has the potential to draw on the financial resources of the state, but, more importantly, can use (political) means that are vastly more effective in protecting itself from competition than those open to purely private firms. Over time, this political advantage would enable the government school to dominate the market in which it operates. Thus, while a nationalized enterprise and a state monopoly are not the same thing, the former has a strong empirical tendency to give rise to the latter.

While it is also true that a nationalized industry and a modern state monopoly both typically employ bureaucratic management as their principal method of administration, this aspect of nationalization is not the concern of the present chapter. This is not to deny that the problems of bureaucratic management – emanating from the absence of priceable outputs and the presence of political constraints – examined in Chapter 3 also confront nationalized industries. These problems, however, are not the only ones that are relevant to this study. Here, I will derive the implications of the nationalization of an industry for the interventionist process that emanate from the unintended consequences that arise from that industry's monopolistic, rather than its bureaucratic, character. Thus, unlike Niskanen's (1971) model, in which the dynamic for bureaucratic growth is internal to bureaucracy itself, my discussion focuses on how bureaucracy promotes conditions, within a nationalized industry *qua* state monopoly, that foster negative unintended consequences in other parts of the system that induce further intervention.

Monopoly and the state

In Chapter 3, I discussed the impact of monopoly on the competitive market process when the scale of the monopoly is large in relation to the entire catallaxy. There I emphasized the effect of monopoly in degrading the capacity of relative prices within the market process *to convey relevant knowledge to the monopolist*. In particular, under monopoly there is only a single mind (the monopolist's) for whom such information would have direct value. Thus, while the added protection that monopoly ownership gives to entrepreneurial-monopoly profits benefits the market process to the extent that it inspires more discovery,[29] the monopolist's growth will negate this benefit when a sufficient number of the profit opportunities that at least one of several independent minds would have discovered in a non-monopolistic setting are overlooked by the monopolist. According to standard theory in contrast, if every industry in the catallaxy were monopolized under uniform demand-price elasticy, there would be no normative effect because the relative prices of all commodities would be unchanged (and, thus, no misallocation of resources would occur). The argument just presented leads to a different conclusion, however, since the likelihood of making discoveries in each of these industries would, according to that argument, now be lower compared to what it might have been were these industries non-monopolistic.

What I did not emphasize in Chapter 3 is the impact of progressive monopolization of social resources on *the conveyance of relevant knowledge within the non-monopolized sector*. In other words, when the monopolist is a "big player"[30] in the catallaxy his impact on the use of knowledge in the market process has two aspects. The first is the sluggish response of the monopolist himself to entrepreneurial opportunities (which I have just briefly reviewed) and the second is the effect of that sluggishness on the responsiveness of the rest of the catallaxy, which in turn ultimately hampers the monopolist's ability to make correct decisions. Both effects lend support to the conclusion of the previous chapter that our worst fears about bureaucracy emanate not from bureaucratic management itself but from the size of government.

The first big-player effect will directly degrade the reliability of a monopolist's own output prices (and, likewise, the reliability of the input prices of a monopsonist) as the monopolist becomes a bigger player in the catallaxy. This is because as the monopolist grows, the limitations of his mind will impinge on an ever larger portion of social resources. When the monopolist owns only a small fraction of these resources, prices generated in the rest of the catallaxy can augment his knowledge of the values of resources that he does own. If, for example, the monopolist owns an oil field, the prices of non-monopolized resources, such as coal or other fuels, can serve as referents that to a degree reflect perceived opportunity costs. These referents would be especially important for a vertically integrated industry, which is what a monopoly would certainly be if it achieved the status of a big player. The closer these referents are as substitutes in use for the monopolized resources, the better their prices can function as surrogates for the monopolist. But as the monopolist acquires a growing proportion of social resources, ever fewer of the resources that might have served as referents will lie outside his direct control, and likewise ever fewer prices of non-monopolized resources will be available to him as referents.

The second big-player effect tends to degrade the information content of the prices in the rest of the catallaxy (and ultimately the monopolist's prices) on which the monopolist relies in the following quite straightforward way. Imagine that only a single market in the entire catallaxy remains outside the direct control of the monopolist. In this case not only the monopolist's prices, but also the prices charged in the single non-monopolized market, would function very poorly as signals to guide plans compared to the opposite situation in which there is only one monopolized market with the remainder of the catallaxy non-monopolized. This is because the non-monopolized markets must depend on the monopolist's prices to guide their plans no less than the latter depends on prices in the former markets. This dependence of non-monopolized markets on monopoly prices increases as the monopolist grows in relative size; and since with this growth monopoly prices will less reliably reflect conditions, the prices of the rest of the catallaxy (which depend on the reliability of all prices, including the monopolist's) will also tend to become less reliable. This, of course, feeds back to the monopolist's pricing decisions and further reduces the reliability of his prices, and so on.

Progressive monopolization thus has a tendency to impair the market process and, beyond a certain point, begins seriously to impede it. Yet the question of central importance to this study is

189

whether we can explain this growth in terms of an unconscious internal dynamic. To this end, it is unnecessary (and perhaps not possible) to say definitively that the negative unintended consequences that result from the degradation of market prices stimulate relatively more nationalization than simply an across-the-board increase in intervention of all kinds. The discoordination resulting from the generation of misleading price-signals that attends nationalization, even when it is small in scale, might very well prompt benevolent public choosers, already inclined to intervene further, to do so through nationalization. But whatever form of intervention they select, nationalization lays the groundwork for further intervention in general, just as regulation or income redistribution may induce them to nationalize.

The discussion up to this point has not specified whether progressive monopolization on the scale needed to be a net detriment to the market process is likely to require the assistance of political means – that is, whether state monopoly or private monopoly without state support is more likely to have the negative impact on the market process described so far. In response one need only consider first of all the well-known problems associated with diseconomies of scale that limit the absolute size of private firms and therefore also limit the magnitude of the big-player effects described here.[31] Second, governmental and state-supported organizations have a wider range of means (i.e., not only voluntary exchange but also taxation, subsidies, and coercive entry restrictions) that they can use to grow compared to those available to a purely private association. Thus, it is not surprising that as an empirical matter the modern state (the national government of the United States, for example) is by far the largest organized entity in society by almost any measure. Third, as should be clear by now from the discussion in previous chapters (Chapter 3 in particular), an organization operating within the governmental process is far less capable of making entrepreneurial adjustments to changing conditions than a private firm of the same size that operates within the market process. Hence, for a given size of organization, one would tend to see the disruption to the catallaxy emanating from state bureaucratic management to be much greater, or to persist for a much longer period of time, than would be the case if it were managed for profit in the market process.

Kinds of transfers and their effects

This section briefly examines a few of the more important contemporary varieties of forced transfers and their effects. The earlier discussion of regulation ranked the significance of the assorted interventions examined there on the basis of their impact on the price system. The following, however, makes no attempt to do so.

Direct income transfers

Much of the criticism aimed at the welfare state is based on the deleterious consequences of transfers from those who produce more to those who produce less. These take the form of welfare and social security subsidies, unemployment insurance, etc. along with an income tax to finance them. This is not to deny that transfers in the opposite direction (e.g., publicly supported higher education, state funding for the arts, and bail-outs of failing financial concerns) or between more or less equally productive individuals or groups (e.g., reduced sentences for criminals living in low-income neighborhoods and real-estate taxes for public schools) do occur. In the latter case, it is still true that in addition to the well-being of the net loser, another casualty of the transfer policy is the respect and faith public choosers have in the institution of private property itself. The erosion of the belief in its inviolability, as we have seen, diminishes the ability of entrepreneurs to detect plan discoordination and weakens the resistance of public choosers against the use of political means to address perceived social problems.

If transfers do bestow a net benefit on the relatively unproductive at the expense of the relatively productive, however, this would seem to only exacerbate these effects. An additional effect of such transfers is to reduce the likelihood that persons in the relatively unproductive group will become more like those in the productive group, and to increase the likelihood that the latter will become more like the former. Interventions that foster a mentality of dependency, contempt for private property, and personal irresponsibility tend to produce the very social ills and injustices they were designed to remove.

191

Budget deficit

A deficit in the finances of the state represents an intertemporal transfer of income from production in the future for the purposes of present consumption. In addition to having the effects on relative values and the ideological fine structure in common with other forms of forced transfer, deficit financing also has a direct macroeconomic impact on current relative prices and intertemporal exchange rates – i.e., rates of interest – as well as on the purchasing power of money and the information content of prices via inflation. To that extent, then, the dynamics of deficit financing has much in common with regulatory dynamics.

The "new" social regulation

This phrase refers to public policy that seeks to regulate health and safety conditions in the workplace, practices considered harmful to the natural environment, and conditions of employment with respect to racial, gender, and other forms of discrimination. As noted in Chapter 1, although regulations of this type are not ordinarily associated with the idea of income redistribution, each is intended to and effectively does, to a greater or lesser degree, favor some groups or individuals to the disadvantage of others, and in that way retains the essential character of a forced transfer. Their bearing on the interventionist process, therefore, is essentially the same as that of any other transfer of income by political means. But as regulations they also impinge on the costs of production, raising them in most cases, and thus, through the resulting production restrictions, distort the relative prices of outputs more directly than other kinds of forced transfers. This is a double-barreled character that they also have in common with deficit financing.

REGULATORY AND TRANSFER DYNAMICS: A COMPARISON

Regulatory and transfer dynamics share a common underlying logic. A set of initial relative-price and ideological conditions encourages the state to intervene at the margin in a particular way, which in turn further distorts relative prices (i.e., explicit prices and implicit opportunity costs), generates negative unintended consequences, and causes a revision in ideological preferences. The result is a new set of conditions that is even more favorable for further intervention. This process will continue unless exogenous ideological forces bring it to a halt.

Understanding the basic dynamics of the interventionist process, however, may not be enough to reveal how public choosers will actually decide between regulation and redistribution at the margin. There appears to be no compelling reason, for example, to expect that the disturbance from a regulatory intervention should tend to call forth additional regulation of the same type, or even that the state's response will take the form of regulation at all, rather than an explicit transfer. Similarly for transfers. Thus, for example, the policy response to greater inequality in pre-tax incomes, created by a tax-subsidy transfer scheme, might be an increase in macroeconomic fiscal spending to stimulate short-term income growth, instead of an escalation in forced redistribution. Which path or variation thereof public choosers take is the result of a number of factors ranging from ideological preference to political expediency.

Interaction between dynamics occurs because of this indeterminacy, but also because regulations and transfers each have some direct influence on relative prices, income distribution, and ideology. All regulations transfer income and may directly influence ideology, and to some extent all forced transfers distort relative prices – the differences are a matter of degree rather than of kind. Once again, for example, deficit spending and the new social regulation, although they primarily represent forced transfers, are also capable of severely distorting relative prices. Thus, in really existing mixed economies, the negative unintended consequences initiated in one dynamic are able to create or reinforce effects in the other. Much depends on the facts of the particular case.

Nevertheless, the present framework does enable us to posit significant differences between the overall patterns that each form of intervention produces. Specifically, the impact of regulation falls primarily on explicit relative prices; and while forced transfers distort the implicit opportunity costs of leisure and to a lesser extent explicit relative prices, they impinge even more heavily on marginal and total ideological preferences. One way to rationalize this difference in expectation is to suggest that, on the one hand, the general approach of regulation is to alter the constraints and incentives facing actors in order to induce them to behave in some sense more efficiently and to control how the competitive process operates. On the other hand, the goal of the welfare state is, again in general, to modify the distributional outcomes of the competitive process by converting the flawed outcome of self-interested behavior into one that public choosers believe is more just, and where changing the incentives and behavior of actors is a secondary concern. Thus, while there are exceptions,[32] the emphasis of regulation tends to be on competitive process and procedure, while for redistribution it is the justice of outcomes.

Now, to the extent that the policies of the welfare state are concerned with outcomes, especially long-range outcomes, produced by social processes, I maintain that the rationale behind these policies tends to be more ideological in nature. A *Weltanschauung* may be more important for sustaining a pure welfare dynamic than a pure regulatory one.[33] That is, although the impact of regulation on the ideological attitudes of businesses, households, and government is an integral part of regulatory dynamics as well, the redistributive policies of the pure welfare state seem, much more than regulation does, to be an expression of a larger conscious purpose,[34] even if the ultimate manifestation of that purpose may not be the one intended. In other words, if the outcomes that welfare policy actually produces are unforeseen (which from the perspective of this study would appear to be more than likely), such an occurrence would still be consistent with an initial vision that is more identifiably ideological in nature than would be the case in a pure regulatory state. The policies that flow from such a vision are more likely to go directly to the very heart of the fine structure of society, perhaps tipping the precarious balance between public choosers' love of freedom and their desire for security away from the former and toward the latter.

In addition, because no well-established market for leisure as such exists (although the labor market and entertainment industry do to some extent indirectly reflect an individual's subjective evaluation of leisure), the relation between implicit opportunity costs and the rest of the price system is more subtle and less visible to public choosers. For this reason, the relation may be weaker than the distortions that occur among the conventional relative prices that are more central to regulatory dynamics. That is, because in the welfare state these distortions may be less apparent, entrepreneurs may also be less likely to perceive and respond to them, and so less likely to generate further distortions, than they would be in the regulatory state (i.e., redistribution generates a greater proportion of class-two than class-one errors than does regulation). Furthermore, modifications in the quality of labor and leisure, because they may be harder to detect than changes in explicit relative prices, might also disguise some of the negative consequences of a transfer, limiting them to deadweight losses.

There is also another way in which the relative-price distortions of a given transfer can appear to be somewhat weaker than those of a regulatory intervention. Specifically, compared to regulatory interventions of similar scope, a transfer's actual impact on the overall structure of relative prices may be more limited. In the extreme case, if the state merely takes from Peter to pay Paul, the new configuration of demand need cause no drastic systematic distortions in relative prices, even though it is the state that chooses who the winners and losers are. To see why this might be true, consider what happens when, instead of a pure transfer, the state itself spends these resources strictly according to its own preferences (i.e., the preferences of public authorities rather than citizens). A systematic distortion in relative prices is more likely here because the state *qua* consumer is probably the biggest player in the catallaxy, and as we have already seen the bigger a player the state is, the more significant and systematic these distortions are likely to be (Koppl and Yeager 1992). But if we assume, as is consistent with a basic presumptions of this book, that authorities in the benevolent state do not act to satisfy their own preferences, narrowly construed (i.e., exploiting political power for personal gain), then forced transfers need not substantially alter the configuration of consumer demand and the structure of relative prices. This is most likely to be the case, though it is of course far from being a certainty, when the transfers occur mainly within income classes,[35] rather than, as assumed in my earlier discussion of transfer dynamics, across income classes.

Based on the comparative sensitivity of the price system to regulation and the dominant role of price distortions in the interventionist process, one can derive at least one possibly significant (and observable) implication. Specifically, a pure welfare state may be more stable and endure longer than a pure regulatory state. Whether it is possible to go beyond this and say that a mixed economy that on balance tends toward a welfare state will be more stable than one that on balance tends toward a regulatory state is more problematic.

6

THE INSTABILITY OF THE
MINIMAL STATE

Does the instability that plagues the interventionist mixed economy also confront the minimal state? Mises, for one, did not think so.

Although he argued that a policy of interventionism is "contradictory and illogical" since "any attempt to introduce it in earnest must lead to a crisis from which either capitalism or socialism alone can emerge" (Mises 1977: 37), Mises also maintained that "measures that are taken for the purpose of preserving the private-property order are not interventions in this sense" (ibid.: 17). Thus, for Mises interventionism obtains only after state activity exceeds the minimum necessary to promote social cooperation and coordination within the market process; state activity within these limits does not constitute interventionism. He evidently believed the minimal state to be immune from interventionism's inherent contradictions, and took it for granted that such a state is both stable and perhaps even in some sense "optimal." Yet notwithstanding Mises's position, the investigations into the dynamics of the mixed economy of the previous two chapters do seem to suggest that similar forces could very well also, under the proper conditions, destabilize[1] the minimal state.

In this chapter, I attempt to identify one possible set of those conditions and to analyze the resulting endogenously generated forces. This is not to deny the possibility that other factors, including non-economic ones (e.g., exogenous shifts in ideology), might also produce the same unstable outcome. Nevertheless, my focus here will be on the prospect that endogenous non-ideological forces *initiate* the growth of the interventionist state, even though subsequent endogenous changes in ideological preferences may come into play, just as they do in the interventionist process, proper. (Indeed, the present chapter should shed additional light on that process.)

To address this concern, I will first present the features of a minimal state of my own construction, and then analyze the circumstances that, given those features, would initiate an interventionist process. I will then discuss the likelihood that those features and circumstances will be present in an actual minimal state.

DESCRIPTION OF THE MINIMAL STATE

In a world of public choosers who must act in the presence of the knowledge problem and who have different views concerning state expansion, what set of politico-economic conditions within the minimal state would tend to initiate the interventionist process?

The following is not an exhaustive listing all of the essential features of any minimal state, but is rather an attempt to specify only those that relate directly to the question of instability. [2]

1 The world is initially under the rule of a state that is "minimal" in the sense that it is limited to protecting its citizens against aggression and fraud, and to providing other non-rivalrous, non-exclusive (pure public) goods that the unhampered market is unable to provide, if any.[3] "Interventionism," then, refers to the state provision of services beyond this minimal level.

Two comments are in order here. First, I will not address the consequences of differences among governments of various states that may compete for the loyalty of citizens, although this may affect the conclusions of the analysis. That is, citizens who "vote with their feet" by deserting a government that displeases them could to some extent offset some of the consequences of state error discussed below. Such Tiebout-type phenomena, however, would probably only serve to delay rather than completely counter the consequences of domestic state error. Second, even among advocates of the minimal state there may be no clear agreement on what does in fact constitute its proper functions. For the purposes of the present chapter, however, it does not matter how we delimit the scope of state activity; it matters only that political power is strictly limited to the provision of public goods, however defined. This approach implicitly excludes so-called anarcho-capitalism from consideration, but it does so only for reasons of methodological convenience, in much the same way that this book has for the most part assumed that benevolence guides political action.

2 A majority of citizens initially agree on the exact quality and quantity of the services that the state should provide, although their ideological preferences at the margin differ.
3 State authorities are aware of this agreement, but are ignorant of citizens' underlying (marginal and total) preferences themselves.
4 State authorities are responsive to the wishes citizens communicate to them through a democratic process (the details of which need not be specified). That is, the state operates in the "public interest." Moreover, citizens are also public-spirited.

It follows from condition (3) that state authorities will be uncertain about the optimal rates of taxation to impose, since they have no direct insight into the ideological preferences of the citizens. The state can avoid disappointing any given citizen only when it charges him a fee equal to his marginal rate of substitution of private for a particular public good. Moreover, if such a fee, the "Lindahl tax-price" (t^*), raises revenues sufficient to cover the cost of the public good, this will produce a "Lindahl equilibrium." Condition (4) eliminates most principal-agent problems and perverse incentives on the part of state authorities from the analysis. We are dealing here, as has mostly been the case up to now, with a benevolent state and citizenry.

The realism of conditions (2) through (4) is of course highly questionable. Together, however, they create a near-best-case for the minimal state in the sense that they endow the minimal state with an unrealistically high degree of accurate knowledge about the wants of its citizens. Indeed, they are important for the conclusions of this chapter, not because of their specific content (e.g., that state authorities are unaware of tax-prices rather than the quantity or quality of public-goods provision), but because if the minimal state is unstable under these conditions, which assign state authorities an extraordinary (though not perfectly complete) level of knowledge, then it is likely to apply *a fortiori* to more realistic situations in which their knowledge is highly imperfect.

In accordance with the goal of analyzing the possibility of the endogenous politico-economic instability of the minimal state, the initial ideological preferences of the citizenry – e.g., their original preferences for state versus private provision of goods in total or at the margin – do not in the present analysis *initiate* the changes that destabilize the minimal state. As noted already, however, marginal changes and shifts in these preferences will play an important role in subsequent stages of the destabilizing process. Creating the possibility of endogenous instability will require one further condition.

5 Most citizens have unique and "convex preferences" over private and public goods at the margin, regarding the former positively and the latter negatively beyond the minimal state.

That is, while the majority of citizens of the minimal state consider privately provided goods desirable, they deem public provision evil but necessary, and, beyond some threshold, not necessary at all.[4] The remaining citizens may regard both publicly and privately provided goods as desirable, or they may be anarcho-capitalists (who regard all levels of public provision negatively), or thoroughgoing collectivists (who regard all or nearly all levels of public provision positively), or something in between. The majority, however, on the whole regards the legitimate functions of the state to be rather limited, although they attach different marginal valuations to additional publicly provided goods, stated in terms of the amount of private provision they would be willing to accept as compensation for more public provision.

Recall that one aspect of the concept of ideology used in this study concerns the "moral aversion" that public choosers generally (though not universally) feel toward the use of political means to redistribute or acquire wealth, while another concerns the effect on this moral aversion of the perception that others are using political means. I have chosen to concentrate on what is perhaps the most significant of the many possible factors that might create such a perception – the *number* of public choosers who engage in political activity.[5] As we shall see, the extensive discussion of the dynamics of ideological change in Chapters 4 and 5 with respect to the interventionist process proper, also plays an important role in the present analysis.

ANALYSIS

I have suggested that since the Mises–Hayek–Lavoie critique of central planning and the Misesian critique of interventionism are both based on the observation that informational constraints frustrate various levels of government intervention, one might reasonably expect difficulties of a similar nature, though perhaps different in degree, to confront even a minimal state in its provision of services. And if the assertions of limited-government advocates are correct – that political means are necessary to provide adequate levels of certain public goods (such as national defense) – then it is possible that, among those citizens who already have relatively high marginal preferences for public provision, governmental error will create enough disappointment significantly to increase their demand for such provision. A benevolent government responding to this demand might then begin to exceed the limits of the minimal state even though a majority of its citizens find the idea of increased intervention, as well as the type and scope of intervention that ultimately occurs, on the whole undesirable. (Of course, if the state were truly minimal, the impact of government errors would probably initially be very small for the majority of citizens. As I show later, however, the effects of bureaucratic administration and monopolistic provision of services by the minimal state, as well as the interaction of error and the number of citizens who eventually favor intervention, may raise the magnitude of these errors sufficiently to initiate the interventionist process.)

The assumption of "convex preferences" over marginal changes in public versus private provision of goods should be further clarified. In the minimal state outlined in the previous section, citizens, in keeping with the Austrian tradition of methodological subjectivism, possess different marginal valuations regarding private versus public provision of goods. That is, while citizens might in general support, or not oppose, the maintenance of the minimal state, the strength of that support may differ widely from person to person depending on a particular citizen's willingness to substitute public for private provision of services at the margin. To the extent, therefore, that public choosers possess unique marginal valuations, they will respond differently to an error in public policy (which I shall describe in a moment). The aggregate outcome of these different responses, of course, depends on, among other things, just how strong the general support is for the minimal state at the outset.

In this discussion, what initiates the instability are governmental errors committed in the execution of the limited public policy of the minimal state in the presence of the knowledge problem. In particular, these are errors that the state makes in attempting to set tax-prices to the level of the underlying marginal valuations (i.e., the marginal rates of substitution (MRS) of public for private goods) of its citizens, about which, by assumption, it is still partially though radically ignorant. What Cordato maintains with regard to the possibility of efficient taxation in the presence of the knowledge problem applies here as well: "The information that would be necessary to first construct the tax and then implement it is impossible even to comprehend let along gather and utilize" (1994: 378). Errors thus endogenously arise owing to the knowledge constraints that public authorities confront when trying to execute their policies. For the purposes of the present analysis, it is important to note that the errors of particular relevance here are of the class-one variety, the negative consequences (though perhaps not the sources) of which will almost inevitably be discovered. And as was true of the analysis of the interventionist process proper, the responses of the public authorities to the discovery of such errors (i.e., class-one learning) become the immediate cause of instability within the system.

Specifically, let us relate an individual citizen's demand for intervention directly to the (absolute)[6] size of the divergence between actual and optimal tax-prices, $t^a - t^*$, which is the "level of error," e, committed by the government. A benevolent state will of course try to set $t_{ij}^a = t_{ij}^*$ for each citizen, i, and for each publicly provided good, j (so that a corresponding error can be designated e_{ij}). If the state has perfect information on its citizens" marginal values, there will be no divergence, enabling it to preserve the original mix of governmental and private goods for each citizen, maximize revenues to pay for the public goods that it provides, and contain the demand for further intervention (i.e., there will be no demand-generating disappointment). Although it might appear counterintuitive, increasing governmental error will stimulate the demand for more, rather than less, government. Given the discussion of the previous chapters, the discovery of the consequences of error need not entail the discovery of their ultimate source. The likelihood of the latter kind of discovery diminishes as intervention increases, until the point of systemic crisis. Moreover, I will show later that individual citizens will tend to encounter difficulties in getting the state to adjust tax-prices to their optimal level in the presence of demand-revelation and selection-bias problems. Under these conditions, citizens will be more likely to seek some form of non-price *compensation* (or, in the case of the beneficiaries of tax-prices, *protection*) from the state.

Whether or not citizens act in such a way as (unintentionally) to foster an interventionist process will depend on the degree to which their actual tax-prices deviate from the optimal (i.e., the magnitude of the state's error with respect to each citizen),[7] on the number of citizens so affected, and, of course, on their individual attitudes toward marginal expansions of state activity. Moreover, as suggested earlier in this chapter, governmental error will affect a given citizen's attitude toward interventionism – his ideological preferences – (a) directly through his taxes, which results in marginal changes in ideological preference,[8] and (b) indirectly through his perception of its influence on the responses of others (i.e., the number of political actors), which modifies his aversion toward the use of political means and causes his ideological preferences to shift.

Even though the scope of governmental error in the present construct is far more restricted than it would be in the real world, there are a number of ways in which such error can occur. Let us begin with a situation in which all tax-prices for each publicly provided good, j, are set correctly, in the sense that $t_{ij}^a = \text{MRS}_{ij}$ for every citizen except one. Let this particular citizen's preferences be those of the majority (i.e., those corresponding to condition (5), above). For the error, e_{ij}, imposed on this citizen, he will have an incentive first to discover it and then to try to bring t_{ij}^a and his MRS_{ij} into equality. Given his configuration of preferences, if $t_{ij}^a > \text{MRS}_{ij}$, he will demand more governmental services until MRS_{ij} has *risen* to match t_{ij}^a.[9] (I shall discuss in a moment the reason why the "correction" will tend to occur in the form of the state adjusting the quantity or quality of services rather than its simply lowering this citizen's tax-price.) Since this citizen is the only one affected by governmental error the number of "public agents" is unlikely to change significantly, so the forces for indirect ideological change (i.e., the number of public agents) do not come into play.

Note that, depending on the nature of the public good in question – that is, whether it is perhaps more like national defense or more like a bridge – the state may or may not be able to accommodate the citizen's increased demand. If it is like a bridge, the accommodation may be relatively easy since the citizen could, if he so desired, consume additional units of bridge services by simply using it more often, the marginal cost of doing so (in the absence of congestion) being nearly zero, without the state having to take any actions. If, however, it is like national defense, additional units of which may be difficult or impossible to supply or consume, the state might have to provide an entirely new kind of service to compensate for its error (one that may or, more likely given the nature of the minimal state, may not be a genuine public good), the marginal cost of which could be high enough to discourage the state from providing it for a single citizen, since the perceived benefit from such provision would likely be too small. A sufficiently large demand for either type of public goods would, of course, eventually come up against capacity constraints at some level of provision, so that marginal costs under these circumstances would be positive. Since, however, we are dealing in this first instance with only one disappointed citizen, the chances of this happening are slight.

A "perfectly" responsive state would not only try sincerely to respond to the demands of its citizens, it would also be able to detect important changes in those demands correctly and in a timely manner. It is likely, however, given the form of the knowledge problem in the present construct, that the state would respond imperfectly in this sense and err because either its perception was incorrect or its response was inappropriate for the problem perceived, or some combination of the two. Under these circumstances, its responses in general would likely be suboptimal.[10]

There are two reasons in particular why the state will tend to err. First, methodological subjectivists know well that the process of acquiring accurate knowledge of each citizen's MRS for public goods would entail problems, beyond those relating to dishonest taste-revelation and other strategic considerations, that may well be insurmountable even in principle. That is, from the standpoint of methodological subjectivism, tastes reveal themselves only through actual choices. Indeed, strictly speaking, one could even argue that tastes do not exist except at the moment of choice (Rothbard 1956), so that, in the absence of an actual choice, a person's preferences are fundamentally inscrutable.

A second source of difficulty is that information from citizens would be subject to a form of selection bias. Because of the state's radical ignorance of at least some relevant facts – among them the preferences of its citizens – some citizens would feel disappointment with current tax-prices (that is, of course, after accounting for the subjective costs of their addressing this problem outside the political process), resulting in disequilibrium. The state may respond in any number of ways, but all perforce rely on the accuracy and completeness of the information it receives from its citizens. This may be problematic since, in particular, those for whom $t^a > t^*$ (i.e., those who are forced to pay a price greater than their MRS for public goods) will have a stronger incentive to complain than those for whom $t^a < t^*$. This can create problems, since the state will have difficulty verifying these claims. For example, a downward adjustment in the tax-prices for those citizens who claim to be paying too much without an offsetting upward adjustment for those paying too little (who may, or more likely, may not fully disclose their actual circumstances) could result in a budget deficit, the financing of which, either through borrowing or taxation, would entail further negative consequences.[11]

The state may thus be reluctant to respond to complaints by adjusting tax-prices.[12] It might instead rely on adjustments in the quantity or quality of the goods it provides, or on some other form of compensation or protection to bring tax-prices back into alignment with marginal preferences. Later in this chapter I argue that bureaucratic provision within the minimal state will be hampered because the type of goods it tends to provide are precisely those whose production is difficult or impossible to monitor. If this is so, then economic efficiency is not the proper benchmark against which to evaluate the performance of the minimal state. This means that the (formerly) minimal state might be able to finance additional public services by inappropriately reallocating resources among its various activities, whose costs it may be relatively easy to absorb or disguise, at least in the early stages of the interventionist process, owing to the absence of a meaningful criterion of economic efficiency.[13]

The (perhaps counter-intuitive) result that the state will adjust along a non-price dimension is also a reflection of the disequilibrium and suboptimal nature of the tax-price that it charges for a given service. That is, a higher-than-optimal tax-price in the present analysis is, to employ a metaphor from static analysis, similar to a commodity price that lies above the point of supply and demand equilibrium. For the reasons just given, tax-prices are difficult to adjust so any adjustment has to operate either through "an outward shift of the demand curve" or "an inward shift of the supply curve." But, since the minimal state is currently providing only those services essential to the operation of the catallaxy, a reduction in the supply of governmental services would not be feasible. Any workable adjustment must therefore take place via an increase in demand (with a corresponding increase in the quantity supplied).

Let us next suppose that the state errs with respect to a majority of its citizens, who have preferences following assumption (5). In this case, the increased demand for governmental services may be great enough among the subset of these citizens who have relatively high marginal preferences for state action actually to justify an increase in the quantity supplied of a range of publicly provided goods. This will be especially true if the state sets incorrect prices over a range of goods that it already provides. In this case, the indirect effect on the ideological preferences of a large number of citizens using political means becomes an important factor. As the state expands its services in response to the increased demand, the perception of an increase in the number of such citizens will, on our assumptions, begin to erode the moral aversion toward the use of political means – on the part of both those already using it and, more importantly, those who have so far refrained from doing so. This means that for a given combination of private and public goods the MRS for all taxpayers, especially "marginal" taxpayers (those who are not quite willing, under the current set of tax-prices, to engage in political activity), will begin to fall. That is, for a particular mix of private and public provision, taxpaying citizens will require less private provision to compensate them for a given increase in public provision. (Recall that in this analysis public provision for the majority is a "bad.") Stated another way, a citizen who would be willing to accept a relatively small increase in public provision for a given increase in private provision, will be transformed into one who would be willing to accept a larger increase in public provision. Under current tax-prices the actual tax rates of marginal taxpayers would then exceed their MRSs, so that they too would now have an incentive to demand a greater role for government intervention than they would have been willing to tolerate under a pure minimal-state regime.[14] For example, a citizen who experiences both increasing politicization in his everyday experience (e.g., more persons whom he knows going on public assistance) and greater frustration as a result (e.g., higher taxes and lower real income), may be more willing to support an expansion in government programs (e.g., increased miliary spending) in the hopes of that this will raise his real personal income. If additional citizens actually do as a result engage in more political activity, this will have the effect of further weakening the moral aversion on the part of the remaining "non-politicized" marginal taxpayers, as well as those already engaged in the political process in a relatively limited way. An initial error in tax-prices can thus create a kind of "snowball" effect that considerably magnifies the consequences of a given error in public policy. Such an error, viewed in isolation, may appear to be of relatively small consequence, but viewed from this broader perspective it can grow to dimensions significant enough to set off an interventionist dynamic by ultimately significantly increasing the demand for government provision of additional public services on the part of citizens in a pure minimal state.

Consider now the case in which the state sets tax-prices too low for a segment of citizens with convex preferences. Referring to the analogy from static analysis, adjustment to a lower-than-equilibrium tax-price will tend to occur in the form of "an outward shift in the supply curve," rather than a decrease in demand, once again because of the constraints on the reduction of governmental services that are peculiar to the minimal state. As already mentioned, citizens subject to this kind of error will have a weaker incentive to let public authorities know about it than those who pay too much. In addition, they have an incentive to fight against efforts to adjust their tax-prices upward, and might even engage in political activity to prevent it. The latter response, according to the present analysis, would serve to weaken the moral aversion toward state expansion further and could add to the increased demand for state intervention.

Lastly, if the state sets tax-prices too high for some goods and too low for some others, the issue then becomes whether on the whole a given citizen is paying too much or too little for the bundle of services he receives from the state. We might expect that for some the errors may just cancel out, so that no incentive exists for them to engage in more political activity than they currently find optimal. But those for whom this happy coincidence does not obtain, which would likely be most of those citizens affected, will in fact have, by the argument presented above, an incentive to engage in political behavior (i.e., become "political agents").

The main point here is that a given citizen would be willing to compromise on his principles by breaking taboos against the self-interested use of intervention and tolerate increases in the size of government (if he expects this to compensate for his loss or to preserve his gain) to the extent of the loss imposed on him (or the gain bestowed on him) by the government's mistake. A further erosion of these taboos also occurs in the form of an actual change in ideological preferences themselves, resulting from a perceived increase in the number of political actors. Both those paying too little and those paying too much will perceive the costs of breaking taboos against the use of political means for private gain (or loss avoidance) to be lower.

As was mentioned earlier in this book, according to developments in game theory, one factor that keeps small-scale social relations from succumbing to anti-social incentives is the repetitive and on-going nature of most of these relations. That is, in the context of a "supergame," players might realize that following certain social rules and conventions will lead all players to choose a Pareto-optimal strategy (Axelrod 1984). While this is a result of what is essentially equilibrium theorizing, it is still relevant to the present (non-equilibrium) discussion. In this context, should the cost of observing social taboos against intervention exceed the benefits of violating them, such as when the tax-prices some agents have to pay (or the loss of rents from having them raised) is very high, the constraints of the "supergame" begin to weaken. (The reader may recognize this as a version of the erosion of Glazer's "fine structure of society.") In our discussion, this is reflected in a reduction in moral aversion.[15] It is, of course possible that governmental errors of sufficient size may themselves reduce citizens' aversion to the use of political means, so that such an error will not only generate marginal changes in ideological preference but also directly produce outright shifts.[16] Should the error rate increase to this extent, the size of government this citizen would be willing to accept in the first instance would be much greater than the analysis up to this point has led us to expect. His responsiveness to a given change in the error rate (his "error elasticity of demand," if you will) would vary, depending on the preferences of the citizen in question. Also, because of the cumulative nature of the process described here, even though a given citizen might tolerate a larger state as a result of a governmental error, the actual increase in state activity would be still greater than he would be willing to tolerate.

There are thus two kinds of "externality" associated with citizen *i*'s tolerance for greater public provision. The first follows from the analysis in previous chapters: increasing the scope of state activity produces adverse unintended effects. The second operates indirectly through the ideological preferences of other citizens. That is, citizen *i*'s taboo-bending or breaking may lower the moral aversion of others – and *ceteris paribus* increase the likelihood of further intervention – if we assume that social pressure, in the form of the number of those perceived to be observing taboos against intervention, serves to reinforce these taboos. Hence, not only will a given state error create negative unintended consequences, the subsequent interventions that take place will generate additional errors (the timing, location, and nature of which will be largely unknown), increasing the number of political actors, lowering the ideological resistance to further intervention, generating further errors, and so on. Therefore, just as in the case of the mixed economy, the state tends to expand to a level greater, and at a rate faster, than the vast majority of citizens would find desirable.

Given the marginal valuations of citizens, the demand for more state intervention will depend on the perceived cost of public relative to private provision of services. As we have seen, when citizens become disappointed with the state's suboptimal tax-pricing, the relative cost to each citizen of favoring intervention will fall. Thus, the *total* demand for intervention will vary positively with the following factors:

1 The dimensions of the knowledge problem facing the state. The greater the state's ignorance with respect to consumer tastes, the greater the discrepancy between t^a and t^* will tend to be in each case and the more frequent these errors are likely to be. As we have seen, a high enough value for e might actually influence the underlying preference structures of citizens themselves, increasing over time the proportion of those who would favor (and thus the total demand for) more intervention.

2 The proportion of the citizenry initially less resistant to intervention (i.e., those whose MRSs are relatively low). Again, whatever the level of resistance to intervention initially it will decline the greater the frequency and magnitude of the state's errors. Moreover, as we have seen, errors large enough to induce only a relative few to seek intervention initially may eventually gener-

ate a sufficient critical mass of support for fairly widespread intervention.

Note finally that one of the central arguments of this book has been that the dimension of the knowledge problem facing the state is not at all static, but depends rather on the size of the public sector relative to the private sector. Thus, as the state begins to expand beyond the limits of the minimal state, we should expect the amount of relevant information that it does not have, but that it needs to have to operate effectively, to increase, so that even in these initial stages of the interventionist process the incidence of governmental error will begin to grow (perhaps non-linearly). Whether this relation is sufficiently strong early in the process (i.e., very near to the minimal-state end of the spectrum) actually to induce a significantly greater incidence of error will depend on factors that I will now address.

PUBLIC GOODS, MONOPOLY, AND BUREAUCRACY

Since the size of errors and the likelihood of their occurrence depend on the level of ignorance on the part of public authorities, let us examine three reasons why this ignorance is likely to be particularly great when the minimal state provides public goods.

First, since the minimal state is a monopolist in the provision of pure public goods (i.e., by assumption there is no possible non-governmental alternative), it will tend to be sluggish in learning about and responding to changes in preferences. (See the discussion of information conveyance and of monopoly in Chapters 3 and 5 respectively.) "Sluggish," that is, relative to how the market process tends to adjust to changes in data. In the market process, when entry is free, entrepreneurial discovery can appear from any quarter to correct errors (Kirzner 1973). Since the government is a public-goods monopolist, it alone is capable of directly discovering any errors it is making.[17] Although it can learn indirectly of its errors through citizens' complaints, we have seen that this would tend to bias the resulting adjustments toward those citizens whose tax-prices were too high.

Second, public administration is usually regarded as generally less efficient than private administration, owing not only to its monopolistic character but also to the political constraints (e.g., equity, fairness, political accountability) that often interfere with efficient management. But as we saw in Chapter 3, when applied to non-profit-seeking governmental activities the very notion of efficiency becomes problematic. To the extent that this is true, then, benevolent bureaucratic managers operating under a budget constraint will in general confront (as well as create) problems of efficient resource allocation more chronic than those that private managers commonly face. Sources of information external to the bureaucracy,[18] such as relative prices generated within the catallaxy, may perhaps help to reduce some of this excess error and discoordination within the governmental process. That is, if governmental activities have fairly close referents in the private sector (i.e., market prices for similar services and for the inputs used to produce them), there is some basis on which to evaluate the economic efficiency of state activity. When such referents are remote – as will typically be the case with the functions that advocates of limited-government concede to the minimal state, since government presumably would be performing just those functions for which the market is least capable of offering sufficiently close substitutes – the value of state activity and the competence of its organization will be difficult or impossible to measure accurately. One could thus argue that a strict notion of economic efficiency is inapplicable to the bureaucratic management of governmental services in general, and to that of the minimal state in particular.[19]

A third factor relevant to the question of the efficiency of bureaucracy in the minimal state is provided by James Q. Wilson. Wilson (1989) classifies bureaucratic organizations according to the observability of their operations and procedures (which he terms "outputs") of public agents within an organization – what the agencies do on a day-to-day basis – and whether that agency's long-term goals or mission (Wilson's "outcomes") are achieved. Wilson terms "production organizations," those agencies in which both are observable. The vast majority of private-sector organizations, and some public-sector organizations, are of this type. It is my contention that the provision of public goods *in the minimal state* will tend to occur through the opposite kind of agency, what Wilson calls "coping organizations," in which neither procedures nor long-term "outputs" are observable, because these entail precisely the kinds of functions that markets are supposed to be unable to carry out efficiently (e.g., public security and foreign policy).[20]

Hence, bureaucratic management in the minimal state faces three kinds of problems. There are, first, problems relating to monopolistic governmental provision *per se*; second, problems that arise owing to the non-profit-seeking objectives of government bureaucracy in the absence of market signals; and third, the inability effectively to monitor (coping) organizations. It would therefore hardly be surprising to find that the level of bureaucratic inefficiency and discoordination in the minimal state is sufficiently high to hamper the decision-making ability of the pubic authorities responsible for setting prices for publicly provided goods. The nature of government bureaucracy itself in the minimal state would thus seem to be conducive to instability.[21]

CONCLUDING REMARKS

Even in a minimal state that possesses an unrealistically high level of accurate information about the demands of its citizens, the existence of the knowledge problem creates the potential for adverse consequences of its limited public policy that may result in instability. What is important, of course, is not the particular variables in the construct of this chapter about which the state is assumed to be ignorant. It is rather that authorities in a really existing minimal state would have to face a governmental knowledge problem of much greater dimensions than the one presented here. Thus, the likelihood, scope, and magnitude of governmental errors will be much higher, and the chances of instability much greater, in a more realistic setting. Moreover, I have abstracted from strategic and public-choice-type considerations (at least on the part of public authorities), as well as other factors (such as exogenous shocks) that would reinforce the destabilizing forces that I have isolated in this chapter. Needless to say, the presence of such factors would provide even more reason to expect that a really existing minimal state would be unstable.

Yet even if the argument of this chapter is correct and minimal states face internal problems that make them unstable, there are at least two reasons why this would be insufficient grounds for rejecting the possibility of limited government as a policy alternative.

First, the private provision of public goods – the anarcho-capitalist alternative – may be even less stable. If the market is incapable of furnishing services essential for the peaceful evolution of capitalist society, such as police protection and some form of common defense, the result may be social disintegration. In the face of this possibility perhaps a minimal state, even an unstable one, is worth having.[22]

Second, for a given level of ignorance on the part of the government, the ideological preferences of citizens at the margin will determine whether or not the demand for state expansion will increase enough to destabilize the minimal state. This in turn depends chiefly on their ideological convictions. That is, if all citizens were staunchly anti-interventionist, this would increase resistance to government growth (by raising their MRS's), so that a given decrease in the cost of intervention, resulting from government error, would have less of an impact on the demand for intervention. Both the intensity (i.e., individual gains from intervention would be less) and extent (there would be fewer citizens willing to tolerate intervention) of the demand for intervention would be lower. The ideological convictions of public choosers are thus, not surprisingly, highly relevant for the political-economic analysis of public policy.[23]

7

IMPLICATIONS AND PATTERN PREDICTIONS

Thus far I have re-examined and reconstructed the traditional Austrian critique of interventionism in light of recent theoretical developments in Austrian market-process theory. The present chapter combines this updated and extended version of that critique with both the analysis of Chapter 6 (of the instability of the minimal state) and the modern Austrian analysis of collectivism into a set of propositions from which I will draw some rather broad empirical implications regarding the overall behavior of mixed economies.[1] The existence of such general but possibly observable patterns (examples of which have already appeared under the heading "The interventionist process as a spontaneous order" in Chapter 4) will hopefully, among other things, further support the claim that the interventionist process is a spontaneous order.

The first section of the chapter sets out the three propositions that will serve as the basis for the derivations that follow. Next comes a discussion of the extent to which the implications so derived are observable. This is followed by sketches of several historical episodes that will serve to illustrate and, to a limited extent, support the framework of analysis outlined in this book, as well as to indicate the possible limits of that framework's predictive power. The final section offers some concluding remarks and observations.

PROPOSITIONS

The critiques of collectivism and of interventionism represent two parts of the Austrian comparative analysis of politico-economic systems. The discussion in Chapter 6 adds perhaps a third component to that framework: the instability of the minimal state.

For the purposes of the present chapter let us express the gist of these three components in the following propositions:

A The minimal state is prone to endogenous expansion.
B Interventionism generates a dynamic that destabilizes the mixed economy.
C Rational economic calculation, and thus a sustainable social order, under collectivism is impossible.

We might view these propositions as themselves the immediate, or first-level, implications of Austrian comparative-systems analysis. Each has empirical content, although in their present very general form that content is somewhat low.

Applying the framework of Austrian political economy outlined in the preceding chapters will help to tease out inferences of greater specificity from these propositions, especially with respect to the behavior of interventionist mixed economies. Indeed, most of the second-level implications that appear in the next section are simply more detailed versions of proposition (B), derived with the help of the logic of interventionism and the method of Austrian market-process theory. In this regard, propositions (A) and (C) will serve for the most part as "background propositions" – i.e., propositions taken as valid without further elaboration in order to assist in extracting the implications embedded in proposition (B). In other words, while one could more precisely restate propositions (A) and (C) in forms with higher empirical content,[2] I will, however, with the exception of the last two implications, refrain from doing so in order to concentrate on the characteristics of the interventionist process implicit in proposition (B).

In deriving implications from this set of propositions, the following analysis thus assumes that I have satisfactorily established the reasonableness of propositions (A) and (B), and that the critiques of collectivism of Mises (1981), Hayek (1948: 119–208), and Lavoie (1985a) that underlie proposition (C) are also well established. As already mentioned, the derivations draw on the extensive discussion of the logic of the interventionist process in Chapter 4, of the dynamics of the welfare and regulatory states in Chapter 5, and of the instability of the minimal state in Chapter 6. Lastly, I initially derive these implications under the assumption that public choosers are benevolent, but I will examine the effects of relaxing this assumption at various points in the text following the next part.

IMPLICATIONS

The following eight implications are arranged roughly in order of decreasing generality and increasing empirical content.[3]

The prevalence of mixed economies

The first implication directly addresses what in Chapter 2 I called the "Misesian paradox": How is it possible to square Mises's characterization of the interventionist mixed economy as inherently unstable with the common observation that it is the most widespread and persistent form of politico-economic system?

The key to resolving this paradox is to realize that to claim the mixed economy is unstable is not the same thing as asserting that it is *transitory*. Recall that in Chapter 2 I defined a mixed economy as any politico-economic system that lies between pure laissez-faire capitalism and complete collectivism, whether the state is expanding or contracting in relation to the catallaxy. By introducing contradictions into the system, interventions generate a process that causes the mixed economy continually to adjust and to evolve into novel and diverse forms over time. And while unchecked state expansion produces excessive complexity and discoordination and depletes the reserve fund to such an extent that systemic breakdown becomes inevitable, there is nothing in proposition (B) that implies the end need come quickly. The roads between the minimal and maximal states can thus be very long and winding, and state expansion very gradual.

Indeed, none of the three alternative systems – minimal-state capitalism, interventionism, or maximal-state collectivism – is "stable" in the sense defined in this book. As we have seen, Mises went so far as to claim that interventionism, unlike the other systems, is inherently contradictory, and for that reason not even a coherent alternative. Yet he also rightly questioned the practicality of collectivism, owing to the impossibility of even approaching a degree of plan coordination that benevolent public authorities themselves would find satisfactory and to the capital-consuming consequences of that fact. Finally, I have argued that the minimal state, while logically coherent in the sense that no inherent catallactic forces *per se* necessarily compromise its operation, is nevertheless highly sensitive to governmental error and to changes in ideological preferences (as well as to exogenous shocks). Somewhat paradoxically, therefore, it appears that the product of interventionism, the mixed economy, though unstable, is likely to be more enduring than the pure forms of either collectivism or capitalism, offering as it does a much wider range of (ultimately futile) adaptive forms than either of its rival systems. The inherent instability of interventionism thus drives the mixed economy through a variety of transformations that are denied to the other systems. Thus,

1. *At any given time, nearly all economic systems will be mixed economies.*

The dynamics of mixed economies

The above analysis produced an implication about what might be observable at a given moment in time. Developed further, it can yield another implication concerning the behavior of political-economic systems over time.

The market process is ever changing, always in flux. The imperfect and contextual nature of catallactic knowledge implies that individual plans are never fully coordinated. The resulting error and discoordination, however, as we saw in Chapter 3, creates opportunities for entrepreneurial discovery that on the whole act as a force that tends to bring the plans of anonymous individuals into harmony. Interventionism, on the contrary, as argued in Chapter 4, distorts the very system of relative prices that entrepreneurs use to guide their (mainly local) activities. The excessive complexity and discoordination that result create perverse incentives that lead to waste (i.e., deadweight loss), thwart entrepreneurship (i.e., create barriers to discovery), and channel entrepreneurship into unnecessary activity (i.e., wholly superfluous discovery). These produce consequences that the supporters of interventionism themselves will sooner or later find unacceptable. In short, with the appropriate changes in ideological preferences, interventionism drives the expansion of state activity toward a point at which the system becomes delegitimized[4] in the eyes of public choosers either because coordination problems become overwhelming or because the accessible portion of the reserve fund can no longer support interventionist policies, or both. If public choosers embrace collectivism rather than capitalism, choosing in effect the principle of organization over the principle of spontaneous order, it will have the consequences examined in Chapter 3 – such a system will not be long lived. If they embark on a radical path of state contraction by choosing minimal-state capitalism they may or may not achieve a stable system, depending on how radical their reforms are and how strong their commitment to them is. Anything less than radical reform almost assures an eventual return to the road to collectivism.

Naturally, not all mixed economies will survive lower-level macro-crises, but some will. Not all extreme collectivist regimes immediately disintegrate, but they do in a relatively short time. Not all minimal-state systems slide into interventionism, but most will. Hence, not only will most systems be mixed economies, but

2. *Nearly all really existing systems will be in flux, cycling somewhere between the extremes of laissez-faire capitalism and complete collectivism. Of these, the majority will tend to move secularly toward collectivism.*

Crises in and of the mixed economy

The analysis in Chapters 4 and 5 of the complex dynamics and internal logic that drive the mixed economy through its transformations, serves as the source of the next four derivations.

For reasons given in Chapter 4, for example, an intervention into the spontaneous forces of the market process generates, through internal and external entrepreneurial responses, consequences that are not only unintended by the benevolent proponents of the general policy of interventionism, but so undesirable from their own point of view that these consequences completely offset the benefit they receive from the intervention. (Note that this is the "weak version" of negative unintended consequence.) The resulting circumstances represent a "crisis" that calls into question the policy or program that may be involved. The knowledge problem and informational complexity, however, abetted by the dynamics of ideological change, tend to induce public choosers to extend interventionist policy to address coordination failures that are in fact merely the inevitable result of prior intervention. Under the persistent application of interventionism, discoordination, complexity, and reserve-fund depletion will continue to increase and intensify until public choosers are forced to question the very legitimacy of interventionism itself. (Note that this is the "general version" of negative unintended consequences.) Thus,

3. *A mixed economy that is in the expansionary phase of the interventionist process will be characterized by a series of micro- and lower-level macro-crises that ultimately culminate in a major system-wide macro-crisis encompassing the entire politico-economic system*

The turning point of the expansionary phase

So long as disruptions in the market and governmental processes that result from progressive intervention fail to derail the ideological dynamics of state expansion, and so long as problems of price distortions and excessive complexity continue to mask the ultimate source of those disruptions from benevolent public choosers, support for interventionist solutions will continue to grow. Yet because a system-wide failure brings on the "legitimation crisis" of interventionism, it is at such a point in the expansionary phase of the interventionist process that public choosers will be best able to achieve radical change.[5] This is so not only because the breakdown of the prior ideological preference structure and the unmistakable appearance of overall policy failure removes the informational and ideological obstacles to such change, but also because the severe and systemic nature of the macro-crisis makes radical and sweeping action imperative.

One might venture to infer from this that during periods of crisis those holding ideas that are outside the mainstream should take heart, as it is at such times that they have the greatest chance of influencing the opinion of the relevant authorities. To take an example from interventionism at the micro-level, Derthick and Quirk (1985) have noted that arguments against irrationalities in airline regulation in the United States that economists had been steadily offering for years, to little effect, eventually became a critical factor (though certainly not the only one) in the deregulation of the airline industry when Senate hearings on the matter finally took place in the late 1970s. While they cite several reasons for the success of airline deregulation, they do not specifically deal with the issue of timing (ibid.: 238–45). Others, however, have noted that chronic, regulation-induced excess capacity and escalating fuel prices (also to an extent regulation-induced) began by the mid-1970s to dissipate airline profits, especially in long-haul markets (Kaplan 1986: 43), not to mention the impact of competition from discount airlines operating in the international market (e.g., Laker Airlines) and from low-cost, less regulated intra-state rivals (e.g., Southwest Airlines), all of which contributed to an atmosphere of impending crisis within the established airline industry. The microeconomic critique of the Civil Aeronautics Board's regulatory policies thus took hold only after public choosers became alert to the urgency of the situation.

It does not follow, however, that simply because public choosers are more receptive to unconventional ideas at a time of crisis, among the many proposals put forward any one in particular (such as one's own) will necessarily prevail. Unless their ideas enjoy a competitive or other advantage over their rivals in the intellectual marketplace, then, crises are not necessarily a time for disaffected and marginalized intellectuals to rejoice. In any case,

4. *If there is a "turning point" at which public choosers in the mixed economy reject the interventionist ideology and take radical steps toward either pure collectivism or the minimal state, it will take place at the point of a macro-crisis.*

The timing of the turning point

Chapter 2 identified another lacuna within the Misesian analysis of interventionism relating to the question of why public choosers, acting in the public interest, would remain committed to interventionism in the face of its accumulating negative effects.

From Chapter 4 we know that the phenomena of discoordination and radical ignorance and of complexity and bounded rationality prevent even benevolent public choosers from realizing that the ultimate source of the various micro-crises that arise across the system is the policy of interventionism itself. Such "myopia" tends to afflict public choosers until at or near the onset of a major macro-crisis, at which point it is too late for them to avert it. This means that the legitimation crisis of the interventionist mixed economy will tend to take place only after the mixed economy has had enough time to evolve to the point where it is ripe for crisis. Such a crisis could occur relatively "early" in the expansionary phase of the interventionist process – when, say, less than half of the system's gross domestic product is under some kind of effective government control. In the interests of maximizing empirical content, however, one might prefer to locate this point of maturation rather "late" in the expansionary phase, perhaps near the collectivist end of the politico-economic spectrum. This would suggest the following (strong) implication:

5. *Turning points will occur closer on the politico-economic spectrum to the maximal-state than to the minimal-state.*

The asymmetry between the expansionary and contractionary phases

Another characteristic of the turning point is that it takes place only after a deliberate self-conscious decision on the part of public choosers to reject interventionism and to adopt an alternative system. This is because a major macro-crisis occurs only when the breakdown of the interventionist mixed economy has become so plain (i.e., it has the nature of a class-one error) that a politically significant proportion of public choosers is able finally to perceive the common origin of their systemic problems. Thus, while the largely unintended consequences of a myriad of independent decisions throughout the system tend to drive the expansionary interventionist process, the turning point of that process comes about as a result of a deliberate decision on the part of public choosers. Hence the following:

6. *State expansion will tend to take place more continuously than state contraction, which, especially in its initial stages, will display change of a more rapid, radical, and sweeping nature.*

The relative stability of the welfare state

According to the analysis in Chapter 5, any given intervention impinges on the three areas of income distribution, ideology, and relative prices. Which of these it has the greatest impact on depends on the kind of intervention it is. Because of the central importance of the price system for coordinating individual plans in the market process, interventions that directly distort relative prices (e.g., monetary manipulation and system-wide price controls) are exceptionally disruptive. While income-transfers do tend to degrade the price system, they do so indirectly as a rule, and their consequences are comparatively more difficult to detect. On the other hand, regulation (as defined in this book) gives rise to negative unintended consequences that are not only more serious on average but also, because more easily discovered class-one errors comprise a larger proportion of the resulting discoordination errors, the expansionary logic of the interventionist process is likely to unfold more rapidly in a pure regulatory state compared to a pure welfare state. This suggests that

7. *The pure welfare state will tend to be less prone to macro-crises and endure longer than the pure regulatory state, although it is still fundamentally unstable.*

Ideology and the stability of the minimal state

Advocates of the minimal state might wonder not only about the veracity of their arguments in support of laissez-faire capitalism, but also about the effectiveness of those arguments in achieving and maintaining their ultimate goal (to the extent that these are separable). To put it very broadly, the two basic alternatives are to ground these arguments either on some sort of essentially non-rational commitment to the principles of limited government (in some sense for their own sake), or on a more or less rational analysis of the consequences of following the principles of limited government. One might think of the former as having an "ethical" basis, emphasizing the rightness of a given action, and of the latter as having a "consequentialist" basis, emphasizing the direct and indirect ramifications of a given action. In this regard, the discussion of the ideological setting of the minimal state may shed some light on which of these might better preserve minimal-state stability.

In Chapter 6, I argued that, for a given set of non-uniform ideological preferences among public choosers, an error on the part of the minimal state with respect to the provision of or taxation for public services can set the interventionist process in motion. Or, viewed the other way around, for an error of a given magnitude, a set of non-uniform ideological preferences exists that will destabilize the minimal state. The latter formulation reveals how important the configuration of ideological preferences is in the preservation of minimal-state stability.

The limitations of the human mind, as manifested for example in bounded rationality and radical ignorance, will prevent public choosers from foreseeing the full negative ramifications (from their viewpoint) of their preferred interventions. A greater emphasis on consequentialist arguments for the minimal state, the advantages of which will tend to be relatively abstract and long term, might for this reason prove too weak a philosophical defense against the more concrete and short-term benefits that the use of political means can promise. I believe it is reasonable to speculate, therefore, that

8. *The more strongly committed public choosers are to the principles of the minimal state and limited government, the less likely it will be that changes in marginal preferences, in response to governmental error, will generate the "critical mass" among the public that is needed to initiate the interventionist process.*

INTERPRETATIONS

It is the purpose of neither the present chapter in particular nor this book as a whole to advance a monocausal explanation of the dynamics of the mixed economy. Politico-economic systems, like all complex social phenomena, are subject to a multitude of forces (e.g., cultural and religious upheavals, war, political impulses), that no single theory, no matter how elaborate, can account for in every significant detail. Rather, as set out in Chapter 1, my overall aim has been to offer an approach to political economy that addresses important questions that have not received the attention they deserve – those pertaining to what I have called the dynamics of the mixed economy. Moreover, I believe this framework has identified tendencies underlying those dynamics that are empirically significant and to some extent observable, under the proper conditions.

This last qualifier is intended to convey the familiar idea that every prediction is to some degree contingent. Like any prediction, each of the above implications presumes a set of *ceteris paribus* conditions. The kinds of "predictions of the pattern"[6] to which we are limited when it comes to complex phenomena such as the interventionist process, however, are notoriously difficult to test or falsify, either because their empirical content is small or because reinforcing and offsetting forces may obscure the empirical content in ways that are difficult or impossible to untangle. The implications presented above embody both kinds of problems.

This typically leads to the circumstance that, even when evidence unambiguously contradicts a pattern prediction, to which a researcher has added auxiliary empirical propositions that narrow the range of permissible outcomes, we cannot say that the formulation is untrue, but only that it is not true of a particular situation. Or, to put it somewhat differently, only the specific formulation that the researcher has constructed has been falsified and not necessarily the general tendency that it is supposed to specify (Hayek 1967a: 7). While it is true that the fewer the auxiliary propositions, the less empirical content the prediction has, this also means that there are fewer opportunities for the researcher to protect a faulty theory against refutation through the use of what Karl Popper has termed "immunizing stratagems" (Popper 1972: 30). Thus, there is a trade-off between increasing the specificity of a prediction to gain empirical content and a growing potential for methodological deception. With these considerations in mind, let us evaluate each of the implications in terms of their observability.

Implication one

The first implication is a pattern prediction of a very general kind. It is the prediction with the least empirical content, and says nothing about the particular point in the politico-economic spectrum at which we should expect to find a given system or of how that system will behave over time. Yet it is also the one that has the fewest number of *ceteris paribus* conditions: It depends for its *logical* validity only on the truth of the simple statement of the three major propositions. This implication is therefore the one most likely to be observed.

Implication two

This claim about the overall behavior of mixed economies depends on the analysis of interventionist dynamics, which in turn rests on the validity of the explanation of the dynamics of negative unintended consequences. After implication one, it has the fewest number of *ceteris paribus* conditions, and is therefore the prediction one is next most likely to observe.

Implication three

In addition to the conditions assumed in implications one and two, implication three also depends on the validity of the dynamics of ideological change, which tend to support further intervention at each nodal point in the interventionist process.

Implications four and six

Here I conjecture that, given the source of public-chooser myopia, the systemic breakdown brought on by interventionism produces a sudden realization of the inner contradictions of that policy. Moreover, I conjecture that this realization is powerful enough to overcome political inertia to the extent of permitting public choosers to support a form of "shock therapy" to purge the system of interventionist elements.[7] Adding public-choice considerations, as argued in Chapter 4, might lead us (and the public affected) to expect a delay in and moderation of the resulting reform,[8] which means with respect to implication six that the movement back toward laissez-faire may not be as radical as it would be in the absence of interest groups and bureaucratic sluggishness.

The reader should note that implication six pertains to the *relative* continuity of the expansionary over the contractionary phase. This implication therefore could be quite consistent with Higgs's (1987) thesis about the episodic growth of American national government. These added conditions naturally make observation more problematic.

Implication five

Once again, depending on the validity of the conjecture that severe discoordination and excessive complexity combine to delay benevolent public choosers' recognition of the inherent flaws in interventionism, we are likely to see radical and sweeping changes in public policy to occur "closer" to collectivism than laissez-faire capitalism. The addition of public-choice considerations reinforces this tendency.

While I am not proposing here a rigorous empirical measure of the relative size of government, the number of activities for which actors in the private sector are required to gain sanction in some form from the state (e.g., through direct command, licensure, means-testing, compulsory reporting, or regulation) might be a rough indicator, at least in principle. Turning points are thus most likely to occur when these sanctioned activities outnumber those over which individuals have complete freedom of choice. In this, I am following to some extent the observation of Higgs that

> What distinguishes the capital-letter leviathan is the wide
> scope of its effective authority over economic decision-

making, that is, the great extent to which governmental officials rather than private citizens effectively decide how resources will be allocated, employed, and enjoyed.

Higgs (1987: 27–8)

The problem of big government, then, is not so much its *size* (as reflected say in the percent of government expenditures in gross domestic product), but what it *does*. One indicator of relevant state expansion, and one that Higgs seems to endorse, is the expansion of state authority as reflected in the number of government agencies, programs, and activities.[9] Once again, however, with respect to the observability of implication five, the difficulty is one of selecting the proper benchmark. Another possible measure that might partly address this difficulty, is the percentage of all government civilian employees out of the total civilian labor-force, which in the United States, for example, has been growing steadily since the early 1950s.

Implications seven and eight

Because of their very hypothetical nature, these implications are the least observable. Implication seven pertains to ideal-typical systems that are unlikely ever to exist. It says nothing directly about systems that might on net tend more toward the welfare state than the regulatory state, or vice versa. Later in the present chapter, however, I venture that my conclusions regarding the relative stability of the pure welfare state are robust. With respect to implication eight, I am not prepared to suggest how, even in principle, one might "measure" levels of commitment.[10] Nevertheless, I believe it does contain the practical claim that on balance arguments grounded in the, in some sense, "inherent virtue" of the principles of the rule of law and the minimal state will be more effective in preserving the stability of laissez-faire capitalism than consequentialist arguments. For example, imbuing public choosers with an attachment to personal liberty (or enmity toward arbitrary state compulsion) will be more effective than economic arguments in support of capitalism that stress material benefits. Looked at in this way, one might be able to test this prediction in principle by examining the kinds of arguments that were used to advocate laissez-faire (i.e., consequentialist or "natural rights") in those societies most successful in avoiding the slippery slope of interventionism.

EXAMPLES

There is much that the eight implications do not attempt to explain (although further investigation might generate additional implications from within this framework). Perhaps the most important omission, especially from the standpoint of empirical observation, is the effect of *war and domestic conflict* on the interventionist process.[11] This means that the rapid growth of government in the United States during the twentieth century owing to war and similar national crises lies outside their scope.[12]

The informal observations that follow are intended only to *illustrate* the potential explanatory power of Austrian political economy at this (macro) level of analysis – i.e., to suggest areas in which this framework can be helpful in explaining anomalous phenomena or historical episodes. They are not meant, by any means, to constitute a rigorous test of the implications derived in this chapter (which, if feasible, would certainly be desirable.) Such an examination, however, would extend well beyond the scope of this book.

Higgs's "crisis hypothesis"

This framework may be able to explain an area that Higgs chose not to address in his important treatment of the role of crises in the growth of American national government, to which I have referred several times.

Briefly, besides arguing against the standard use of government expenditures to measure governmental control, the central theme in Higgs (1987) is that "under certain conditions national emergencies call forth extensions of governmental control over or outright replacement of the market economy" (p. 17). This is his "crisis hypothesis." There would appear then to be the potential for considerable overlap between the issues Higgs addresses and those addressed in this book. Higgs, however, chooses to direct his attention to the important task of substantiating the historical significance of crises in "ratcheting-up" the pace of government growth (rightly measured) beyond the secular rate of growth that would have obtained in their absence. Higgs thus discusses system-

226

atically neither the reasons for the emergence of crises nor the underlying causes of the secular trend in government growth (some clues for which his investigations have nevertheless uncovered.) The present framework, as we have seen, accounts for both of these factors.

On the prevalence of mixed economies

By any measure, there are currently no examples of really existing systems in the world that are either pure minimal states or thoroughly collectivist regimes.[13] There are in fact roughly three kinds of politico-economic systems in the world today: Systems in transition that have rejected the attempt to centrally plan their economies (Eastern Europe and most of Asia); still highly collectivist systems on the verge of similar radical change (the remaining communist regimes); and interventionist mixed systems in which, despite temporary deviations, the trend is toward more rather than less government participation in the economy (the United States and the rest of the world). Hence, observation most strongly corroborates implication one. Although it is the pattern prediction with the least empirical content, it is also somewhat counter-intuitive, at least insofar as it can give rise to the Misesian paradox.

Modern Germany

The German experience during the late nineteenth and early twentieth centuries seems to support implication two, regarding the cyclical and expansionary behavior of mixed economies. Few other countries have experienced such dramatic shifts in politico-economic structure, even though, especially from the Anglo-American perspective, Germany has always appeared to embody an authoritarian and statist orientation.[14] Nevertheless, the transitions from Bismarckian Germany to Weimar to the Third Reich to the German Miracle to Unification, trace a path of fluctuating state power. Germany is, in a way, a country that at least twice in the twentieth century confronted macro-crises that took place near the point of totalitarian rule, which is consistent with implication five, and made a different choice at each juncture. The collapse of Weimar, the result of an accumulation of micro-crises,[15] drove the system toward collectivist *Zwangswirtschaft*, while the military defeat of Hitler led to Erhard's largely successful return to a market economy.

The Soviet and Chinese experiences

Like Germany, the former Soviet Union might provide a good example of a system in a cyclical interventionist process, lending some support to implication three. It has experienced dramatic changes in its politico-economic landscape since 1917, through the impetus of moderate to highly statist policies (although both systems tended to remain near the maximal-state end of the spectrum). In addition, the early Soviet experiment with thorough-going central planning, the period of so-called "war communism," according to Boettke (1990) and Lavoie (1985a: 152–8), confirmed Mises's pattern prediction about the unworkability of such a system (which is proposition (C), above). The macro-crisis the Soviet Union confronted in the 1980s, the culmination of a decades-long series of lesser, but nonetheless enervating, micro- and macro-crises also appears to corroborate implications four and five.

It would be more difficult to argue, however, at least at this early date, whether the contractionary phase (if indeed that is what we are seeing) has been any more discontinuous than the earlier movement toward collectivism, which would cast some doubt on implication six. As Boettke (1995) has observed, however, the piecemeal reforms undertaken by Russia and the Confederation of Independent States, compared to the more radical steps that Poland and the Czech Republic have implemented, probably doomed those reforms to failure, which was one of the conclusions of Chapter 4, above.

Similarly, the Chinese Revolution of 1949 and early collectivist movements (e.g., the "Great Leap Forward") might prompt us more carefully to scrutinize implication six's prediction of asymmetrical development in the interventionist process. The experience of the People's Republic of China, however, does seem to support implications four and five. While one could justifiably view the circumstances surrounding many of the dramatic changes in economic policy that took place in China between 1975 and 1989 as having been driven by political considerations, the economic conditions that preceded Deng Xiaopeng's radical movement toward the free market in agriculture in the late 1970s could also with justification be described as one of system-wide economic failure. And during the early 1970s, China represented one of the most totalitarian regimes on the face of the earth.[16]

Introducing a public-choice insight discussed in Chapter 4, one might further speculate that the much greater success of the PRC in carrying out reform in the 1970s and 1980s compared to the more recent ineptness of the former USSR, owes something to the comparatively less established interests in the former than in the latter. That is, turmoil in Chinese society and politics during the Great Leap Forward and especially the Cultural Revolution destabilized the Chinese bureaucratic and interest-group structure, which may have been very important in permitting a more radical reform to take place in China than in the USSR. (Whether the more dramatic reforms undertaken in the Czech Republic and Poland owe their success to similar considerations is an open question.)

The United States and Great Britain

It is problematic how well the citizens of any nation understand the philosophical foundations that underlie the form of government under which they live, or how widely and sincerely they embrace those foundations. Yet there is reason to believe that in Britain and the United States such understanding may be stronger and more widely held, given the history of their constitutional structures, compared to other countries in which the sanctity of life, personal liberty, and private property are also outwardly honored.[17] If that is true, then this would seem to be consistent with implication eight. Among all countries in the world, Britain and the United States not only boast the oldest surviving governments, but, more importantly for the present study, they have both shown remarkably steady economic development for most of their histories. Moreover, according to some Austrian scholars the more serious economic instability that has occurred during the twentieth century has been the result of precisely the kind of destabilizing intervention (particularly macroeconomic policy) that is the focus of this book.[18]

As a possible counter-example, however, consider the case of India, as discussed in Olson (1982), who observes that

> the fact remains that more than a half-century of laissez-faire
> did not bring about the development of India or even get it

229

off to a good start. The laissez-faire ideology in its focus on the evils of government alone clearly leaves something out.

(ibid.: 179)

That "something," according to Olson, is allowance for "distributional coalitions" (as embodied in India's caste system) of the kind public-choice analysis, broadly understood, would postulate. Thus, not only does Olson provide a counter-example, he also appears to be pointing out an area of conflict between the conclusions of Austrian political economy and public choice.

It would be very surprising indeed if two quite different approaches to the study of politico-economic phenomena were not to conflict at all, and I am willing to entertain the possibility that the discussion in Chapter 4, on the limited consequences for the conclusions of the theory of interventionism of relaxing the benevolence assumption, was perhaps overly optimistic. I would question, however, Olson's presumption of the depth to which in less than a century deeply held beliefs about the relation of the individual to society in India, an important center of non-Western thought, gave way under British influence to Western notions of individualism and liberty. Nevertheless, a general theory of interventionism, which I have argued should unify Austrian and public-choice insights into a common framework (but not necessarily obliterate their unique qualities), would leave a researcher the freedom to emphasize whichever aspect of the theory best fits the facts at hand. In other words, the common framework should strive to explain as many significant historical facts as possible, even though no smaller subset of that framework would be monocausal.

The case of Sweden

Sweden's economic performance through the 1950s and 1960s has presented something of an enigma to critics of interventionism. According to the aggregate data Olson provides, for example, during this period Sweden's measured per capita growth rate outstripped many other Western democracies including the United States (Olson 1982: 6). Notwithstanding the problems that plague nearly all aggregate statistics (after all, similar data masked the dismal performance of the Soviet Union during this same period of time (Boettke 1993: 57–72)), this apparently impressive achievement by what many considered a model welfare state has tended to put such critics on the defensive.

In this regard, the present framework *could* be of some assistance, although, strictly speaking, it pertains to pure forms of the welfare state. If we are willing, however, to allow that implication seven is sufficiently robust and to assume that Sweden was in fact during this period a welfare state in the sense defined in Chapters 2 and 5 (i.e., it employed political means mainly to redistribute directly income and wealth to achieve greater income equality or security), then it would seem to be consistent with the pattern prediction contained in implication seven. Thus, rather than a potential source of chagrin, Sweden could turn out to be an important illustration of the utility of Austrian political economy. We must not forget either, that since the early 1970s Sweden's economic performance had slipped considerably (one could argue because of the contradictions within its system), and that its government has recently undertaken a serious re-evaluation and potential redirection of its welfare policies.[19]

Other possible counter-examples

Besides those counter-examples already cited, the experiences of Britain and Argentina in the twentieth century, while they appear to support some aspects of the framework, appear also to contradict others.

In the 1980s, Britain under Thatcher undertook a dramatic shift in its policy of nationalization, although in other significant respects it remained a highly interventionist mixed economy. Thatcher's public support came after years of dismal British economic performance – "stagflation" – which threatened the collapse of the economy (Paul Johnson 1991: 740). Hence, this fact could be seen as lending support to implication four. Yet, that this policy shift took place in a mixed economy that many would not consider "close" to the maximal state tells somewhat against implication five. Similarly, the Argentine experience from the first Peron regime in 1945 to Carlos Menem's largely successful market-based reforms of the early 1990s corroborate implication three, yet the Menem reforms could not be said to have taken place in a country with anything approaching a maximal state. Since Argentina had, for example, seven military coups between 1920 and 1966, one might be advised also to look to non-economic reasons for its highly uneven economic performance (ibid.: 616).

A different version of implication five, one that stands on somewhat firmer theoretical ground but is "weaker" in terms of empirical content, would simply assert that "a major legitimation crisis will take place when state intervention has gone on for so long that it has produced a mixed economy 'ripe' for crisis." This implies that the relevant measure is temporal rather than politico-economic in nature. Thus, such a crisis need not necessarily occur "close" to the maximal state, but only after sufficient time has elapsed for the mixed economy to have suffered significant interventionist disruption, chaos, and crises. Under this interpretation, the experiences of England and Argentina, as well as those of other countries,[20] appear to be consistent with the weaker form of implication five.

CONCLUDING REMARKS

The purpose of this chapter was to present and discuss certain pattern predictions, testable in principle, that Austrian political economy is capable of generating. The usefulness of the central message of this book, however, does not depend on the testability of these particular predictions. Indeed, whether they are testable in fact is a question I have only briefly touched on, and did so only to the extent of providing examples to illustrate the potential predictive power and empirical content of several (though not all) of the implications that might be derived from it. These examples were suggestive only, and not meant rigorously to test these highly conditional implications. A much more thorough historical study would be required to pursue some of the lines of inquiry suggested in this chapter, especially those cases that appear to contradict one or more of the implications. Such an inquiry, however, might be more fruitful were its object not to formulate predictions of sufficiently high empirical content so as to be refutable using standard techniques (which, given the nature of the phenomena under study, could well turn out to be a futile exercise, anyway), but to examine the kinds of institutions, incentives, and discoveries that might work either to reinforce or to modify these predictions. Nevertheless, this more modest undertaking could, I believe, make significant and valuable contributions to our understanding of the mixed economy.

8

WHITHER THE MIXED ECONOMY?

I have attempted in these pages not only to explain why the inner contradictions of interventionism make it inherently unstable as a system and vulnerable as a doctrine, but also to tell a story about the prevalence and persistence of the mixed economy. I have thus striven to resolve the "Misesian paradox" – i.e., why, despite its grave defects, interventionism has been and continues to be the most widespread politico-economic system in the world, and why benevolent public choosers remain myopically committed to it even when the repercussions that inevitably follow from its policies and doctrine are, from their own viewpoint, ultimately destructive.

In the course of doing so I have also sought to tackle a number of related questions. These included the nature of the governmental process, why it is that the consequences of intervention do turn out to be undesirable on balance, why public choosers tend systematically to commit errors that destabilize the system, how this instability can lead to a major system-wide crisis, the timing of that crisis, the conditions under which sweeping and radical correction is most likely to occur, and the character and role of ideological change. Other issues addressed were how the framework presented here applies to the level of individual or groups of markets, the similarities and differences between the processes of state contraction and expansion and of the dynamics of the regulatory and welfare states, the place of non-price regulation and nationalization within these dynamics, and the instability of the minimal state. Finally, I have attempted to tease out pattern predictions from what I have called Austrian political economy, as envisioned in the present study, in order to explicate possible regularities in the general behavior of all mixed economies. Whether and the extent to which any of these explanations have been persuasive is, of course, for the reader to decide. Nevertheless, I believe that each of these explanations – or at least each of the phenomena that I have attempted to explain – constitutes an aliquot part of a coherent and useful (though perhaps still incomplete) framework within which to analyze the mixed economy.

LIMITATIONS AND QUESTIONS FOR FURTHER RESEARCH

While I maintain that the logic of this framework applies to any age, owing to the extraordinary advances in more recent times in what might be called the "technology of totalitarianism," that logic has possibly found in the twentieth century its most congenial setting. Before the advent of modern methods of organization, monitoring, and information processing, that is, an authoritarian state's effective control over its citizens was limited to a comparatively small area of its nominally held territory. More recent innovations in these fields have significantly increased this control and in so doing have amplified those dynamic tendencies that culminate in major system-wide crises.[1] That mixed economies in the more-distant past may have been able to endure for extended periods of time at particular stages in the interventionist process, therefore, probably owes much to the technical limitations that then constrained the growth of state activity. But this is no longer the case.

It is probably worth repeating that this framework is not intended to be monocausal. Indeed, one of the lessons we can draw from it is that the enormous complexity of the social phenomena with which it deals effectively rules out the possibility of meaningful monocausality. No single theory can explain in a non-trivial way the impact on the dynamics of the modern mixed economy of, for example, wars, the personalities and whims of political leaders, and changes in cultural and ethical norms. The theory of interventionism developed here is no exception. As I have suggested earlier, however, it may yet be profitable to integrate some aspects of alternative approaches to political economy, especially but not exclusively those of public choice, with Austrian political economy into a more general theory of interventionism.

Along similar lines, another possibility not explored is that the impetus for the interventionist process could stem, not from government intervention, but from public choosers' responses to drastic and often painful catallactic adjustments to entrepreneurial discoveries and innovations in the pure market process. Developments in computer technology, for example, that tip the scale of comparative advantage toward, say, the programmer and away from the machinist may provoke the latter, out of the sheer desire to preserve his real income, to seek through political means to resist or thwart such change. There is scarcely any doubt that in the proper setting "economic change produces political issues" (Hughes 1991: 95), and it is not my aim to deny that catallactic forces do sometimes play an initiating role in interventionist processes. The problem facing those who claim they are paramount, however, is to explain why public choosers should have a greater proclivity at a given time to pursue redress through political means rather than to develop catallactic responses to catallactic changes, and why, moreover, these actions should then produce additional "political issues" by means of further "economic change." An explanation for such endogenous tendencies was, of course, the chief burden of the approach taken here.

Finally, an important task for future research would be to study the interaction between interventionist dynamics and the evolution of judicial (i.e., "judge-made") law, as well as to pursue the relation of changes therein to the rest of the politico-economic system. Others have examined the history of judicial law with great skill, although naturally not with the theory of interventionism as presented here in mind.[2] While integrating the dynamics of the judicial process into the present framework, as with insights from the public-choice school, would help to achieve a more general theory of interventionism, it would also promise to be a very challenging undertaking. For it would have to address issues such as the American court's struggle over the last hundred years to interpret and enforce progressive-era legislation, given judges' contrasting attitudes toward *stare decisis* and other legal principles, and how that struggle has impinged on the multi-layered, multi-faceted interactions of the governmental and market processes. That this is an extremely complex subject matter anyone could attest who is familiar with the long and tortuous development of American antitrust law (to take but one aspect of that legal history). There, the conflict between the evolving economic and legal analyses of competitive behavior and its implications for actual competition – and thus for further governmental and judicial interventions – has been and continues to be a variable but ever-present force.[3] Nevertheless, being familiar with the history of some areas of antitrust law and economics,[4] I would be willing to conjecture that the findings from research in this area would be consistent with the present study's theme that interventions tend inadvertently to produce harmful systemic consequences over the long term.[5] As one student of government has put it, "All political action has unintended consequences; the kind of political action practiced by judges is no exception" (Wilson 1989: 287). The links between actions and their effects can be just as indirect, obscure, and unintended in the judicial process as they are in the interventionist process, though often taking more time to operate, and for the same reasons (i.e., dispersed knowledge, radical ignorance, and systemic complexity). Integrating all of this into the framework of relative-price and ideological dynamics, in the manner outlined here, is therefore a project best left for another time.

THE PROSPECTS FOR THE MIXED ECONOMY

It is too tempting to conclude a book such as this by indulging in a bit of speculation, or at least commenting on what others have speculated, about the future of really existing capitalism.

Francis Fukuyama for one has suggested that we have come to the "end of history" (Fukuyama 1989). That is, we can expect the global politico-economic landscape of tomorrow to look essentially like that of the West today because the contest over which ideas will shape events to come has ended, with the ideology of liberal democracy having defeated communism, socialism, and every other serious contender. (His concepts of ideology and ideological change are much richer than the very simple ones used in the present study, and his analysis takes place along a strictly ideological dimension. Nevertheless, we both view ideology as a prior factor determining the direction of capitalism – either primarily, as in Fukuyama's case, or as a co-determinant along with relative-price distortions as in mine.) His vision, of course, is not one in which literally nothing happens in the realms of thought and action. But in it radical thinking and the process of ideological synthesis have stopped and non-liberals have abandoned "their ideological pretensions of representing different and higher forms of human society" (ibid.: 13). The most significant task left to intellectuals will instead be merely "the perpetual caretaking of the museum of human history" (ibid.: 18) and its showpiece, the doctrine of (classical) liberalism.[6] According to Fukuyama, the absence of ideological contradictions and passionate doctrinal conflict at the end of history will make it "a very sad time" (ibid.).[7]

It might appear as though Fukuyama is right about our present situation. Today, with ever fewer exceptions, intellectuals around the world are rejecting the theory and practice of collectivism, while acknowledging the merits of capitalism (with, of course, varying degrees of enthusiasm, understanding, and devotion). In short, their disagreements tend to be over whether interventions that are deemed necessary do not at the same time endanger the viability of the "free market."[8] The discussion of the previous chapter, however, indicates that the struggle over ideas and the drama of history will be unlikely ever to end. Even if the *doctrine* of liberal democracy were truly free of fundamental contradictions (ibid.: 15) and the vast majority of intellectuals now believed in it, it does not follow that the system to which at present it is practically everywhere linked (i.e., the mixed economy) would be equally free of contradiction. For example, "liberal democracy" in the United States *in practice*, with total government expenditure currently (cir. 1996) some 43 percent of gross domestic product, contains more than enough politico-economic (rather than ideological) contradictions to continue to generate the kinds of distortions that will in turn tend fundamentally to alter ideological preferences. It is thus prudent to expect that the ideological preferences of public choosers will remain highly changeable within a wide spectrum of beliefs, given the high levels of intervention and policy error in most countries at present. Consequently, the viable alternatives to capitalism are still as diverse as they ever were. Communism, in new garb, may very well again emerge as a legitimate rival to liberal democracy even if no one really wants this to happen.

The great Viennese economist, Joseph Schumpeter, has given a rather different prognosis of the capitalist process on which I also feel obliged briefly to comment. While Fukuyama's thesis is based on the proposition that the struggle of ideas propels historical events, Schumpeter, like Kirzner, views capitalism as driven by an entrepreneurial quest for profit. Unlike Kirzner, however, the forces of entrepreneurship for Schumpeter give rise to a process, not of coordinating discovery, but rather of discoordinating "creative destruction" (Kirzner 1973: 125–31) that operates not only to fuel competition within the market process, but, perversely, to erode over time the very social fabric that supports it. Eventually, as investment opportunities steadily vanish, this process sets the stage for its own demise. Specifically, the creative–destructive process generates a growing hostility on the part of intellectuals against capitalists and capitalism and a spreading *ennui* among entrepreneurial innovators that in the long term turns activity within the capitalist process into mere routine. His outlook for capitalism is thus infamously gloomy: "Can capitalism survive? No. I do not think it can" (Schumpeter 1950: 61). The gales of creative destruction abate and history comes to an end for Schumpeter, not in a liberal democracy under capitalism, but in a workable, if uninspiring, form of socialism (ibid.: 131–86).

Both Fukuyama and Schumpeter envision a future for really existing capitalism that is discouraging (with the latter's outlook, to a classical liberal at least, much more so than the former). Of course, the thrust of the previous chapter might also be interpreted in a similar light (or gloom). An underground joke making the rounds in eastern Europe just before the momentous events of 1989 declared that "communism . . . is the longest and most painful route from capitalism to capitalism" (Gwertzman and Kaufman 1990). We have seen that it might also be equally correct to say that capitalism is the longest and most painful route from communism to communism. Many would probably find disagreeable the prospect of politico-economic systems around the world perpetually cycling between (although perhaps never quite reaching) laissez-faire capitalism and totalitarian collectivism and back again, punctuated by episodes of acute dislocation and severe systemwide crises. In any case, collectivist central planning need not be our final destination as Schumpeter reluctantly concludes, but merely a possible stage in what *may* be a journey without end.

Is escape from the interventionist process possible? In spite of what has just been said, I believe the answer is yes. One quite radical way out would be to eliminate the inner contradictions of interventionism entirely by abolishing the state altogether. From the viewpoint of political pragmatism, of course, such a policy would be in many ways highly problematic, since a majority of public choosers undeniably harbor serious concerns over whether the market process, without the threat of effective state coercion to govern it, would be sufficiently self-regulating or produce outcomes of which they would approve (e.g., a "fair" distribution of wealth).[9] Leaving these admittedly important pragmatic issues to one side, however, there is no doubt from a purely theoretical standpoint that so-called anarcho-capitalism would eradicate most if not all of the important sources of instability identified in this book.

A less drastic course, though potentially a less stable one, is toward that of the minimal state. The final proposition of chapter seven asserts that a sufficiently strong commitment to the minimal state among public choosers can hold the number of actual political agents below "critical mass" and thereby keep the inherent tension between governmental and market forces in check. Whether it is reasonable to expect this to happen is, as we have seen, still problematic, possibly more so than even anarcho-capitalism. Nevertheless, among the alternatives examined in the previous chapters, the minimal state, or a close approximation to it, seems to offer the best hope for systemic stability. Accordingly, if liberalism does enjoy unprecedented support throughout the world today, this could signal not the end of the last dramatic historical contest but perhaps the beginning of the end. The next great challenge would then be to make the practice of liberalism conform more closely to liberal principles, thereby calming the turbulence that otherwise threatens perpetually to upset social cooperation. Stability might then endure, if that is what we want and want badly enough.

APPENDICES

APPENDIX A: ON KNOWLEDGE AND MOTIVES

To clarify the differences among Austrian and alternative approaches to political economy compared in Chapter 1, figure A.1 may be useful:

Motive

		Narrow interest	Benevolence
Knowledge Assumption	Perfect knowledge	*Chicago public choice*	*Public interest* Kelman/Wilson
	Partial ignorance	*Virginia public choice* Habermas/Offe	*Austrian political economy*

Figure A.1 Knowledge–motive matrix of politico-economic systems

As discussed in the text, there are basically two assumptions analysts have made regarding motivation – i.e., public choosers are motivated either by narrowly selfish or political interest or by benevolence and a desire to promote the general welfare. Similarly, we can assume either that public choosers possess perfect knowledge in some sense or that they are subject to at least partial radical ignorance. Each of the four quadrants in the above matrix, then, represents a different combination of one of the two motive assumptions with one of the two knowledge assumptions. Thus, for example, the approach of "Chicago public choice" tends to combine the assumptions of perfect knowledge and narrow self-interest, while "Austrian political economy" tends to combine the opposite assumptions.

Note that in presenting this classification, I have made no attempt to be either exhaustive or especially representative. For instance, there is no mention here of Marxian or of so-called radical political economy (aside from Habermas and Offe). That is because only those approaches that are particularly germane to the discussion in the text are included. Also, my intent in constructing this classification has been to indicate the characteristic emphasis of the approaches listed, rather than to argue that there is no common ground among some or even all of them. Mises and Hayek, for example, recognized and contributed insights from a "Virginia" perspective, just as some of the work of certain public-choice theorists (e.g., Olson, Wagner, and the early Tullock) could meaningfully be classified as "Austrian." And I have already noted the parallels between Austrian political economy and the Habermas–Offe critique of welfare-state interventionism.

APPENDIX B: MISES ON NATIONALIZATION AND SUBSIDIES

Why did Mises omit nationalization and price subsidies from the concept of interventionism? Working from Mises's own definition of interventionism, it might be possible to provide a reasonable explanation. Specifically, his exclusion of nationalization and partial socialization is consistent with his view, especially in 1929 when *A Critique of Interventionism* was first published, that intervention is first and foremost a method of industrial and commercial *regulation* (i.e., a form of regulatory statism), and it is for that reason distinct from the outright appropriation of private business and industry.

Furthermore, recall that for the purposes of this study I defined an intervention, following Rothbard, simply as violent interference with the market process, typically through the use of political means. Mises, however, defined it rather differently as follows:

> [I]ntervention is a decree issued directly or indirectly, by the authority in charge of society's administrative apparatus of coercion and compulsion which forces the entrepreneurs and capitalists to employ some of their factors of production in

a way different from what they would have resorted to if
they were only obeying the dictates of the market.

(Mises 1966, 718–19)

Hence, when the state employs for its own purposes the factors
of production that it has appropriated, it does not "intervene"
in Mises's sense, and thus such activity does not constitute an
intervention.

Yet the act of appropriation itself would seem to conform to
Mises's definition, since it would certainly be contrary to the
dictates of the market (unless the state were to purchase the assets
in question in the open market, although Mises makes no mention
of this possibility). Also, when private entrepreneurs attempt to
compete with a nationalized industry they typically encounter
legal barriers, enforced by political means, that block their way.
Furthermore, Mises seems to contradict himself when, in the same
part of *Human Action* in which he again denies that nationalization
is an intervention, he states:

> If the government itself owns and operates plants, farms,
> forests, and mines, it might consider covering a part or the
> whole of its financial needs from interest and profit earned.
> But government operation of business enterprise *as a rule* is
> so inefficient that it results in losses rather than in profits.
> Governments must resort to taxation, i.e., they must raise
> revenues by forcing the subjects to surrender a part of their
> wealth or income.

(Mises 1966: 737; emphasis added)

The implication here is that state-run enterprises, such as nationalized whole industries and heavily regulated legal monopolies,
apparently contrary to his denial, do "as a rule" require intervention (in Mises's sense), since such firms would tend to incur
persistent budget deficits that the state would then be obliged to
finance through some form of taxation. One way to resolve this
paradox, and to clear Mises of this charge of contradiction, is to
interpret him as suggesting that a nationalized industry would
likely entail intervention as a *practical* matter, though not as a
matter of *logical* necessity.

It might also have made sense for Mises to isolate nationalization
from what he regarded as interventionism, proper, if *relative-price
distortions* were at the core of his critique. That is, because

nationalization does not at first appear to disrupt the price mechanism, at least in the same way that price and quantity controls do, Mises may have considered it somewhat removed from the price-based dynamic of the interventionist process. Mises described that dynamic as consisting mainly in the responses of actors in the market to shortages and surpluses resulting from relative-price distortions. Mises may have reasoned that the presence of nationalized industries in the market process does not significantly affect relative prices in this manner. (This, of course, is a rational reconstruction of Mises's reasoning. In Chapter 5, I argue that nationalization and legal monopoly *do* have significant relative-price effects of a kind that Mises, even in his later work, did not envision.)

This means, however, as Rothbard (1977) and Lavoie (1982) have shown, that Mises's categories of alternative economic systems is non-exhaustive, since a situation in which the state has nationalized almost all, but not the entire, total domestic production capacity would be, on Mises's terms, neither interventionism nor collectivism, and certainly not capitalism. (See Lavoie (1982) for an excellent critique both of this part of Mises's argument and of minor aspects of Rothbard's typology.) For this reason I have found it more convenient to adopt Rothbard's definition of "intervention" for the present study. Under this definition, nationalization and partial socialization would be considered interventions. Note that I still retain the Misesian definition of interventionism, so that only interventions that go beyond the minimal state or that fall short of the maximal state (because it is a species of collectivism), would be regarded as elements of interventionism.

With regard to price subsidies, Mises in his earlier work took a rather curious position. There he wrote, for example that

> Government measures that use market means, that is, seek to influence demand and supply through changes of market factors, are not included in this concept of intervention. If government buys milk in the market in order to sell it inexpensively to destitute mothers or even to distribute it without charge, or if government subsidizes educational institutions, there is no intervention.
>
> (Mises 1977: 19–20)

The argument that I used to resolve the paradox of Mises's conflicting statements about the interventionist character of nationalization is not relevant here. That is, while it is an empirical question whether state-run enterprises run deficits that require coercive taxation to finance them, the state's reliance on coercion to finance price subsidies is entirely a matter of logical necessity. Price subsidies, or any other kind of benefit provided through political means, perforce depend on direct or indirect taxation, which is inherently interventionist (in either Mises's or Rothbard's terms).

Although Mises rectified this problem by the time he wrote *Human Action* in 1949, it is possible to imagine that he might have wanted to exclude income transfers from his concept of interventionism had he, once again, intended to place the effects of relative-price distortions at the center of his critique of interventionism. That is, while Mises's critique of the welfare state relies *implicitly* on a logic similar to that underlying regulatory statism (explicated in Chapters 4 and 5), relative-price distortions play no role at all in his analysis of the welfare state's transfer activities. Perhaps the source of this difficulty lies in the absence in Mises's theory of the "hampered economy" of an *explicit* principle or logic that unifies the analysis. In his critique of collectivist planning, for example, Mises singles out the impossibility of rational economic calculation in the absence of market prices that emerge when privately owned assets are freely exchanged.

In his critique of interventionism Mises does say that private and public control of the means of production "can never be confounded with one another; they cannot be mixed or combined; no gradual transition leads from one of them to the other; they are mutually incompatible" (1966: 716). Elsewhere he says that "those authors who do not totally reject economics and yet assert that price control can attain the ends sought lamentably contradict themselves" (ibid.: 761). And throughout his entire analysis the notion of "consequences of intervention undesirable from the viewpoint of its supporters" appears again and again. While such statements hint at a central theme, especially the last thesis, it remains implicit. Thus, Mises, in a discussion of the welfare state, declares that "There is no need to add anything to the disquisitions of the preceding chapters [which discussed price dynamics and the welfare state among other things] concerning the effects of *all* varieties of interventionism" (ibid.: 834–5; emphasis added). Interpreted liberally, this could mean that Mises did indeed envision transfer and regulatory dynamics as simply two manifestations of a common interventionist process. If so, it is a pity that he felt no need to elaborate further, since the connection between relative-price distortions and the problems of the welfare state remains obscure. It should be clear by now that I believe that the place to begin the search for a unifying principle is in the logic of the relative-price distortions that underlie regulatory dynamics.

APPENDIX C: ROTHBARD'S TYPOLOGY OF INTERVENTION

While using the Misesian framework as his starting point, Murray Rothbard, one of Mises's most influential American students, has devised a typology, which has the great virtue of encompassing most if not all of the phenomena normally associated with intervention, including nationalization and state-sponsored monopolization. He divides intervention into three categories: *autistic intervention*, i.e., state interference with private, non-exchange activities; *binary intervention*, i.e., forced exchange between private individuals and the state; and *triangular intervention*, i.e., state-mandated exchange among private individuals. (In comparison, Nicholas Barr in his survey article, "Economic theory and the welfare state," reflects general professional opinion when he gives as the four generic types of government intervention regulation, price subsidy, public production, and income transfers (Barr 1992: 743–4).) Rothbard's convenient typology readily accommodates interventions connected with both the regulatory and welfare states, and thereby eliminates the gaps and inconsistencies that appear in Mises's original formulation. Autistic interventions, for example, include "compulsory enforcement or prohibition of a salute, speech, or religious observance" (Rothbard 1970: 767). Examples of binary intervention encompass state activities such as taxation, compulsory education, publicly provided goods and services, and the nationalization of industries. Lastly, among interventions of the triangular type are income-transfer programs, price controls, fiscal and monetary policy, trade and contract restrictions, and environmental, safety, health, and civil rights regulations.

Note that, with the exception of autistic interventions, intervention entails direct or indirect income transfers. Indeed, this typology favors an income-transfer interpretation of government intervention similar to that which we have found in public-choice analysis in the previous chapter. It is even possible to consider autistic interventions as transfers to the extent that the, presumably onerous, restrictions on private behavior that they represent benefit some for whom political means were employed, whether they are in government or the market, at the expense of others. Prohibitions on the use of "indecent" language or dress, for example, usually have winners and losers in the political process no less than explicit income-redistribution programs.

Regrettably, while I agree with Don Lavoie's favorable evaluation of this reformulation to the extent that the changes Rothbard made "are extensions of the scope of the concept of interventionism to an increasing variety of categories of government policy to which [Mises's] original form of argument was applicable" (Lavoie 1982: 169), I believe they add very little to our understanding of the nature of the interventionist *process*. (On the other hand, recall that Rothbard's redefinition of the concept of intervention itself, which I have adopted for this study, has been quite helpful.) Beyond a much needed improvement in expositional tidiness, it is hard to see how Rothbard's richer typology, alone, enhances the analytical power of Mises's critique so as to advance significantly the research program on interventionism, at least in the direction I have chosen. (According to Jeffrey Friedman (1990: 703), "But no unintended consequences of intervention are being elucidated by Rothbard's all-purpose arguments against intervention; he is simply cloaking the moral claim that the *intended* consequences are undesirable in the economistic garb of utility functions" (emphasis original). While I have scruples with the tone of this statement, I believe its basic point is very similar to mine.) What, for example, does the fact that income transfers, credit expansion, and price control all fall under the category of triangular intervention tell us about the differences, if any, in the way in which each of these work themselves out in the interventionist process? How does it deepen our understanding of the nature of interventionism to know that nationalization is a binary intervention, whereas an environmental regulation is a triangular intervention? What have we gained in the analysis of taxation, which is a binary intervention, by *calling* it a binary intervention? In other words, in the absence of analytical differences that are uniquely associated with each category (as is the case, for example, in the difference between externalities and, say, increasing returns), how do the categories *per se* increase our knowledge about the interventionist process at all? Because my own responses to these questions fall against Rothbard's typology, it will, accordingly, not play a significant role in the present analysis.

To reiterate, the claim I am disputing here concerns the analytical power of Rothbard's *typology* alone, and not with Rothbard's analyses of the various kinds of intervention so classified. The latter (e.g., the incidence of taxation (Rothbard 1977: 88–108)) do demonstrate considerable analytical power.

NOTES

1 THE CHALLENGE OF THE MIXED ECONOMY

1 See Mises (1920). While not a prediction in the sense of conventional falsificationist methodology, Mises's claim may be seen as an example of what Friedrich Hayek would later term a "pattern prediction," a prediction relating to the behavior of an entire class of phenomena rather than to a specific event within that class. For further discussion and examples of pattern prediction, see Chapter 7, below.

2 As we will see, there are striking parallels between Claus Offe's post-Marxian analysis of the contradictions of the welfare state and the framework presented here. For example, with respect to welfare-state capitalism, Offe declares that

> Today, by contrast, the tantalizing and baffling riddle... is why capitalist systems have so far been able to survive – in spite of all existing contradictions and conflicts – even though an intact bourgeois ideology that could deny these contradictions and construct the image of a harmonious order no longer exists.
> (Offe 1984:36)

David Prychitko, however, in his valuable critique of the Habermas –Offe analysis, argues that despite these similarities in diagnosis "Offe is trapped, by his assumption of the objective need for the welfare state, into being unable to offer any more realistic solutions" (Prychitko 1990: 627). Nevertheless, Prychitko concludes that their analysis "might explain a good deal about the failings and dynamics of the welfare-state version of interventionism that appears as the century turns" (Ibid.: 628).

3 There are those who acknowledge Mises's vision but not his analysis. See, for example, Heilbroner (1989).

4 Even within the Austrian tradition the theoretical basis of Mises's critique has received relatively little attention. Among those who have more recently attempted to address some of the fundamental issues are Hagel (1975), Grinder and Hagel (1977), Rothbard (1977), Littlechild (1979), Lavoie (1985b), and Kirzner (1985:119–49).

Charles Wolf (1990), dean of the RAND Graduate School of Policy

Studies, offers an enlightening non-public-choice alternative to the critique of intervention that is also outside the Austrian tradition, narrowly defined. Wolf's concept of "derived externalities" is very similar to this study's analysis of negative unintended consequences. "Derived externalities in the nonmarket domain," he states, "are side effects that are not realized by the agency responsible for creating them, and hence do not affect the agency's calculations or behavior" (ibid.: 77).

Also extremely relevant to the present study is Jonathan Hughes's excellent history of American economic regulation. Hughes argues that the haphazard development of American regulation is nonetheless based on a set of regulatory principles that date back to Colonial America and feudal England. Concerning the present muddled state of regulation in particular, Hughes writes:

> In the pervasive economic troubles of the 1990s we face general economic problems with a bag of tools for government interference with economic processes that were fashioned piecemeal, over a long period of time, to cope only with specific problems. The mechanisms of control are not coordinated where they are effective; their effects spill over into areas of economic life that are not subjected to the same controls, and the consequences are generally disruptive.
>
> (Hughes 1991:14)

Unlike Wolf, however, Hughes does not aim to explain how the "mass of controls" fail to produce their desired outcome. He simply assumes, quite reasonably but for my purposes unsatisfactorily, that without an "overall logic" such a "congeries" could only produce on net undesirable consequences.

5 Lavoie (1982) offers a brief but highly useful overview of this development.

6 Hence, I can agree with Lavoie (1982: 180) when he claims that "The proliferation of new forms of government interference into the market is certain to present many new challenges for the analyst in the future. . . . But I believe all these will prove susceptible to the Misesian critique of interventionism . . .," to the extent that this refers to the basic *logic* of Mises's critique and not to the form in which he left it. On whether Rothbard's typology of intervention really improves on Mises's critique in the sense of more adequately fitting the concept of interventionism "into the analytical role that Mises tried to make it play in his overall theory of economic policy" (ibid.: 169), see Appendix B.

7 Richard Wagner is an example of someone working within the public-choice tradition who has undertaken this task head on. As a public-choice scholar, however, his emphasis is exactly the reverse of the one taken in this study. According to Wagner, (1989: 108),

> Since any regulation can be translated into an equivalent budgetary operation, and vice versa, an examination of the welfare state that

is restricted to budgetary operations must be seriously incomplete. [This study] makes an effort to incorporate aspects of the regulatory state into an examination of the welfare state.

I, on the contrary, am concerned with how to explain the dynamics of the welfare state largely in terms of the dynamics that underlie the regulatory state. Later in this chapter, I compare and contrast Austrian political economy with public choice.

8 The terms "regulatory state," "welfare state," "socialism," etc. are defined in Chapter 2.

9 I discuss the meanings of these terms in Chapter 3.

10 Boettke (1990) in fact argues that the Soviet Union's experiment with pure socialism ended in 1922, after which it was more akin to a mixed economy. Similarly, Prychitko argues that East European socialism, "was but a vastly exaggerated version of the Western interventionist welfare state." Indeed, he goes to say that "the fact that socialism has failed does not imply that the welfare state is a viable alternative, for the welfare state differs only in degree, and not in kind, from its miserable East European counterpart" (Prychitko 1990: 628).

11 As I will be using the term, "government growth" will refer to both state expansion and contraction, in both absolute and relative terms.

12 Although "neoclassical economics" covers a range of approaches, its defining methodological features are the primacy of equilibrium analysis, the widespread use of the concept of optimization, and perfect information (probabilistic or otherwise). For a more complete discussion, see Ikeda (1990; 1991; 1992), as well as the discussion in Chapter 3, below.

13 For an example of the kind of problems addressed in the traditional approach, see Scherer (1980).

14 Of course, still another approach to regulation economics would recognize only very broad limits, if any, on the scope of effective state activity. This view is critiqued elsewhere in this book, especially in Chapter 3.

15 In fact Dennis Mueller traces the development of public choice as a separate field to Arrow's 1951 article on social-choice theory, and places public choice "within the stream of political philosophy extending at least from Thomas Hobbes and Benedict Spinoza, and within political science from James Madison and Alexis de Tocqueville" (Mueller 1989:2). The articles cited in the following three notes, however, better reflect the beginnings of the particular aspect of public choice that I am concerned with here.

16 Notably Stigler (1971), Posner (1975), and Peltzman (1976).

17 Especially Buchanan and Tullock (1962) and Tullock (1967).

18 See especially Mancur Olson (1965) and Anthony Downs (1957).

19 For a more precise differentiation among the approaches that I have placed under this rubric, see Appendix A, in which I try to show schematically how Austrian political economy relates to public choice and other approaches to the economics of regulation, broadly construed. In addition, Charles K. Rowley's essay on "Public choice

economics" in Boettke (1994) is also helpful in de-homogenizing the varieties of public choice.

20 Buchanan (1979) notes that public choice should not claim full credit for the recent widespread skepticism toward politics, and that in particular "for members of the general public, the simple observation of failure on the part of government to deliver on their promises, these failures have been much more important in modifying attitudes than any set of ideas or any ideology" (p.20).

21 General introductions to these and other propositions in public-choice theory can be found in Mueller (1989), David Johnson (1991), and Buchanan and Tollison (1984).

22 Also along these lines see Charles T. Goodsell's (1985) deliberately polemical defense of bureaucracy.

23 Strictly speaking, rent seeking refers to a type of rational behavior having as its object the capture of rents – typically though not exclusively monopoly rents created by state-erected or sanctioned barriers to competition – the normative outcome of which is usually additional deadweight losses. See Buchanan, *et al.* (1980).

24 According to Thomas Sowell, to those who hold an "unconstrained" vision of how human reason can direct social processes, "deliberate obstruction and obfuscation account for many evils, and... what is crucially needed on the part of the public-spirited reformers is commitment" (Sowell 1987: 73).

25 See Ikeda (1990) for a discussion of these foundations of neoclassical economics.

26 Chapter 3, below, includes a more detailed comparison of market-process with neoclassical economics. This is perhaps an appropriate place to mention an article by Thomas DiLorenzo (1988), who takes public choice to task for its sometimes too rigid adherence to the large-numbers assumption underlying the neoclassical model of perfect competition.

27 Jonathan Hughes criticizes a particular example of this kind of reasoning thus:

> Antitrust laws, applied for a century now, have not stopped the growth of massive industrial concentration and oligopolistic behavior. Hence it is argued by some that such results must have been the object of antitrust policy. The observed result identifies the motivation. Such ideas are naive.
>
> (Hughes 1991:15)

28 In a manner fully in accord with the framework adopted here, Charles Wolf also argues that "a complete theory of nonmarket failure requires more than is provided by public choice alone." Specifically, with reference to the production of nonmarket outputs, Wolf points out that (among other neglected factors), "the frequency of 'derived' or unanticipated externalities resulting from these outputs [is] ignored or inadequately explained by existing public choice theory" (Wolf 1990: 5).

29 In this vein, Jeffrey Friedman (1990: 703) writes: "If we accept Mises's

dictum that the economist as such is indifferent to the desirability of the goals pursued by an economic policy, it is clear why his or her only role should be to investigate whether goals would in fact be achieved by the means proposed. This implies that the economist should look into the 'invisible,' unanticipated and unintended consequences of intervention."

30 In contrast to Wagner, for example, according to whom, "in the welfare state income redistribution is regarded as an intentional activity" (Wagner 1989: 8).

31 These concepts and their relation with each other will be discussed in Chapters 2 and especially, 5.

32 This may be wise from an empirical standpoint, as well. Mueller, for example, comments:

> But if redistribution is the primary activity of government, then some additional logical arguments are missing to explain the growth of government to the sizes now observed in different countries. Alternatively, government activity is not exclusively redistributive. Government has grown to far greater size than is necessary just to achieve redistribution.
>
> (Mueller 1989: 330)

33 Gary M. Anderson (1994: 298), however, argues that "the recent experience of deregulation can be adequately explained within the framework of the economic theory of regulation," which in this context refers to the "Chicago" variant of public choice represented in particular by Peltzman and Becker. Still, Anderson acknowledges that "loose ends" remain, and suggests that this is "an important problem for future research" (ibid.).

34 This debate is reviewed later, in Chapter 3.

35 For recent scholarship on the importance of constitutional constraints for safeguarding against unlimited democracy, see the articles contained in Gwartney and Wagner (1988).

36 See Chapter 2 for additional documentation on this point. Significantly, Mises went on to say in the very next sentence: "But for the inefficiency of the law-givers and the laxity, carelessness, and corruption of many of the functionaries, the last vestiges of the market economy would have long since disappeared" (Mises 1966: 859). Because "inefficiency, laxity, carelessness, and corruption" in public choice often constitute the very engine of government growth and not the brake that Mises is here asserting they are, the latter passage suggests Mises had in mind a very different role for these phenomena to play.

37 Relations may be even closer than this. Thus, a highly regarded Austrian economist has recently offered an analysis of the regulatory process that is indistinguishable from public choice. See High (1991). Some of the central ideas developed in the present book were in fact first published in response to this essay. See Ikeda (1991).

38 One of the most notable examples of a public-choice theorist whose work approaches (but does not quite coincide with) that of market-process theory is James Buchanan. See especially (Buchanan 1985:

71–120). Even Buchanan, however, characterizes public choice as "the extension of the economists' utility-maximizing framework to the behavior of persons in various public-choosing roles" (ibid.: 87).

39 This section draws heavily though not exclusively from Mueller (1989) and his excellent survey of the growth of government literature.

40 In addition, public goods contain an "assurance problem." In the context of the prisoners' dilemma game, in which public-goods problems are frequently analyzed, David Schmidtz explains that an assurance problem "arises if a person believes it would be futile to contribute because the good will not be provided anyway" (Schmidtz 1991: 56). Schmidtz claims that assurance contracts may be voluntarily entered into, thus overcoming this particular obstacle to the private provision of pure public goods.

41 For a persuasive case that the prisoners' dilemma rationale for the existence of the state contains a self-defeating paradox (because the state is itself a public good), see Kalt (1981).

42 E. C. Pasour (1991) offers a subjectivist rebuttal of Lee's welfare-maximization calculus.

43 Although an aspect of Lee's (1989) analysis of the suboptimality of the minimal state plays a role in the discussion of the instability of the minimal state in Chapter 6.

44 Robert Higgs has recently observed that no single theory (including his own) tells the whole story; and of those that are the most popular (market failure, safety-net, redistributionist) "each fails to depict the *process*" (Higgs 1987: 258; emphasis original) whereby big government has developed.

45 As discussed there, however, other factors may have also been at work implicitly, especially those relating to informational problems.

46 I would like to thank Israel Kirzner for bringing this argument to my attention.

2 THE MEANING OF INTERVENTIONISM

1 What I call the "micro" aspect of interventionism is somewhat different from traditional regulation economics because of its focus on spillover effects. See Chapter 4.

2 In particular, see Appendix C for a discussion of Murray Rothbard's contribution.

3 To promote organizational tidiness, I will be dividing this chapter, and each of the remaining chapters of this book, into segments called, in order of decreasing generality, "parts," "sections," and "subsections."

4 This definition of government is consistent with those found in Rothbard (1970: 766) and implicitly in Nozick (1974: 22–5). The distinction between political means and economic means is from Oppenheimer (1975: 12). Also, according to Mises (1966: 719), "The essential feature of government is the enforcement of its decrees by beating, killing, and imprisoning."

5 This is different from though consistent with what Wagner (1989: 2)

calls the *contractarian state*, in which "the state undertakes only those activities that its members agree to and only to the extent that they are willing to pay for them."

6 Wagner, employing Buchanan's terminology, would perhaps refer to this kind of state, depending on what portion of its duties is taken up with addressing externalities and public goods, as either a "protective" or a "productive" state. See Wagner (1989: 3–8); also Nozick (1974: 26).

7 However, Hayek observes that "socialism so long as it remains theoretical is internationalist, while as soon as it is put into practice ... it becomes violently nationalist" (ibid.: 141).

8 For a wide sample of the various meanings given to this term, see James J. Martin's "The unresolved question of fascism" in Martin (1971: 53–70).

9 See also Prychitko (1990: 628).

10 Because so-called anarcho-capitalism is not directly relevant to the present discussion, I have chosen not to address it here. I try to do so to a very limited extent in Chapter 8, below.

11 In Chapter 3 I discuss the meaning of the market and governmental processes.

12 While the terms "interventionism" and "mixed economy" are often used interchangeably (as in this book), Mises, for one, appears to make a subtle distinction between the two. He defines interventionism in terms of its relation to laissez-faire capitalism and is concerned with how the state might intervene into the catallaxy while preserving its essential capitalist nature. Mises expresses this, using somewhat different terminology, as follows:

> If one considers the idea of placing by the side of these two systems [capitalism and socialism] or between them a third system of human cooperation under the division of labor, one can always start only from the notion of the market economy, never from that of socialism. The notion of socialism with its rigid monism and centralism that vests the powers to choose and to act in *one* will exclusively does not allow of any compromise or concession; this construction is not amenable to any adjustment or alteration.
> (Mises 1966: 716; emphasis in original)

The concept of the *mixed economy*, however, appears to make no such presumption and refers simply to any politico-economic system that lies between the extremes of laissez-faire capitalism and pure collectivism. In this book, I have found it convenient to let interventionism also refer to the set of policies that attempt to shape and guide the mixed economy, regardless of whether the interventionist process moves toward laissez-faire or collectivism. Interventionism, then, will refer to a system, the underlying dynamics of which drive it in the direction of either more or less state control.

13 As we have seen, this is the approach that Wagner (1989) has explicitly taken.

14 As Wolf observes, "nonmarket activity is rarely undertaken without a

case being first made on normative grounds, based on market failure or distributional equity" (Wolf 1990: 96–7, n30).

15 Save in cases of the second-best type, in which, for example, imperfections that restrict output in a given market might be offset completely by other imperfections in that same market or in markets elsewhere in the economy. See Mishan (1981: 289–300).

16 Harold Demsetz's classic article (1969), on the fallacy of the "Nirvana approach" of 1960s-vintage public-policy economics, is relevant here. Indeed, despite important theoretical differences, the present study is very much in the spirit of Demsetz's critique.

17 This last phenomenon is a market failure in the technical economic sense, according to one authority, only if voluntary contribution is the principal method of redressing these disparities and "there is reason to believe that voluntarism will be suboptimal" (Barr 1992: 748).

18 Nicholas Barr in his survey of welfare economics asserts that one aspect of the notion of efficiency in neoclassical theory is *macro-efficiency*, which dictates that "the efficient fraction of GDP should be devoted to the totality of welfare state institutions, e.g., policy should seek to avoid distortions which lead to cost explosions" (1992: 745).

19 See Chapter 3 for the importance of genuine or radical ignorance for the understanding of the market process and also for the governmental and interventionist processes.

20 With respect to the particular example of a price ceiling, Mises later recognized two exceptions: rent-control may lower rental rates without diminishing the supply of rental space if there is a significant difference between urban and agricultural rent; and a price ceiling may lower prices without creating a shortage if significant monopoly power is present. See Mises (1966: 765, 766).

21 In Chapter 4, I point out three ways to interpret the statement that the outcomes of interventionism are contrary to expectations.

22 When Mises explains how intervention exhausts the reserve fund (see below, Chapter 4), he does so in the context of redistributive transfers rather than price or quantity controls. See Mises (1966: 855–8).

23 Similarly, with regard to the payment of taxes, Mises (1966: 745) states: "As far as the government fulfills its social functions and the taxes do not exceed the amount required for securing the smooth operation of the government apparatus, they are necessary costs and repay themselves."

24 See Appendix B for a possible explanation of why Mises made these exceptions.

25 Chapter 3 outlines the modern Austrian theory of the market process insofar as it illuminates the nature of interventionism; it also defines such terms as "radical ignorance."

26 I have occasion for example to draw on the work of Henry Simon and his concept of "bounded rationality" in the more detailed analysis of this problem in Chapter 4.

27 While it is possible that Mises may have tacitly relied on these ideas, the distinction that is made in Chapter 4 between "class-one" and "class-two" errors and the corresponding concepts of "inevitable"

and "dynamic" learning, which is so important in the explanation of the discoordinating effects of interventionism, was in Mises inchoate at best. Indeed, in neither his earlier price-control example nor in later writings, does Mises display clear awareness of what Kirzner has called "radical ignorance," which is more closely associated with class-two errors. Especially when discussing interventionism, Mises included only class-one errors i.e., errors, such as a shortage, that alert actors will "almost inevitably" discover. See the discussion in Chapter 4.

28 In an earlier work, Mises states that "no legal precautions are strong enough to resist a trend supported by a powerful ideology. The popular ideas of government interference with business and of socialism have undermined the dams erected by twenty generations of Anglo-Saxons against the flood of arbitrary rule" (1969: 16).

29 Recall from Chapter 1 that this is similar to Wolf's (1990) concept of a "derived externality."

3 THE USE OF KNOWLEDGE IN GOVERNMENT AND CATALLAXY

1 This chapter borrows heavily from Ikeda (1995a).

2 According to Hayek,

> What distinguishes the rules which will govern action within an organization is that they must be rules for the performance of assigned tasks. They presuppose that the place of each individual in a fixed structure is determined by command and that the rules each individual must obey depend on the place which he has been assigned and on the particular ends which have been indicated for him by the commanding authority. The rules will thus regulate merely the detail of the action of appointed functionaries or agencies of government.
>
> By contrast, the rules governing a spontaneous order must be independent of purpose and be the same, if not necessarily for all members, at least for whole classes of members not individually designated by name. They must... be rules applicable to an unknown and indeterminable number of persons and instances. They will have to be applied by the individuals in the light of their respective knowledge and purposes; and their application will be independent of any common purpose, which the individual need not even know.
>
> (Hayek 1973: 49, 50)

The term "spontaneous order" is attributable to Michael Polanyi (1951).

3 These institutional differences, however, need not imply complete incompatibility. Recall that Mises (1977), for example, argued that the minimal state, operating in relation to a market economy, maintains an uneasy though stable balance between the forces of voluntary exchange and coercion, which is nevertheless a necessary condition for

peaceful social cooperation in complex societies. He further claimed that state expansion beyond its minimal duties upsets this balance, destabilizes the system, and thereby sets into motion the dynamics of the interventionist process.

4 Gordon Tullock's (1965) pathbreaking, though somewhat neglected, study of bureaucracy contains a thoughtful and lucid explanation of the practical difficulties involved in communicating relevant information up and down a typical bureaucratic hierarchy. See especially pp. 137–56.

5 This is also the judgment of Tullock (1965), who argues that Hayek's objection to the centrally planned economy "clearly has wider applications. . . . Administrative problems in other fields could also be of such complexity that the centralization of information necessary to make decisions effectively in a bureaucracy might not be possible" (p. 124).

6 From this perspective, then, the method of inquiry into the nature of the interventionist process in mixed economies would be distinct from either of these, since it would explicitly focus on the interaction between the public and private sectors when both are outside of full plan coordination and the knowledge problem prevents rapid adjustment. In short, the method would entail examining the consequences of the interaction between the market and governmental *processes* that are examined in this chapter.

7 This section draws heavily from Ikeda (1994). This essay contains a comparison between competition in market-process theory and the neoclassical concept of perfect competition.

8 My point here is more than a mere logical one. Rather, it is epistemological, having to do with the kind of knowledge that actors acquire and that is essential to the operation of the market process.

9 As I explain in Chapter 4, these actually constitute two distinct classes of error, and have two distinct learning procedures corresponding to them.

10 Non-economists are usually surprised to learn that the concept of entrepreneurship is absent from the core of modern neoclassical theory and the role of profit and loss correspondingly marginalized.

11 See Ikeda (1983). Thomsen (1992) provides a thorough discussion of the role of non-equilibrium prices in coordinating market behavior, especially as it contrasts to the more mainstream treatments of the informational role of prices in the manner of Grossman, Stiglitz, *et al.* The standard reference is still Kirzner (1973).

12 For further discussion of normative market-process theory, see Kirzner (1992: ch. 11) and Ikeda (1990).

13 See Hayek's essay, "Economics and knowledge," in Hayek (1948).

14 Here, "input" should be interpreted broadly to include such things as reputation, skill, and experience. According to this concept of monopoly, what control over an essential input grants is a monopoly over a particular production process, which differs from standard monopoly theory in which a monopolistic firm is said to dominate the market for a particular product. See Kirzner (1973: 88–134) and Ikeda (1988).

For an alternative Austrian viewpoint on monopoly, see Rothbard (1977).

15 While this statement is modified somewhat below, it is consistent with Kirzner's (1973) treatment.

16 This bears some relation to one of the lessons of what used to be called the "new learning" in industrial organization, although the latter retained a fundamentally equilibrium orientation (Ikeda 1990). See, for example, Goldschmidt *et al.* (1974).

17 As an example, consider the general competitiveness of the telecommunications industry in the United States during the past twenty years, which made impressive progress despite very significant legal protection granted to its incumbents.

18 This point is also related to the "new learning."

19 As I explain in Chapter 4, the forces of discoordination consist of (1) radical ignorance *per se* and (2) relative-price distortions that interfere with the discovery of plan inconsistencies owing to radical ignorance. The relation between monopolization and relative-prices distortions is discussed in Chapters 4 and 5.

20 This assumes that sellers can overcome some other formidable obstacles, which I discuss in note 27, below.

21 In Chapter 5 I address the question of whether the private or the public sector would be able to achieve monopoly on this scale.

22 This is his "Economic calculation in the socialist commonwealth," reprinted in Hayek 1975c: 87–130.

23 Lavoie (1985a, especially chs 3 and 6) does provide such an historical context for the argument.

24 Though not the entire scope, since, as I will explain below, to the extent that the central authority is constant, it will have an incentive to act entrepreneurially.

25 See for example Taylor (1964) and Dickenson (1933). Lavoie (1985a, especially chs 4 and 5) provides a thorough critique of these proposals from an Austrian perspective.

26 A similar case arises with respect to Olson's concept of an "encompassing organization." See Olson (1982), and especially Olson (1992), in which he argues that the encompassing interests of a dictator could explain some of the limited economic success of the former Soviet Union.

27 Moreover, the nature of information as a commodity presents an obstacle to trading. With most commodities, it is possible for buyers and sellers to trade, in part, because learning about the commodity in question, a car for example, is not the *same thing* as consuming it (even in the case of so-called experience goods). It is otherwise with information, however. The demand for a unit of information, of course, depends on the evaluation of potential buyers. Yet buyers will not know how to evaluate this information unless they already know something about it, which would, however, "pull the rug out" from under the demand for the information. That is, buyers will not buy unless they know what they are paying for, but, in the case of information, if they already know it, they have no need to buy it.

Another constraint on the ability of entrepreneurs under collectivism to sell information to a monopsonist-dictator is that much of the "knowledge of time and place" relevant to the achievement of plan coordination is tacit or non-articulable, and thus largely non-transferable (at least in the manner advocates of collectivist planning usually have in mind). On this see Polanyi (1962) and Lavoie (1985b, especially pp. 247–65).

28 See Mueller (1989: 384–99) for a definition of these terms (à la Vickrey) as well as a thorough discussion of the theorem and its postulates.

29 Indeed, this is the central message of *The Road to Serfdom*. Although Hayek made a few remarks regarding the perils of interventionism in this early book, he addresses the actual dynamics of interventionism only tangentially. His later writings, which focus on the concept of the knowledge problem, are more relevant to the concerns of the present study.

30 Note that unlike the narrow aspect of this definition, which is intended to enrich later discussion of related topics, the broad aspect is a consequence of the distinction between bureaucratic and profit management, which we will examine later in the present chapter. See Mises (1969).

31 The emphasis here is on the organizational structure of the public sector. If my concern were with the nature of governmental relations, then the defining feature would of course be the use of political means.

32 Another difference that results more from the *ad hoc* nature of the governmental response to diverse interests, which is relevant to the present study although not to the particular point being made here, is reflected in Robert Hughes's observation that "the mass of controls that had come to exist by the end of World War II had no overall logic, but each separate control had its own reasons" (Hughes 1991: 184). In general he blames this "congeries" of federal controls, which has no direct parallel in the catallaxy, on "the belief in the efficacy of piecemeal supervision, the origin of separateness of each agency of control from the others" and on the tendency for government controls to live far beyond their original mandate (ibid.: 226).

33 Hayek (1973: 36) defines an order as "a state of affairs in which a multiplicity of elements of various kinds are so related to each other that we may learn from our acquaintance with some spatial or temporal part of the whole to form correct expectations concerning the rest, or at least expectations which have a good chance of proving correct."

34 This is based on a perusal of the 1991–3 edition of *The World Almanac of US Politics*. See Wagman (1991).

35 Once again, this appears to be closely related to Wolf's (1990) concept of derived externalities.

36 In this connection Hughes has observed that "the [United States] federal control structure is a halfway house, without the virtues of either economic planning or free-market economy" (Hughes 1991: 19).

37 See Max Weber's authoritative statement of this proposition in Gerth and Mills (1958, especially, pp. 209–11).

38 Once again, in order to remain as close as possible to the assumption

of benevolence in government, I will not discuss explanations of this deviation between intentions and actual outcomes that are not based on the Hayekian knowledge problem, such as that of Niskanen (1971) or Terry Moe (1989).

39 In Chapter 5, however, I focus on a different aspect of the relation between a nationalized industry, *qua* legal monopoly, and the knowledge problem.

40 Bribery is a (frequently monetary) payment and as such does represent an explicit price for services rendered. To the extent that bribery is an important part of the governmental process, then, a kind of crude price mechanism is at work. Empirically, however, payments for political services are more commonly made in kind (as occurs, for example, in vote-trading or mutual favors granted between public agents) or in indirect or earmarked money payments (as in the case of campaign contributions). This state of affairs in the "political market" is similar to that of a barter economy in a market context, the inefficiency of which, compared to a money economy, is well known. See, for example, the early but excellent discussion of the evolution and role of money in economic development in Menger (1981, ch. 8).

41 Indeed, Rizzo (1980) argues, for similar reasons, that with respect to the law a more "static" conception may be preferable to one that is "dynamic."

42 It is perhaps appropriate to mention at this point an alternative Austrian concept of political entrepreneurship to the one offered here, which claims that "the essence of political entrepreneurship is to *destroy* wealth through negative-sum-rent-seeking behavior" (DiLorenzo 1988:66; emphasis original). Since that concept relates to the interface between the political and the catallactic, while mine concerns activity strictly within the political, I see no necessary conflict between the two.

43 Note that there is no presumption that the state is minimal or maximal, limited or unlimited.

44 For Olson, however, it is not necessary for an encompassing organization to be benevolent in order to serve the interests of society. That is, the more encompassing the organization becomes, the more its interests will naturally coincide with those of society.

45 While I am for the moment assuming public-spiritedness or benevolence on the part of public choosers, this is not the same thing as the deliberate sacrificing of one's own interest to those of others. Benevolence, as understood in the present context, simply refers to the purposeful action of helping and not harming others. This is why I have been careful in the text to distinguish between this broader concept of self-interest and *narrow* or *political* self-interest. Thus, the desire to become (re)elected is consistent with the desire to serve the general public interest.

46 Even in a world of benevolent public choosers, of course, differing views of what is in fact in the public interest might exist. Hence, the passage of this measure could meet with some public-spirited opposition (e.g., perhaps by non-smokers who believe citizens should retain

the right to smoke where and whenever they desire, or by citizens who believe that smoking is in fact healthful).

47 When consumers spend their incomes in the market, they are not *directly* expressing their valuations of the inputs or "higher-order goods" that go into the production of the consumption or "lower-order goods" they purchase (Hayek 1948:90). Neither are they *necessarily* demonstrating a preference for the supplier from whom they buy specific items of consumption (i.e., if I buy brand X produced in plant A, I am not necessarily expressing a direct preference for plant A). Yet this is precisely what is supposed to happen in the political process. With respect to elected offices, the voting mechanism, in accordance with a particular set of voting rules, helps to elect officials (higher-order goods) whom citizens then hope will provide services (lower-order goods) for which the possibilities of effectively expressing approval or disapproval are quite limited. Admittedly, there is some similarity between politicians (who may be characterized as "experience goods" composed of uncertain bundled services) and private agents such as building contractors, stock brokers, and durable goods in general. But the possibility of (horizontally or vertically) disintegrating market services into separate and competing units, and the impracticability of doing this with respect to relations based on political power (Mises 1969: 6) suggests another important difference in the way the voting mechanism and the price system operate.

48 The normative theory of rent-seeking is concerned, in good neoclassical fashion, with the value of the *resources* expended to capture rents that are (typically) politically generated, rather than with pecuniary transfers. The discussion in the text is not meant to dispute the correctness of this approach, but only to point out that the existence of a cash price for governmental services may have implications for plan coordination in the public sector. To the extent that public choosers pay for political favors in kind, the situation once again approaches that of a cumbersome barter economy.

49 Terry Moe observes, however, that political incentives can induce bureaucrats to build unnecessary complexity and labyrinthine procedures into the administrative structure of bureaucracy. From an interest-group perspective,

> democratic government gives rise to two major forces that cause the structure of public bureaucracy to depart from technical rationality. First, those currently in a position to exercise public authority will often face uncertainty about their own grip on political power in the years ahead, and this will prompt them to favor structures that insulate their achievements from politics. Second, opponents will also tend to have a say in structural design, and, to the degree they do, they will impose structures that subvert effective performance and politicize agency decisions.
>
> (Moe 1989: 277)

The upshot of these phenomena is that within the governmental process there may actually be gains from promoting plan discoordination.

261

50 Indeed, the situation is even graver than this, since, as previously noted, private property in the governmental process is extremely limited.

51 Moreover, as we have seen, within the bureaucracy the existence of a meaningful criterion of efficiency is problematic, especially as government takes over more and more functions within the economy.

4 TOWARD A THEORY OF INTERVENTIONISM I: THE FRAMEWORK

1 DeBow (1991) reaches the same conclusion by a similar argument in his insightful analysis of interventionism.

2 See Appendix B.

3 As I explain below, although suppliers of substitutes in both factor and output markets will tend to benefit, their gains are "superfluous" from the viewpoint of the unhampered market process.

4 The same phenomenon can operate in reverse; that is, an unanticipated change in the private sector can result in spontaneous responses in the public sector that then have further repercussions in the private sector, and so on. This does not mean, however, that market activity initiates the interventionist process.

5 This example is adapted from one used in Kirzner (1979: 230–4).

6 This does not rule out the possibility that someone might eventually notice a profit opportunity in changing or removing the speed limit.

7 See Chapter 5 for a discussion of the relative potency of different kinds of regulation for disrupting and hampering the market process.

8 In the first scenario, you would commit the same kind of error if you decided to sell it for $5,000 thinking (pessimistically) that no one would pay a higher price, and then got a better offer. Thus, I disagree with Rizzo (1990: 21) when he attributes what I will call a class-two error to overpessimism.

9 It is an error because were you to learn of it, you would feel genuine disappointment. You would regret your decision because the possibility of avoiding the error was simply a matter of alertness and not high transactions costs of some kind.

10 These correspond for the most part with what Kirzner (1963) calls "type-one" and "type-two" errors. I avoid these terms because they are used in statistical inference to refer to concepts whose meanings are close enough to those presented here to cause confusion.

11 If, say, both buyers and sellers expected the price of gasoline under present-day conditions to range between $1,000 and $2,000 per gallon, eliminating pockets of ignorance might be harder than if their expectations agreed more closely with actual scarcities.

12 Recall that this is consonant with Charles Wolf's analysis of "derived externalities" in the non-market sector. According to Wolf,

> Government intervention to correct market failure may generate unanticipated side effects, often in areas remote from that in which the public policy was intended to operate. Indeed, there is a high likelihood of such derived externalities, because government tends

to operate through large organizations using blunt instruments
whose consequences are both far-reaching and difficult to forecast.

(Wolf 1990: 77)

Similarly, Jonathan Hughes has argued that in American public policy,

the problem is that each control policy is targeted to a specific
problem, without regard for its macroeconomic spillover effects ...
The Federal Reserve System fights inflation ... while tariff policies,
federal spending, agricultural subsidies, and labor and management
policies sanctioned by federal agencies are all designed to *raise*
prices.

(Hughes 1991:14–15; emphasis original)

13 Also, in his account of the growth of government in the United States
during the twentieth century, Robert Higgs observes:

Because of the complexities of tax liability, incidence, and
shifting ... modern taxation is likely also to produce unintended
consequences such as a diversion of resources toward greater use
of accountants, lawyers, and investment advisers – diversions that
sap the economy's potential to produce goods valued by consumers

(Higgs 1987:29).

14 Littlechild (1979) explains why it is difficult to measure deadweight
loss in a market outside of equilibrium.

15 I attempt to clarify the meaning of this phrase on pages 110–12.

16 This discussion raises the related point that, from the viewpoint of
Austrian political economy, even if property rights are completely
specified and transactions costs are zero, externalities might still exist
for the same reason that unexploited profit opportunities can exist even
when information costs are zero.

17 Thus Kirzner (1985: 145) states: "Unless, quite fantastically, the regulatory authorities (somehow all acting in completely coordinated
fashion) are perfectly informed on all relevant data about the market,
they will *not* generally be able to perceive what new profit opportunities they create by their own regulatory actions."

18 To anticipate possible confusion, recall that radical ignorance
encompasses both class-one and class-two errors. Think of it as a
generic term for the source of both classes of errors. The discovery
effect (i.e., stifled or superfluous discovery) will then manifest itself
through either class-one or class-two errors, depending on the circumstances.

19 See Chapter 7.

20 Notice that I am not arguing that intervention can never produce
outcomes that might be a net benefit to society, but rather that there
are very strong reasons to doubt that this could consistently be the
case, and that systematic error is much more likely. See also the discussion of the meaning of "frustrated intentions," on pages 110–12.

21 Clearly, rent-seeking agents would be even less likely to do so, unless
their interests are "encompassing" (Olson 1982: 53).

22 Mark Thornton (1991) has written a detailed and up-to-date theoretical treatment of prohibition from an Austrian perspective, which analyzes the dynamic responses of the market participants to government controls along many of the same lines followed in this book.

23 Wolf provides several others, including "recent efforts to impose 'voluntary' quotas on South Korean and Brazilian steel exports into the United States" without regard "to the effect that such restrictions would have on South Korean and Brazilian ability to service the enormous debts they owe to American commercial banks" (1990: 107–8). Wolf's point here, it should be noted, is that these are consequences analysts should be better able to foresee.

24 See for example Williams (1978).

25 William Tucker, however, argues that the economic rationale for imposing rent controls in New York City during World War II was actually less than compelling. He points out that in the face of relatively high vacancy rates and moderate rent increases New York was the last major city to implement rent controls. See Tucker (1990: 253–67).

26 Recent empirical studies by Katz and Krueger (1992) and Card and Krueger (1994) have cast some doubt on this rather well-accepted conclusion. See, however, the studies by Zycher (1995), Neumark and Wascher (1995), and Deere et al. (1995), which detect flaws in the empirical methods used by Card/Krueger/Katz sufficient to overturn most of their results.

27 About the effectiveness of the Environmental Protection Agency during the 1970s, however, Wilson (1989: 288) argues that "to the states, the federal government had displayed a head-in-the-clouds ignorance of the complexity and variety of local pollution problems," which tended to weaken the enforcement of anti-pollution laws.

28 Among these the socially and politically influential are disproportionately represented. According to Tucker (1990: 273), "For more than a generation, most of the political, social, and cultural leaders have been permanent beneficiaries of rent control." He also cites the findings of a 1988 study by the Arthur D. Little Corporation that "71 percent of the apartments in affluent neighborhoods were regulated, while only 47 percent were regulated in lower-income neighborhoods" (p. 274). This fact is consistent with many versions of public-choice analysis.

29 William Tucker (1990: 34–67) conducts a statistical analyses of these other factors.

30 I would like to thank David Harper for bringing this to my attention. This aspect is particularly relevant in regard to the ideological trade-off between freedom and security discussed in Chapter 5.

31 Although the narrow self-interests of public choosers may lead them to resist radical reform, I will continue to abstract from this important aspect of the actual interventionist process until later in the chapter.

32 Likewise, a predisposition against intervention may result in state contraction when the evidence of "government failure" manifests itself to a sufficient number of public choosers who are entrepreneurially

alert enough to realize the net benefits of jettisoning the offending intervention, or who are unwilling to oppose such a move. (Granted, there are positive externalities associated with such a change, but there are also entrepreneurial profits associated with their internalization.) As I explain in the next part of this chapter, the contractionary phase of the interventionist process is likely to be accompanied by negative unintended consequences of its own, owing to "bottlenecks" and other obstacles to the market process that newly emerge during this phase. If the ideological change toward less intervention is strong enough, the governmental response is likely to be further decontrol to remove these bottlenecks.

33 Douglass North (1990) also employs relative price changes to describe a different form of dynamic change, in particular the response to relative-price changes that produce cumulative evolutionary changes in social institutions. For a critique of North's analytical framework, see Steel (1995).

34 Only when this chapter was in its penultimate form did a very recent article by Assar Lindbeck with the intriguing title "Hazardous welfare-state reform" come to my attention. Apart from the very similar subject-matter, significant portions of Lindbeck's analysis of welfare-state dynamics exhibit striking parallels to the present study. I refer to this short article again elsewhere in the present study, but I believe it is worth quoting one particularly relevant passage here at length:

> More specifically, it is reasonable to assume that the individual experiences disutility when breaking existing habits and violating social norms – because of a loss of reputation... *and* because of a subjectively *felt resistance* to violating habits and norms that he or she believes should be obeyed. It is also likely that a single individual is more inclined to conform to traditional habits and social norms the greater the *number of individuals* in society who do so – an example of the importance for individual behavior of a "critical mass" of people with similar behavior patterns.
>
> (Lindbeck 1995: 10; emphasis original and added)

35 Once again, compare with Lindbeck (1995: 10), who says that adjustments in the observation of existing habits and norms "may be modeled either as changes in the frequency of the adherence to formerly existing habits and norms or as changes in the prevailing habits and norms themselves, or a combination of both."

36 I have already referred to Robert Higgs's *Crisis and Leviathan* (1987), in the context of endogenous theories of ideological change. Higgs's central argument is that crises, economic and political, have accelerated the growth of government in the United States, especially during the twentieth century. While there is much in common between his thesis and mine, and we are both attempting to address much the same phenomenon, I do not believe Higgs attempts to explain the underlying causes of these crises, nor does he address the underlying causes of state expansion (or contraction), in general. Nevertheless, his book

has been an important source of insight as well as historical examples for the present study.

37 In Chapter 6 I raise the question of whether any combination of government and catallaxy will produce instability. I should point out for clarification that, unless otherwise stated, the term "instability" refers to the unstable nature of the interventionist process and not to the nature of state expansion between periods of sudden and dramatic changes in the rate of that expansion. That is because this study identifies as a prime cause of government growth of all kinds the inherent instability of the mixed economy itself.

38 This accords with Claus Offe's definition of "crises" as "processes in which the structure of a system is called into question" (Offe 1984: 36).

39 In his recent biography of Maynard Keynes's early career, for example, Robert Skidelsky observed the following with respect to Britain in the early 1930s:

> [Historians] argue that the kind of fiscal deficits and adverse trade flows needed to make any substantial impact on employment figures would rapidly have brought on a major financial and political crisis requiring either the reversal of the policy or the move to a completely state-controlled economy like in Nazi Germany.
>
> (Skidelsky 1992: 475)

40 Thus, Higgs (1987: 78) argues: "crisis alone need not spawn Bigger Government. It does so only under favorable ideological conditions."

41 Traditional neoclassical economic theory views agents as finding the constrained optimal solution when the ends and means they face are fully known. Herbert A. Simon provides one alternative to this approach, his "bounded rationality." According to Simon (1987: 266), "the term 'bounded rationality' is used to designate rational choice that takes into account the cognitive limitations of the decision-maker – limitations of both knowledge and computational capacity." (See also Simon 1972.)

42 Note that, while micro-crises within the mixed economy are recurrent, system-wide failures or macro-crises, which are the topic now under investigation, are relatively few in a given regime. The collapse of Czarist Russia, of Weimar Germany, of the Labour Government in Great Britain, and, most recently of all, of the various communist states, are examples of macro-crises of this sort.

43 Compare Offe (1984: 52–3): "The economic system depends on continuous state intervention for the elimination of its internal malfunctions; for its part, the economic system transfers – by means of taxation – portions of the value produced in it to the political-administrative system."

44 As one Soviet analyst has recently remarked, "the Soviet economy was not a centrally planned economy radically different from any other economic system witnessed in history. It was over-regulated, abused and distorted, but it was, nevertheless, a market economy" (Boettke 1993: 69). See also Prychitko (1990).

45 See the revealing discussion of the real Soviet economy in Boettke (1993, especially pp. 65–9).

46 Hughes, for one, is less than optimistic: "The private sector has no way to free itself from the tentacles of nonmarket control except by a major reform movement at the national level, hardly a promising prospect" (1991: 226).

47 Barr (1992), in his survey article on the welfare state makes the interesting point that government failure *per se* does not justify the faith in catallactic forces to perform better and more cheaply than collectivism – a sort of Demsetz's "Nirvana fallacy" in reverse. What is intriguing is that just as the Nirvana fallacy tends to help promote the growth of government, the reverse Nirvana fallacy should tend to accelerate market reforms in former collectivist countries.

48 I am indebted to Peter Boettke for this point.

49 Again, this does not imply that perfect competition prevails under laissez-faire capitalism. See the discussion of the market process in Chapter 3.

50 For a more thorough explication of the Mises–Hayek theory in its traditional form, see Mises (1971) and (1966: 538–86); and Hayek (1975a, 1967b, 1975c, and 1984).

51 In Chapter 5, I compare and contrast the dynamics of these and other forms of intervention.

52 Some economists, however, appear to be more certain. According to Assar Lindbeck, for example: "Next to bombing, rent control seems to be the most efficient technique so far known for destroying cities" (Quoted in Tucker 1990: 265).

53 A good source of material on these issues is Goodman and Musgrave (1992).

54 Wilson (1993) has an enlightening discussion on the importance of families in instilling a sense of morality in children. (See especially pp. 141–63; see also Murray 1988: 287–90.)

55 Moreover, recall from Chapter 2 that a state that has the power to intervene at will in the catallaxy but merely refrains from doing so of its own accord would be a mixed economy in appearance; without effective constraints on that power, it would actually be latently collectivistic.

56 Murphy *et al.* (1992) in a recent article on the dynamics of partial reform appear also to support this view: "When some, but not all, resources are allowed to move into the private sector, and state prices remain distorted, the result may be ... bottlenecks and shortages in the state sector" (pp. 905–6).

57 The following item appeared in the *Wall Street Journal* on 19 January 1988, a decade after Deng Xiaoping's reforms and over a year before the Tienanmen Square incident: "Because of government price controls on grain, celery earns Mr. Ju about twice what he would get from planting wheat. It is this disparity that is helping to produce China's grain shortage." The article goes on: " 'Prices are the most sensitive issue in China,' says a middle-aged Beijing office worker. 'If the government starts raising prices more, there could even be riots'."

58 See Chapter 3 for a definition of Hayekian order.

59 McCormick *et al.* (1984) provide another rationale for this inertia. They argue that if rent-seeking transforms all or most of the monopoly profits from intervention into rents, the social gains from dis-intervention will be relatively meager, which would contribute to a "disinterest" in reform even on the part of public-spirited officials.

60 Here I believe there is much common ground on which to build in Tullock's (1965) pioneering study.

5 TOWARD A THEORY OF INTERVENTIONISM II: ROADS TO COLLECTIVISM

1 In most cases, this blend will characterize the road to collectivism. The one exception is the abrupt, revolutionary transformation of capitalism into collectivism (or vice versa).

The classic method for achieving this radical shift is the sudden and swift nationalization of privately held market resources. Instances of radical politico-economic change that have transformed a minimal state directly into a maximal state are rare. More commonly, the "distances" that revolutions take societies are much shorter, and the "initial conditions" from which revolutions begin contain numerous interventions.

In any case, because the transformation involved is so rapid and the scale of intervention so vast, revolution stands largely outside the present analysis. There is, however, an important analytical link between similar radical change that one might broadly construe as revolutionary, and the interventionist process. Specifically, one can regard the outcome of a politico-economic crisis as a kind of revolutionary transformation.

2 While I am not suggesting that redistribution and regulation exhaust all possible forms of government intervention, they may include much more than might at first appear to be the case. That is, one might initially view these two categories as encompassing interventions of only the binary and tertiary type, to use Rothbard's taxonomy (see Appendix C), but largely excluding interventions of the autistic type. Yet if an autistic restriction on, say, eating red meat merely amounts in practice to reducing the utility of those on whom the state imposes the restriction as it raises the utility of those who favor it (which one could loosely regard as a kind of "transfer"), then these categories might well be exhaustive.

3 See Hayek (1948:33–56), who employs the terminology of "objective" and "subjective" facts in his pathbreaking essay on knowledge acquisition in economic theory.

4 I use the more general term "intervention" rather than regulation here because the political response to the situation does not perforce take any particular form of intervention.

5 One might reasonably object that this first approach is a straw man, since less narrowly neoclassical positions might well lead to a different conclusion from the one I am about to draw, below. Yet the claim

that there are a wealth of neoclassical theories of the market that incorporate the possibility of ignorance and persistent non-equilibrium should not be taken at face value. For a critique of several such "dynamic" theories from an Austrian market-process perspective, see Ikeda (1990; 1992).

6 For more on this point, see the discussion on insecurity under transfer dynamics in the next part of the present chapter.

7 See the discussion of the "dynamic trade-off thesis," below, for further details.

8 One might envision the basis of the following ranking as a three-tiered pyramid, in which the lowest tier represents regulations that have the most widespread and disruptive influences on the catallaxy. From the lowest (primary) to highest (tertiary) tier, then, would be monetary manipulation (primary), macroeconomic price controls and widespread nationalization (secondary), and microeconomic price, quantity, and quality regulations (tertiary).

9 Recall from Chapter 2 that it is consistent in particular with the rationales for state intervention presented in Barr's (1992) survey article. This does not mean, of course, that Barr or others in the field would necessarily agree with my definitions of welfare- and regulatory-state capitalism.

10 Needless to say, confiscating wealth rather than income also serves to discourage labor-force participation if wealth represents accumulated labor income. Conversely, I am also assuming that changes in income correlate positively with changes in wealth.

11 Similarly, the standard microeconomic treatment of the social cost of an increase in theft concentrates on the deadweight losses that accrue from it (e.g., more and stronger locks on doors), rather than on its impact on the propensity to steal in the future, the long-term social consequences of which may be much more serious.

12 The following draws on Wagner (1989). Given my earlier criticisms of this work, my acknowledgement perhaps calls for some explanation.

Wagner faults standard approaches to the study of the impact of policy on the market process for typically assuming that the pre-policy environment is free of intervention, when in reality when a new program is introduced into the mixed economy it becomes "part of a package of programs" (Wagner 1989: 106) with which the new program interacts in complex ways (ibid.: 77). Therefore, a proper analysis of the impact of a particular welfare program on the market process should not ignore the reinforcing and offsetting effects of other programs that coexist within the mixed economy, including the redistributive forces of regulations that could dramatically alter the conclusions of that analysis. In this sense, I am largely in agreement with his approach to public-policy analysis.

Although this is useful for some purposes, it does not justify subsuming the regulatory state into the welfare state for all purposes – in particular, for the purpose of analyzing the knowledge-based dynamics of the interventionist state. My complaint, then, is not simply that Wagner treats them as equivalent, but that his approach, which as I have argued earlier is fairly typical of public choice, has tended to turn attention away from the kinds of questions that I am addressing here. Nevertheless, his treatment of the unintended incentive effects of redistributive policies is both insightful and highly relevant for our purposes.

13 The former depends on the average tax rate and the latter on the marginal tax rate, under a given set of preferences (including ideological ones).

14 For the analysis of the proportional-tax case, see Wagner (1989: 81–2).

15 A flat, proportional tax will avoid this perverse outcome only if the income differential is stated in percentage terms. If, however, workers prefer an income differential in terms of an absolute monetary amount, say $5,000, the perverse outcome remains, although it will be less severe than a progressive income tax would be in this situation. An absolute-income premium arguably makes more sense intuitively than a proportional one. For an analysis of the absolute case, see Wagner (ibid.).

16 Those who are forced to pay for subsidies need not be better off financially than those who are in many cases "forced" to receive them. It is well known that the beneficiaries of redistributive programs can have on average the same or higher real incomes than their benefactors (Goodin and LeGrand 1987). This perverse outcome is consistent with the assumption of benevolence on the part of the state. Nevertheless, I will assume H-income earners are taxed to subsidize L-income earners.

17 This issue is not precisely the same as, but it is related to, the one addressed in the debate surrounding the so-called "culture of poverty." To some extent, however, the latter is related to the discussion of how transfers affect what Glazer calls the "fine structure of society," which we will examine later in the analysis of ideological change.

18 This might be a good place to mention Roy Cordato's interesting suggestion that income taxes, by penalizing saving, shortens the time horizon of investors and thereby distorts the structure of production, which is very much in line with traditional Austrian concerns, but which unfortunately I cannot pursue in the present study. See Cordato (1994) and the references contained therein.

19 I am not claiming that Glazer himself would agree with the inferences that I draw from (and the uses to which I put) his analysis of the fine structure, although his reasoning and conclusions, especially regarding the welfare state, largely parallel those of the present study.

20 Compare with Lindbeck: "a very active redistribution policy focuses the political debate on distributional issues, and people then may become more aware of existing inequalities" (1995: 12–13).

21 For an informative mutual commentary between Murray and Glazer see Murray (1990) and Glazer (1990).

22 This is the flip side of what Murray has termed the "destruction of status rewards." See Murray (1984: 178–91).

23 It is true that private charity can have similar deleterious effects. As I see it, however, there are at least three differences between private giving and public subsidies, all of which stem from the advantages of

decentralized organization and local information: First, perhaps because the nature of the relationship between giver and receiver is more personal, the psychological stigma associated with charity may be greater than with public welfare payments; second, private persons and groups tend to be more familiar with the local conditions and the circumstances of their clients, and tend also to be better motivated than public institutions; and third, errors are less likely to be discovered in the case of a public program, and are more likely to be orders of magnitude larger, than in a private program.

24 One could cite nearly any standard text in microeconomics. See, for example, Landsburg (1992: 483–99).

25 Once again, compare with Lindbeck: "tolerance of income inequality may very well fall when it becomes apparent that the distribution of income is to a large extent determined by 'arbitrary' political decisions rather than by market forces that reward productive contributions" (1995: 13).

26 If these persons share certain recognizable characteristics in common that would make the group within which they operate easily identifiable – e.g., the poor, the low-skilled, agricultural workers, infant industries, mature industries, manufacturing labor – this might reduce some of the per capita costs to them of using the political process to gain protection for their group (Olson 1982: 17–35). The formation of such groups, however, is not essential for the process in question.

27 The extraordinarily alert reader will recognize this from Chapter 4 as the second aspect of the weak version of unintended consequences.

28 This is not to argue that these are the only or even the primary constituents of the fine structure.

29 Static deadweight losses, however, may somewhat offset even this benefit.

30 For a more developed discussion of so-called "big-player" effects, though along somewhat different lines, see Koppl and Yeager (1992).

31 There are of course what might be called diseconomies of large scale in government, to which the socialist-calculation debate first drew our attention and the discussion of the governmental process in Chapter 3 was meant to be an extension. The next sentence in the text, however, addresses this concern.

32 To take but one example, imposing penalties and sanctions on businesses in order to end alleged discrimination against women is an attempt to achieve a more just outcome by altering constraints on behavior.

33 Charles Wolf's observation that "distributional issues are usually more influential than efficiency ones in shaping judgments about the success or shortcomings of market outcomes" (Wolf 1990: 19) appears to lend some support to this position.

34 One might cite as a prominent counter-example to this statement the so-called "Progressive Era" in the United States, which covers roughly the first third of the twentieth century. In this period, "the rise of big business, large-scale technological change, and a shift of emphasis in production and distribution from capital goods to consumer goods"

(Keller 1990: 2), led to a correspondingly dramatic rise in the expansion of business regulation that some scholars argue was the result of deliberate, perhaps conservative, ideological forces of one kind or another. Gabriel Kolko (1963) is representative of this view.

My position receives some support from the Harvard historian, Morton Keller, who argues that rather than reflecting any particular ideological agenda the Progressive Era is best portrayed as the expression of two themes: *persistence*, with respect to "preexisting [nineteenth-century] values, interests, procedural and structural arrangements"; and *pluralism*, encompassing "an expanding, roiling aggregate of interests, issues, institutions, ideas" (Keller 1990: 3). Given the environment that Keller describes, unlike that of the 1930s and 1960s when American public policy underwent dramatic redirection, it appears doubtful that an overarching vision was the prime mover of public policy during this time. (Jonathan Hughes (1991: 137), however, appears to cast doubt on whether even New Deal legislation marked a radical departure from traditional American political values.)

35 Some of the essays in Goodin and LeGrand (1987) appear to lend empirical support to this postulate. Obviously, however, preferences can differ radically among consumers in the same income and wealth class.

6 THE INSTABILITY OF THE MINIMAL STATE

1 Stability in standard economics usually refers to the idea of "convergence to a neighborhood of equilibrium" (Fisher 1983: 2). Stability in this study relates, as we have seen, more to the capacity of the relations between government and catallaxy within a particular politico-economic system to remain relatively unaffected by endogenous change.

2 Discussions of optimal public-goods provision frequently entail an auctioneer who facilitates either the calculation of the optimal tax-price given a quantity of a public good, or vice versa. In other models, the optimal quantity and tax-price of a public good are both determined endogenously. See, for example, Mueller (1989: 49–50). The first approach is inappropriate here because auctioneer-driven processes sidestep the problems of ignorance and dispersed information (Lavoie 1985a:120–4), while the second approach does not apply to a minimal state in which the quantity and quality of pure public goods are a given.

3 Mueller (1989: 9–39) presents the public-goods rationale for the existence of the state. (For a persuasive case that this rationale contains a self-defeating paradox, see Kalt (1981). More generally, see the essays contained in Cowen (1992).) Of course, public goods and publicly provided goods (i.e., goods that the state provides) bear no necessary relation to each other. Thus, in the United States private firms produce television broadcasts (a pure public good) and the US Postal Service is granted a legal monopoly on first-class mail delivery (a private good).

4 This might be approximated in standard choice-theoretic terms by upward-sloping and convex indifference curves that begin some (relatively short) distance to the right of the origin, with public and private provision of goods measured along the horizontal and vertical axes, respectively.

5 Other highly relevant factors that I do not examine here, however, are the kind of intervention sought, the intensity with which it is pursued, and the frequency with which a given actor employs political means.

6 I assume that citizens regard those governmental errors that favor and those that harm them with equal significance. An important asymmetry emerges, however, in the different *responses* that they make to these two types of errors. See below.

7 Considerations similar to those mentioned in note 5, would also apply here. That is, a more complete analysis might also look at, for example, the frequency with which the actual tax for good j deviates from the optimal for citizen i. Thus, although nothing essential would be added in doing so, it might make it possible to discuss the decision facing a particular citizen in terms of the "expected value" and "variance" of the error.

8 Later, I consider the possibility that errors in tax-pricing might themselves result in a shift in ideological preferences.

9 Given the convexity and upward slope of the "indifference curves" hypothesized in note 4, increases in the consumption of publicly provided goods will *increase* rather than decrease the MRS of a citizen with the preferences of the majority.

10 This is a genuine suboptimality, since what prevents the state from responding optimally is not a cost of any kind but sheer ignorance.

11 Suboptimal tax-pricing essentially represents a transfer of wealth from those paying too much to those paying too little. While citizen responses to this transfer will create deadweight losses, recall that the latter are not the focus of the present analysis. Rather it is that these responses will encourage further intervention, which in the presence of knowledge-type problems and bounded rationality, will create additional difficulties.

12 One partial solution might be for the state to provide additional services (if this is feasible) to those who complain about higher-than-optimal tax-prices and finance these services by raising taxes on the remaining non-complainers. Unfortunately, even if this resulted in a balanced budget it would clearly encourage false complaints.

13 The corollary to this would seem to be that in some sense the minimal state, because of the very nature of the goods it provides, is somehow less efficient than a state that has taken over a larger portion of the functions that the private sector could perform. This is discussed in the next section of the chapter.

14 It also means, of course, that some of those citizens who were paying too little could have their marginal preferences lowered just enough to bring them back into equilibrium with respect to their original tax-prices. There appears to be, however, no reason to expect this to happen systematically.

15 This weakening moral aversion is not confined to the destabilization of the minimal state, since we saw in Chapter 4 that the same ideological forces operate in the dynamics of the ensuing interventionist process.

16 That is, to employ the analogy of indifference curves once again, not only will a change in the cost of consuming additional public services cause a movement along a given set of indifference curves, a particularly large error – e.g., an especially egregious act of injustice – may actually alter the shape of the indifference map.

17 As mentioned at some point in each of the chapters 3 through 5, while *many sellers* of information may have an incentive to uncover error and sell this information to the state monopoly, it is still the case that, unlike the competitive market-process, there is ultimately only *one buyer* who has an incentive to buy it.

18 The administration of the minimal state, of course, need not be bureaucratic. First, however, some functions are likely to be bureaucratic for reasons of transactions cost. Second, "privatized" functions (such as a private army, post office, or court system) would probably still be subject to a high degree of regulation to meet non-economic goals (e.g., fairness and equity). The administrations within the firms performing these functions would be constrained to behave bureaucratically.

19 Some have attempted to measure the efficiency of bureaucratic performance on the basis of questionnaires that purport to reveal levels of satisfaction. See for example Goodsell (1985). Of course, even if citizens report being "satisfied" with bureaucratic service, the bureaucracy in question may still be doing its job either too poorly or too well.

20 If it turns out, contrary to my argument here, that "in practice" the functions of the minimal state do not entail a coping organization, then of course the propensity of the minimal state to become unstable is lessened. However, the destabilizing tendencies that emanate from the monopolistic character of state provision and from the irrelevance of efficiency within bureaucracy would be largely independent of this finding.

21 In Chapter 1, I referred to Dwight Lee's analysis of the impossibility of a desirable minimal state as an example of a class of models that purport to analyze the optimal size of the state. This analysis, I believe, broadly supports the conclusion of the present chapter in a manner that also invokes endogenous forces. Specifically, Lee (1989) argues that the "lack of public (as opposed to special interest) control over government that makes the minimal state desirable also renders it impossible to achieve" (p. 279). However, should the public manage to gain the level of control necessary to achieve a minimal state, this would make the minimal state less desirable from the viewpoint of optimality than a more expansive one. Thus, he maintains: "Even if somehow we started with a minimal state, it would yield soon to special interest pressure to expand beyond minimal state limits" (ibid.). The potential for such an expansion, in the context of the present

analysis, represents yet another endogenous force that could destabilize the minimal state.

Subjectivist objections, such as those of E. C. Pasour (1991), to Lee's use of comparable utilities to reach his normative evaluations, while well taken, do not, I think, necessarily alter his positive conclusions.

22 In Cowan (1992), however, are arguments that tend to support the possibility of the private provision of pure public goods. Nozick (1974) argues that anarcho-capitalism would, in fact, be unstable, but does not compare this with the problem of instability in the minimal state.

23 This second point would seem to suggest that those who combine ideological elements – broadly conceived to include political philosophy, morality, religion, etc. – with consequentialist arguments for limited government stand to be not only more effective advocates for their position, but, at least from the perspective of the present analysis, possibly more consistent ones than we (or they) might have at first believed.

7 IMPLICATIONS AND PATTERN PREDICTION

1 Note that these implications are not the only ones that I have derived in the course of this book. Rather, I argue that they follow chiefly from the three propositions (presented in the next part of the chapter) *taken together*. For more specialized implications, see especially Chapters 4 and 5.

2 For example, about pure collectivism one could say that "vast economic control by the government leads to resource waste and a destruction of wealth," or that "socialism, as a limit, is not feasible because of the difficulties in economic calculation outside of the private property order and price system." For the original statement of these propositions, see Rizzo (1992).

3 These implications pertain chiefly to macro-level phenomena. Recall, however, that Chapter 4 presented what amounted to empirical implications regarding behavior at the level of markets and particular lines of activity, also. (For example, the concept of reserve-fund depletion had a micro-level counterpart.) But we are now engaged in an exploration of the implications derived from the three propositions set down at the beginning of this chapter. Our present goal, therefore, does not include an elaboration of those micro-level implications, which may warrant further investigation in another study.

4 To reiterate, I have borrowed this terminology from Claus Offe, whose critical examination of the contradictions of the welfare state from a post-Marxian perspective, as mentioned in Chapter 1, parallel to a surprising degree those of Austrian political economy. See, in particular, Offe (1984).

5 There is a parallel here with Thomas Kuhn's theory of scientific change or "paradigm shifts" (Kuhn 1970).

6 I am using the concept of pattern prediction of Hayek (1967a: 22–42). It can be defined as prediction regarding the behavior of an entire class of phenomena rather than a specific event or pattern within that class. This means that if a theory

> yields a determinate implication for a *class* of phenomena, each element of that class will be perfectly consistent with the explanatory schema. Thus, with respect to the specific event itself, the schema is not deterministic.
>
> (O'Driscoll and Rizzo 1985:27; emphasis original)

If, in a theoretical construct, we are unable to specify the values of the unknowns, the empirical content of a pattern prediction derived from that construct will reside chiefly in statements about what cannot happen. That is, predictions drawn from a construct that, owing to a lack of knowledge, permits a broad range of possible outcomes may be most conveniently expressed in terms of the outcomes that they rule out. For example, we should not expect a doubling in the supply of money and credit to result in a fall in the average price level in the long run.

7 Boettke (1993: 129–30) has recently argued that with respect to the former Soviet Union, shock therapy of this kind would have been the policy most likely to produce a successful transition to a more laissez-faire economy. The actual consequences of the faltering and half-hearted policies Soviet authorities did implement would seem to support Boettke's view.

8 If the public has had experience with such wavering in the past, credibility problems of the kind that Boettke (1993: 88–105) describes can arise, which would further jeopardize the success of radical reform.

9 See the appendix to ch. 2 in Higgs (1987: 263–71) for a list of federal agencies.

10 The discussion of ideological preferences in Chapters 4 and 5 related to conditions that could generate changes in ideology, and the direction in which those changes were likely to move under the conditions specified. There I referred to the content of ideological preference as if it were a measurable dimension. Here the discussion concerns the very different though related issue of the intensity of the commitment to a given ideology.

11 Indeed, in a recent study of the British experience (Cronin 1991), war is seen to play a crucial role in the ability of the state to expand in the face of what the author claims were vastly superior institutional forces. See also Higgs (1987: 123–58, 196–236).

12 In the next and final chapter of this book, I again discuss these omissions, which, in addition to those already mentioned, include the importance of judicial change to the interventionist process.

13 The closest at present (1996) are probably Hong Kong near one extreme and North Korea and Albania near the other. None, however, represent pure examples. One of the few that comes to mind in this regard is the United States (and the American Confederation) immediately after the American Revolution, although even in this case

the historical evidence provided by Jonathan Hughes may cast some doubt. He argues, for example, that "the New Deal's social legislation had precedents back to colonial times and beyond" (1991: 137). Yet, relatively speaking, the early days of the United States certainly were closer to laissez-faire than any nation today.

14 For example, Paul Johnson's assertion about Wilhelmine Germany that it was "in many ways the most militarized on earth" (Johnson 1991:108).

15 On this see Peukert (1989), although Peurkert's history of the Weimar era chronicles a much broader array of social and cultural problems and tensions than those treated in the present study.

16 On the heavy-handedness of Chinese communist rule in this period, see Leys (1978) and the personal account of Cheng (1988); and for a report on the lasting impact of the Cultural Revolution on Chinese attitudes after the death of Mao, see Butterfield (1982). For short and highly readable overview of the period, see Paul Johnson (1991: 544–74).

17 For a somewhat contrary view, see Hughes (1991), who argues that modern interventionism in the United States and Britian has an ancient pedigree. He states: "But in fact the powerful and *continuous* habit of nonmarket control in our economy reaches back for centuries" (p. 5; emphasis original). This is not the same as saying, of course, that these controls have at each point in history threatened the foundations of economic liberty as some have argued that they do today.

18 For an examination of the Great Depression era from the Austrian perspective, see Rothbard (1975) and Anderson (1979).

19 Goran Persson, Sweden's finance minister, has for example recently proposed "tax rises and spending cuts that will equal 7% of GDP by the time they take full effect in 1998. . . . Much of the reduction is to come from taking a scalpel to the welfare state" (Quoted in *The Economist*, 14 January 1995, p. 46.)

20 Alan Bollard's account of the circumstances that led New Zealand to undertake radical liberalization policies, under the leadership of David Lange beginning in 1983, also support many of the implications contained in the present chapter, including implication seven. On this see especially the section on "crisis as catalyst" in Bollard (1993).

8 WHITHER THE MIXED ECONOMY?

1 Hayek offers another reason for the correlation between modern times and totalitarian state control that emphasizes the extent to which individual actions have a social dimension when he writes that "Even during the periods of European history when the regimentation of economic life went furthest . . . it extended only to those activities of a person through which he took part in the social division of labor" (Hayek 1972: 99). In the modern era, in contrast, "almost every one of our activities is part of a social process" (ibid.: 100), and thus potentially subject to regimentation.

2 See, for example, Keller (1990) and Hughes (1991, especially pp. 92–135).

3 See, for example, Posner (1976) and Neale and Goyder (1982). For an analysis of the effect of antitrust enforcement on competition from a market-process perspective, see Armentano (1982) and Ikeda (1988).

4 See Ikeda (1988).

5 With respect to the remainder of progressive-era legislation, the evolution of the *Munn* and *Nebbia* doctrines in American judicial history might provide a good sense of what such an analysis could be. For this, I recommend Hughes's (1991: 98–117) discussion. It is highly pertinent to the theory of interventionism, not only because it presents the social and legal context of the doctrines set out in these landmark cases, but more importantly because Hughes carefully examines the tendencies latent in the *Munn* doctrine (as well as, he argues, the *milieu* of English jurisprudence since before the establishment of the American colonies) that led inexorably though unintentionally to *Nebbia* and beyond. Also germane is James Q. Wilson's (1989: 277–94) analysis of the unintended effects of judicial decisions with respect to the interpretation of bureaucratic decrees.

6 That Fukuyama has in mind the doctrine of classical or nineteenth-century liberalism is clear: "The state that emerges at the end of history is liberal insofar as it recognizes man's universal right to freedom, and democratic insofar as it exists only with the consent of the governed" (ibid.: 5).

7 Hughes offers a vision that is in some ways very similar to Fukuyama's, though without the Hegelian underpinnings: "A slowly growing, slowly inflating economy may be our foreseeable future, since neither a movement to a planned economy nor a return to significantly greater reliance on the price mechanism has been among the options produced by our leaders" (Hughes 1991:214).

8 Robert Skidelsky, biographer of Maynard Keynes, thus comments: "Capitalism may have vanquished socialism, but the debate between *laissez-faire* and Keynes's philosophy of the Middle Way is still fiercely joined" (Skidelsky 1992:229).

9 Schmidtz (1991), however, reviews some interesting non-coercive solutions to prisoners' dilemma and public-goods-type problems. See also Cowen (1992).

REFERENCES

Anderson, Benjamin M. (1979 [1949]) *Economics and the Public Welfare: A Financial and Economic History of the United States, 1914–1946.* Indianapolis: Liberty Press.

Anderson, Gary M. (1994) "The economic theory of regulation." In Peter J. Boettke, *The Elgar Companion to Austrian Economics.* Brookfield, VT: Edward Elgar.

Apple, R. W. jr. (1993) "Surprise! When you talk as President, people listen." *New York Times,* 17 January: A1, A3.

Armentano, Dominick T. (1982) *Antitrust and Monopoly: Anatomy of a Policy Failure.* New York: John Wiley & Sons.

Arrow, Kenneth J. (1951) *Social Choice and Individual Values.* New York: John Wiley & Sons.

Axelrod, Robert (1984) *The Evolution of Cooperation.* New York: Basic Books.

Barr, Nicholas (1992) "Economic theory and the welfare state: a survey and interpretation." *Journal of Economic Literature,* 30(2): 741–803.

Baumol, William J. (1967) *Welfare Economics and the Theory of the State.* Second edn. Cambridge, MA: Harvard University Press.

Becker, Gary (1983) "A theory of competition among pressure groups for political influence." *Quarterly Journal of Economics,* 98 (August): 371–400.

Bennett, James T. and Thomas J. DiLorenzo (1983) *Underground Government: The Off-Budget Public Sector.* Washington DC: Cato Institute.

Berkowitz, Edward D. (1991) *America's Welfare State: From Roosevelt to Reagan.* Baltimore: The Johns Hopkins University Press.

Birnbaum, Jeffrey H. and Alan S. Murray (1987) *Showdown at Gucci Gulch: Lawmakers, Lobbyists, and the Unlikely Triumph of Tax Reform.* New York: Vintage Books.

Boettke, Peter J. (1995) "Credibility, commitment, and Soviet economic reform." In Edward P. Lazear (ed.) *Economic Transition in Eastern Europe and Russia: Realities of Reform.* Stanford: Stanford University Press.

—— (ed.) (1994) *The Elgar Companion to Austrian Economics.* Brookfield, VT: Edward Elgar.

—— (1993) *Why Perestroika Failed: The Politics and Economics of Socialist Transformation.* New York: Routledge.

—— (1990) *The Political Economy of Soviet Socialism: The Formative Years, 1918–1928.* Boston: Kluwer.

Bollard, Alan (1993) *The Political Economy of Liberalisation in New Zealand.* Working Paper 93/2. Wellington, New Zealand: NZ Institute of Economic Research.

Brennan, Geoffrey (1986) "Public choice and the socialist calculation debate." Unpublished manuscript.

Buchanan, James M. (1986) *Liberty, Market and State: Political Economy in the 1980s.* New York: New York University Press.

—— (1985) *Liberty, Market and State: Political Economy in the 1980s.* New York: New York University Press.

—— (1979) "Politics without romance: a sketch of positive public choice theory and its normative implications." *Institute for Humane Studies Journal,* 3: B1–11. Also in Buchanan and Tollison (1984).

—— (1969) *Cost and Choice: An Inquiry in Economic Theory.* Chicago: University of Chicago Press.

Buchanan, James M. and Robert Tollison (eds) (1984) *The Theory of Public Choice – II.* Ann Arbor: University of Michigan Press.

Buchanan, James M., Robert Tollison, and Gordon Tullock (eds) (1980) *Toward a Theory of the Rent Seeking Society.* College Station; Texas A & M Press.

Buchanan, James M. and Gordon Tullock (1962) *The Calculus of Consent: Logical Foundations of Constitutional Democracy.* Ann Arbor: University of Michigan Press.

Butterfield, Fox (1982) *China: Alive in the Bitter Sea.* New York: Bantam Books.

Caldwell, Bruce J. and Stephan Boehm (eds) (1992) *Austrian Economics: Tensions and New Directions.* Boston: Kluwer.

Card, David and Alan B. Krueger (1994) "Minimum wages and employment: a case study of the fast food industry in New Jersey and Pennsylvania." *American Economic Review* (September): 772–93.

Cheng, Nien (1988) *Life and Death in Shanghai.* New York: Penguin Books.

Cordato, Roy (1994) "Taxation." In Peter Boettke (ed.), *The Elgar Companion to Austrian Economics.* Brookfield, VT: Edward Elgar.

Cowen, Tyler (ed.) (1992) *Public Goods and Market Failures: A Critical Examination.* New Brunswick: Transaction Publishers.

Cronin, James E. (1991) *The Politics of State Expansion: War, State and Society in Twentieth-Century Britain.* New York: Routledge.

DeBow, Michael E. (1991) "Markets, intervention, and the role of information: an 'Austrian school' perspective, with an application to merger regulation." *George Mason Law Review,* 14(1): 31–98.

Deere, Donald, Kevin Murphy, and Finis Welch (1995) "Sense and nonsense on the minimum wage." *Regulation,* (1): 47–56.

Demsetz, Harold (1969) "Information and efficiency: another viewpoint." *Journal of Law and Economics,* 12: 1–22.

Derthick, Martha and Paul J. Quirk (1985) *The Politics of Deregulation.* Washington, DC: The Brookings Institution.

Dickenson, Henry Douglas (1933) "Price formation in a socialist community." *Economic Journal,* 43: 237–50.

DiLorenzo, Thomas J. (1988) "Competition and political entrepreneurship: Austrian insights into public choice theory." *Review of Austrian Economics,* 2: 59–71.

Downs, Anthony (1957) *An Economic Theory of Democracy.* New York: Harper & Brothers.

Ebeling, Richard M. (ed.) (1991) *Austrian Economics: Perspectives on the Past and Prospects for the Future.* Hillsdale, MI: Hillsdale College Press.

England, Catherine and Thomas Huertas (eds) (1988) *The Financial Services Revolution.* Boston: Kluwer.

Fisher, Franklin M. (1983) *Disequilibrium Foundations of Equilibrium Economics.* Cambridge: Cambridge University Press.

Friedman, Benjamin M. (1989) *Day of Reckoning: The Consequences of American Economic Policy.* New York: Vintage Books.

Friedman, Jeffrey (1990) "The new consensus II: the democratic welfare state." *Critical Review,* 4(4): 633–708.

Fukuyama, Francis (1989) "The end of history?" *The National Interest,* 16 (summer): 3–18.

Fund, John H. (1990) "Czechoslovakia's free-market minister." *The Wall Street Journal,* 2 March.

Gerth, H. H. and C. Wright Mills (1958 [1946]) *From Max Weber: Essays in Sociology.* New York: Oxford University Press.

Gifis, Steven H. (1984) *Law Dictionary.* Second edn. New York: Barron's Educational Series.

Glazer, Nathan (1990) "Is welfare a legitimate government goal?" *Critical Review,* 4(4): 479–91.

—— (1988) *The Limits of Social Policy.* Cambridge, MA: Harvard University Press.

Goldschmidt, H.J., H.M. Mann, and J.F. Weston (eds) (1974) *Industrial Concentration: The New Learning.* Boston: Little, Brown & Co.

Goodin, Robert E. and Julian LeGrand (eds) (1987) *Not Only the Poor: The Middle Classes and the Welfare State.* London: Allen & Unwin.

Goodman, John C. and Gerald L. Musgrave (1992) *Patient Power: Solving America's Health Care Crisis.* Washington, DC: Cato.

Goodsell, Charles T. (1985) *The Case for Bureaucracy: A Public Administration Polemic.* Second edn. Chatham, NJ: Chatham House.

Grinder, Walter E. and John Hagel III (1977) "Toward a theory of state capitalism: ultimate decision-making and class structure." *Journal of Libertarian Studies,* 1(1): 59–79.

Gwartney, James D. and Richard Wagner (eds) (1988) *Public Choice and Constitutional Economics.* Greenwich, CT: JAI Press Inc.

Gwertzman, Bernard and Michael T. Kaufman (1990) *The Collapse of Communism.* New York: New York Times Co.

Hagel, John III (1975) "From laissez-faire to Zwangswirtschaft: the dynamics of interventionism." Unpublished manuscript.

Hayek, Friedrich A. (1984) *Money, Capital, and Fluctuations: Early Essays.* Ed. by Roy McCloughry. Chicago: University of Chicago Press.

—— (1976) *The Mirage of Social Justice.* Vol. 2 of *Law, Legislation and Liberty.* Chicago: University of Chicago Press.

—— (1975a [1939]) *Profits, Interest and Investment, and Other Essays on the Theory of Industrial Fluctuations.* Clifton, NJ: Augustus M. Kelley.

—— (1975b [1933]) *Monetary Theory and the Trade Cycle.* Clifton, NJ: Augustus M. Kelley.

—— (ed.) (1975c [1933]) *Collectivist Economic Planning: Critical Studies on the Possibilities of Socialism.* Clifton, NJ: Augustus M. Kelley.

—— (1973) *Rules and Order.* Vol. 1 of *Law, Legislation and Liberty.* Chicago: University of Chicago Press.

—— (1972 [1944]) *The Road to Serfdom.* Chicago: University of Chicago Press.

—— (1967a) *Studies in Philosophy, Politics and Economics.* Chicago: University of Chicago Press.

—— (1967b [1931]) *Prices and Production.* New York: Augustus M. Kelley.

—— (1948) *Individualism and Economic Order.* Chicago: Regnery.

—— (1937) "Economics and Knowledge." *Economica,* 4 (ns.): 33–54. Reprinted in Hayek (1948).

Heilbroner, Robert (1989) "The triumph of capitalism." *The New Yorker,* 23 January.

Higgs, Robert (1987) *Crisis and Leviathan: Critical Episodes in the Growth of American Government.* New York: Oxford University Press.

High, Jack (1991) "Regulation as a process: on the theory, history, and doctrine of government regulation." In Richard M. Ebeling (ed.), *Austrian Economics: Perspectives on the Past and Prospects for the Future.* Hillsdale, MI: Hillsdale College Press.

Hughes, Jonathan R.T. (1991) *The Governmental Habit Redux: Economic Controls from Colonial Times to the Present.* Princeton: Princeton University Press.

Ikeda, Sanford (1995a) "The use of knowledge in government and market." *Advances in Austrian Economics,* 2A: 211–40.

—— (1995b) "Bureaucracy matters." Unpublshed manuscript.

—— (1994) "Market process." In Peter J. Boettke, *The Elgar Companion to Austrian Economics,* Brookfield, VT: Edward Elgar.

—— (1992) "L'analyse du processus de marché dans l'organisation industrielle: Kirzner, la contestabilité et Demsetz." *Journal des Economistes et des Etudes Humaines,* 2(4) (December): 479–98.

—— (1991) "Regulation as a process, a comment." In Richard M. Ebeling (ed.), *Austrian Economics: Perspectives on the Past and Prospects for the Future.* Hillsdale, MI: Hillsdale College Press.

—— (1990) "Market-process theory and 'dynamic' theories of the market." *Southern Economic Journal,* 57(1): 75–92.

—— (1988) "The Theory of Resource Monopoly and Antitrust Economics." Unpublished manuscript.

—— (1983) "An essay on equilibrium prices, disequilibrium prices, and information." Unpublished manuscript.

Johnson, David B. (1991) *Public Choice: An Introduction to the New Political Economy*. London: Bristlecone Books.

Johnson, Paul (1991) *Modern Times: The World from the Twenties to the Nineties*. Revised edn. New York: Harper Perennial.

Kalt, J. (1981) "Public goods and the theory of government." *Cato Journal*, 1(2): 565–84.

Kaplan, Daniel P. (1986) "The changing airline industry." In Leonard W. Weiss and Michael W. Klass (eds), *Regulatory Reform: What Really Happened*. Boston: Little, Brown, & Co.

Katz, Lawrence F. and Alan B. Krueger (1992) "The effect of the minimum wage on the fast-food industry." *Industrial and Labor Relations Review*, 46(1): 6–21.

Keller, Morton (1990) *Regulating a New Economy: Public Policy and Economic Change in America, 1900–1932*. Cambridge, MA: Harvard University Press.

Kelman, Steven (1987) *Making Public Policy: A Hopeful View of American Government*. New York: Basic Books.

Kirzner, Israel M. (1992) *The Meaning of Market Process: Essays in the Development of Modern Austrian Economics*. London: Routledge.

—— (1985) *Discovery and the Capitalist Process*. Chicago: University of Chicago Press.

—— (1979) *Perception, Opportunity, and Profit: Studies in the Theory of Entrepreneurship*. Chicago: University of Chicago Press.

—— (1973) *Competition and Entrepreneurship*. Chicago: University of Chicago Press.

—— (1963) *Market Theory and the Price System*. Princeton: D. van Nostrand.

Kolko, Gabriel (1963) *The Triumph of Conservatism: A Reinterpretation of American History, 1990–1916*. Glencoe, IL: The Free Press.

Koppl, Roger and Leland B. Yeager (1992) "Big players and the Russian ruble: lessons from the nineteenth century." Unpublished manuscript.

Kornai, János (1990) *The Road to a Free Economy, Shifting from a Socialist System: The Example of Hungary*. New York: Norton.

Krueger, Anne O. (1974) "The political economy of the rent-seeking society." *American Economic Review*, 64 (June): 291–303.

Kuhn, Thomas (1970) *The Structure of Scientific Revolutions*. Second edn. Chicago: University of Chicago Press.

Landsburg, Steven E. (1992) *Price Theory and Applications*. Second edn. New York: Dryden.

Lange, Oskar and Fred M. Taylor (1964 [1938]) *On the Economic Theory of Socialism*. New York: McGraw-Hill.

Lavoie, Don (1985a) *Rivalry and Central Planning: The Socialist Calculation Debate Reconsidered*. Cambridge: Cambridge University Press.

—— (1985b) *National Economic Planning: What Is Left?* Cambridge, MA: Ballinger.

—— (1982) "The development of the Misesian theory of interventionism." In Israel M. Kirzner (ed.), *Method, Process, and Austrian Economics: Essays in Honor of Ludwig von Mises*. Lexington, MA: Lexington Books.

Lee, Dwight R. (1989) "The Impossibility of a desirable minimal state." *Public Choice*, 61: 277–84.

Leys, Simon (1978) *Chinese Shadows*. New York: Penguin Books.

Lindbeck, Assar (1995) "Hazardous welfare-state dynamics." *American Economic Review, Papers and Proceedings*, 85(2): 9–15.

Lindblom, Charles E. (1977) *Politics and Markets: The World's Political-Economic Systems*. New York: Basic Books.

Littlechild, S. C. (1979) *The Fallacy of the Mixed Economy: An "Austrian" Critique of Conventional Economics and Government Policy*. Cato Paper No. 2. San Francisco: Cato Institute.

McCormick, Robert E., William Shughart, and Robert D. Tollison (1984) "The disinterest in deregulation." *American Economic Review*, 74 (December): 1075–9.

Martin, James J. (1971) *Revisionist Viewpoints: Essays in a Dissident Historical Tradition*. Colorado Springs, CO: Ralph Myles.

Meltzer, A. H. and S. F. Richard (1978) "Why government grows (and grows) in a democracy." *Public Interest*, 52 (summer): 111–18.

Menger, Carl (1985 [1883]) *Investigations into the Method of the Social Sciences with Special Reference to Economics* (Untersuchen über die Methode der Socialwissenschaften und der Politischen Oekonomie insbesondere). Trans. by Francis J. Nock. New York: New York University Press.

—— (1981 [1871]) *Principles of Economics* (Grundsätze der Wolkswirthschaftslehre) Trans. by James Dingwall and Bert F. Hoselitz. New York: New York University Press.

Merton, Robert K. (1957) *Social Theory and Social Structure*. Revised and enlarged edn. New York: Free Press.

Mises, Ludwig von (1981 [1932]) *Socialism: An Economic and Sociological Analysis*. Trans. by J. Kahane. Indianapolis: Liberty Classics.

—— (1977 [1929]) *A Critique of Interventionism* (Kritik des Interventionismus) Trans. by Hans F. Sennholz. New Rochelle: Arlington House.

—— (1972 [1956]) *The Anti-Capitalistic Mentality*. Spring Mills, PA: Libertarian Press.

—— (1971 [1912]) *The Theory of Money and Credit*. Trans. by H. E. Batson. Irvington-on-Hudson, NY: Foundation for Economic Education.

—— (1969 [1944]) *Bureaucracy*. Westport, CT: Arlington House.

—— (1966 [1949]) *Human Action: A Treatise on Economics*. Third edn. Chicago: Regnery.

—— (1920) "Die Wirtschaftsrechnung im sozialistischen Gemeinwesen." *Archiv für Sozialwissenschaften*, vol. 47. Also in Hayek (1975c).

Mishan, E. J. (1981) *Introduction to Normative Economics*. New York: Oxford University Press.

Moe, Terry M. (1989) "The politics of bureaucratic structure," in John E. Chubb and Paul E. Peterson (eds), *Can the Government Govern?* Washington, DC: Brookings.

Morrison, Steven and Clifford Winston (1986) *The Economic Effects of Airline Deregulation*. Washington, DC: Brookings.

Mueller, Dennis C. (1989) *Public Choice II: A Revised Edition of Public Choice*. New York: Cambridge University Press.

—— (1979) *Public Choice*. Cambridge: Cambridge University Press.

Murphy, Kevin M., Andrei Shleifer, and Robert Vishney (1992) "The transition to a market economy: pitfalls of partial reform." *Quarterly Journal of Economics*, 107(3): 889–906.

Murray, Charles (1990) "The prospects for muddling through." *Critical Review*, 4(4): 493–504.

—— (1988) *In Pursuit: Of Happiness and Good Government*. New York: Simon & Schuster.

—— (1984) *Losing Ground: American Social Policy, 1950–1980*. New York: Basic Books.

Neale, A. D. and D. G. Goyder (1982) *The Antitrust Laws of the USA: A Study of Competition Enforced by Law*. Cambridge: Cambridge University Press.

Neumark, David and William Wascher (1995) "The effects of New Jersey's minimum wage increase on fast food employment: a reevaluation using payroll records." *Employment Policies Institute Working Paper* (March), Washington, DC: Employment Policies Institute.

Niskanen, William A. Jr. (1971) *Bureaucracy and Representative Government*. New York: Aldine/Atherton.

North, Douglass C. (1990) *Institutions, Institutional Change and Economic Performance*. New York: Cambridge University Press.

Nozick, Robert (1974) *Anarchy, State and Utopia*. New York: Basic Books.

O'Driscoll, Gerald P. and Mario J. Rizzo (1985) *The Economics of Time and Ignorance*, New York: Basil Blackwell.

Offe, Claus (1984) *Contradictions of the Welfare State*. Ed. by John Keane. Cambridge, MA: MIT Press.

Olson, Mancur (1992) "The hidden path to a free economy." In Christopher Clague (ed.), *Emergence of Market Economies in Eastern Europe*. New York: Blackwell.

—— (1982) *The Rise and Decline of Nations: Economic Growth, Stagflation and Social Rigidities*. New Haven: Yale University Press.

—— (1965) *The Logic of Collective Action*. Cambridge, MA: Harvard University Press.

Oppenheimer, Franz (1975 [1914]) *The State*. Trans. by John Gitterman. New York: Free Life Editions.

Owen, Bruce M. and Paul D. Gottlieb (1986) "The rise and fall of cable television regulation." In Leonard W. Weiss and Michael W. Klass (eds), *Regulatory Reform: What Really Happened?* Boston: Little, Brown & Co.

Pasour, E. C. (1991) "The possibility of a desirable minimal state." *Public Choice*, 69: 107–10.

Peltzman, Sam (1976) "Toward a more general theory of regulation." *Journal of Political Economy*, 19(2): 211–40. Also in Stigler (1988).

Peukert, Detlev J. K. (1989) *The Weimar Republic: The Crisis of Classical Modernity*. Trans. by Richard Deveson. New York: Hill & Wang.

Polanyi, Michael (1962) *Personal Knowledge: Towards a Post-Critical Philosophy.* Chicago: University of Chicago Press.
—— (1951) *The Logic of Liberty: Reflections and Rejoinders.* London: Routledge & Kegan Paul.
Popper, Karl R. (1972) *Objective Knowledge: An Evolutionary Approach.* Revised edn. Oxford: Clarendon Press.
Posner, Richard A. (1976) *Antitrust Law: An Economic Perspective.* Chicago: University of Chicago Press.
—— (1975) "The social costs of monopoly and regulation." *Journal of Political Economy,* 83(4): 807–27. Also in Stigler (1988).
—— (1971) "Taxation by regulation." *Bell Journal of Economics,* 2: 22–50.
Prychitko, David L. (1990) "The welfare state: what is left?" *Critical Review,* 4(4): 619–32.
—— (1988) "Marxism and decentralized socialism." *Critical Review,* 2(8): 127–48.
Przeworski, Adam (1990) *The State and the Economy Under Capitalism.* New York: Harwood Academic Publishers.
Rawls, John (1971) *A Theory of Justice.* Cambridge, MA: Harvard University Press.
Rizzo, Mario J. (1992) "Austrian economics for the twenty-first century." In Bruce J. Caldwell and Stephan Boehm (eds), *Austrian Economics: Tensions and New Directions.* Boston: Kluwer.
—— (1990) "Hayek's four tendencies toward equilibrium." *Cultural Dynamics,* 3(1): 12–31.
—— (1980) "Law amid flux: the economics of negligence and strict liability in tort." *Journal of Legal Studies,* 9: 291–318.
Rosenberg, Nathan and L. E. Birdzell, Jr. (1986) *How the West Grew Rich: The Economic Transformation of the Industrial World.* New York: Basic Books.
Rothbard, Murray N. (1977) *Power and Market: Government and the Economy.* Kansas City: Sheed Andrews & McMeel, Inc.
—— (1975) *America's Great Depression.* Third edn. Kansas City: Sheed & Ward, Inc.]
—— (1970) *Man, Economy and State: A Treatise on Economic Principles.* Los Angeles: Nash.
—— (1956) "Toward a reconstruction of utility and welfare economics." In Mary Sennholz (ed.), *On Freedom and Free Enterprise.* New York: Van Nostrand Co.
Rowley, Charles K. (1994) "Public choice economics." In Peter J. Boettke (ed.), *The Elgar Companion to Austrian Economics,* Brookfield, VT: Edward Elgar.
Scherer, Frederic M. (1980) *Industrial Market Structure and Economic Performance.* Second edn. Boston: Houghton Mifflin.
Schmidtz, David (1991) *The Limits of Government: An Essay on the Public Goods Argument.* Boulder, CO: Westview Press.
Schumpeter, Joseph A. (1950 [1942]) *Capitalism, Socialism and Democracy.* New York: Harper Torchbooks.
Sharp, Ansel M., Charles A. Register, and Richard Leftwich (1994) *Economics of Social Issues.* Boston: Irwin.

Simon, Herbert A. (1987) "Bounded rationality." In John Eatwell, Murray Milgate, and Peter Newman (eds), *The New Palgrave Dictionary of Economics*, vol. 1. London: Macmillan.

—— (1972) "Theories of bounded rationality." In C. B. McGuire and R. Radner (eds), *Decision and Organization*. Amsterdam: North-Holland.

Skidelsky, Robert (1992) *John Maynard Keynes: The Economist as Savior, 1920–1937*. New York: Penguin Books.

Smith, Hedrick (1988) *The Power Game: How Washington Works*. New York: Ballantine Books.

Solomon, Caleb (1993) "What really pollutes? Study of a refinery proves an eye-opener." *The Wall Street Journal*, 29 March: A1, A6.

Sowell, Thomas (1987) *A Conflict of Visions: Ideological Origins of Political Struggles*. New York: Quill.

—— (1980) *Knowledge and Decisions*. New York: Basic Books.

Steele, Charles N. (1995) "Discovery, transaction costs, and growth: review of Douglass C. North's *Institutions, Institutional Change and Economic Performance*." *Advances in Austrian Economics*, 2B: 447–59.

Stigler, George J. (ed.) (1988) *Chicago Studies in Political Economy*. Chicago: University of Chicago Press.

—— (1971) "The theory of economic regulation." *Bell Journal of Economics and Management Science*, 2(1): 1–21. Also in Stigler (1988).

Tanzi, V. (1980) "Toward a positive theory of public sector behavior: an interpretation of some Italian contributions." Washington, DC: International Monetary Fund, mimeo.

Taylor, Fred M. (1964 [1929]) "The guidance of production in a socialist state." In Benjamin E. Lippencott (ed.), *On the Theory of Socialism*. New York: McGraw-Hill.

Thomsen, Esteban F. (1992) *Prices and Knowledge: A Market-Process Perspective*. London: Routledge.

Thornton, Mark (1991) *The Economics of Prohibition*. Salt Lake City: University of Utah Press.

Tucker, William (1990) *The Excluded Americans: Homelessness and Housing Policies*. Washington, DC: Regnery Gateway.

Tullock, Gordon (1967) "The welfare costs of tariffs, monopolies, and theft." *Western Economic Journal*, 5 (June): 224–32.

—— (1965) *The Politics of Bureaucracy. Washington, DC: Public Affairs Press*.

Wagman, Robert (ed.) (1991) *The World Almanac of US Politics*. New York: Pharos Books.

Wagner, Richard E. (1989) *To Promote the General Welfare: Market Processes vs. Political Transfers*. San Francisco: Pacific Research Institute for Public Policy.

Wasley, Terree P. (1992) *What Has Government Done to Our Health Care?* Washington, DC: Cato.

Weiss, Leonard W. and Michael W. Klass (eds) (1986) *Regulatory Reform: What Actually Happened*. Boston: Little, Brown, & Co.

Williams, Walter E. (1978) *Youth and Minority Unemployment*. Palo Alto: Hoover Institution Press.

Wilson, James Q. (1993) *The Moral Sense*. New York: Free Press.

—— (1989) *Bureaucracy: What Government Agencies Do and Why They Do It*. New York: Basic Books.

Winston, Clifford (1993) "Economic deregulation: days of reckoning for microeconomists." *Journal of Economic Literature*, 31 (September): 1263–89.

Wolf, Charles Jr. (1990) *Markets or Governments: Choosing between Imperfect Alternatives*. Cambridge, MA: MIT Press.

Zycher, Benjamin (1995) "Minimum evidence." *Reason*, (June): 44–7.

INDEX

absolute dictatorship 68–9
actions 106, 108, 155–6, 256
anarcho-capitalism 197, 239, 254, 275
Anderson, G.M. 252, 277
anti-trust laws 251
Argentina 231–2
Armentano, D.T. 278
Arrow, K.J. 61, 70, 250
Arthur D. Little Corporation 264
Austrian political economy 1, 9–14, 28–9, 42, 50, 110, 149–50, 213–14, 226, 230, 231, 275; *see also* market process
Averch-Johnson effect 101
Axelrod, R. 116, 207

Barr, N. 245, 255, 266, 269
Baumol, W.J. 19
Becker, G. 16–17
benevolence *see* public-spiritedness
Berkowitz, E. 182
big-player effects 188–90, 271
black markets 130
Boettke, P.J. 34, 65, 130, 228, 230, 250, 251, 266, 267, 276
Bollard, A. 277
boom/bust cycle 96, 98
bottlenecks 140, 265
bounded rationality 21, 23, 100, 121, 124, 125, 219, 221, 255, 266
Brennan, G. 87
bribery 260
Buchanan, J.M. 107, 251, 252, 254;

et al. 251; and Tollison, R. 6, 251; and Tullock, G. 250
bureaucracy 20, 23, 147–8, 178, 187, 210–11, 257, 274; as inefficient 80; nature of 77–80
business cycle 39, 96, 98, 131–2
Butterfield, F. 277

calculation debate *see* socialist-calculation debate
capitalism 3, 4, 32, 35–7, 115, 128, 182, 217, 236, 237–8, 278
Card, D. and Krueger, A.B. 264
catallaxy 32, 125; as antagonistic/compatible 58; political tension with 43; theory and practice 55–8
central planning 3, 29, 34, 56–7, 65–6, 93, 108, 124, 138, 199–200, 257; bottom up 69–71; failure of 66–8; top down 68–9
change 118–19; marginal 115–16, 173, 177, 186; total unanticipated 74
Cheng, N. 277
China 228–9, 277
collectivism 1, 3, 24, 29, 32–5, 42, 45, 56, 65–6, 69, 70–2, 75, 93, 115, 124, 213, 215, 224, 237, 258–9, 268, 275; failure of 66–8; property rights under 68–72
communism 1, 3, 237, 238
comparative-systems analysis 92–3
competition 62, 63–5, 90, 183, 235, 238, 257

complexity 3, 20, 22, 106, 109, 121, 122–4, 126, 127, 215, 217, 224
confiscated surplus 45–6
constructivism 28
contractarian state 253–4
control 12, 16, 17, 43–4, 56, 92, 274; ambiguity of term 105; catallactic 104–5; of resources 92–3
coordination 56, 89, 146; limitations of non-price devices 86–9; meaning of 82; mechanisms of 81–9; problems 65–6, 80
coping organizations 210
Cordato, R. 201, 270
cost/benefit analysis 107–8
Cowen, T. 272, 275, 278
credit expansion 132
crises 25–6, 45, 54, 99, 118–19, 130, 132, 144, 217–18, 226–9, 266; hypothesis 226–7; macro-crises 123, 131, 132, 133, 138, 140, 144, 148, 151, 217–18, 219, 220, 266; micro-crises 123, 131, 133–6, 148, 151, 218, 219, 266; timing of 122–3
Cronin, J.E. 276
culture of poverty 135–6, 270

DeBow, M.E. 262
decision-making 65, 74, 89, 92, 121
Deere, D. et al. 264
demand see supply and demand
Demsetz, H. 255, 267
Deng Xiaoping 228, 267
derived externalities 109, 249, 256, 262–3; see also externalities
Derthick, M. and Quirk, P.J. 218
Dickenson, H.D. 258
difference principle 39
DiLorenzo, T. 251, 260
dis-intervention 142; piecemeal 139–41
discontinuity 138–9
discoordination 63, 65, 66, 103, 105, 109, 114, 122, 123–4, 127, 128, 132, 137, 190, 210, 215, 216, 217, 219, 224, 237, 256, 258

discovery effect 52, 59, 60, 81, 88, 103–6, 155, 168, 216, 237; pure 59; stifled 96; superfluous 96
distributional coalitions 22
domestic conflict see war/domestic conflict
Downs, D. 250
dynamic trade-off thesis 28, 49, 181–5, 269

education 19
efficiency 255, 262
efficiency/equity dilemma 38
encompassing organization 258, 260
endogenous/exogenous explanations 17–25, 35–8, 115, 117, 131–2, 159, 186, 196, 198–9, 211, 216, 265
England, C. and Huertas, T. 123
entrepreneurial, alertness 97, 146; discovery xi, 74, 88, 95–6, 105, 122, 155; profit 124, 172–3, 237
entrepreneurial-competitive process 67, 124, 128
entrepreneurs/entrepreneurship 22, 24, 57, 60, 62, 94, 108, 194, 216, 237, 257, 258–9; political 81–3; pure 63
equilibrium 9, 59, 61–2, 63–4, 107, 125, 129, 273; learning outside of 98–9
Erhard, L. 228
errors 61, 64, 66, 74, 114, 116–17, 137, 233; class-one/class-two 97–8, 111, 122, 125, 130, 155, 201, 220, 255–6, 262, 263; reasons for 203–4; relation to stifled and super-fluous discovery state 197, 200–7, 209–10, 211, 216, 273
evolutionary approach 23
exchanges 60, 85, 88
expansion/contraction, asymmetry between 220; timing of turning point 219–20; turning point in expansion 218–19; turning points 224–5
expenditure, and tax 169–74

externalities 16, 17, 101–2, 109, 249, 256, 262–3

fascism 33
feedback process 133
fiscal illusion hypothesis 16
Fisher, F.M. 272
freedom 27, 93, 161, 181–4, 194, 264
Friedman, J. 246, 251
frustrated intentions 263; general version 112; strong version 110–11; weak version 111–12
Fukuyama, F. 236–8, 278
Fund, J.H. 142

game theory 207
Germany 227–8, 277
Gerth, H.H. and Mills, C.W. 259
Gifis, S.H. 66
Glazer, N. 2, 25–6, 27, 49, 116, 176–8, 182, 207, 270
Goldschmidt, H.J. et al. 258
Goodin, R.E. and LeGrand, J. 270, 272
Goodman, J.C. and Musgrave, G.L. 136, 156, 267
Goodsell, C.T. 110, 150, 251, 274
government 32; as antagonistic/ compatible 58; as benevolent 195, 259; and coordination mechanisms 75–80, 81–9; defined 72–3; differences with market process 73–5; endogenous growth 19–24; errors 197, 200–7, 209–10, 211, 216, 273; exogenous growth 17–19; expansion/contraction xi, 3, 53, 137–43, 151; failure of 5, 9, 10, 21, 53, 264, 267; growth of 14–15, 18–19, 250; process of 58, 72–5; and role of ideology 24–8; size of 15–17, 77, 80, 224; as spontaneous order 89; theory and practice 55–8; (un)limited 32–3
gradual-acceptance thesis 26, 49, 176–9
Great Britain 229–30, 276

Grinder, W.E. and Hagel, J. 248
Grossman, et al. 257
Gwartney, J.D. and Wagner, R. 252
Gwertzman, B. and Kaufman, M.T. 238

Habermas, J. 241
Hagel, J. 248
Harper, D. 264
Hayek, F.A. (Hayekian) 2, 3, 9, 24–6, 28, 32–33, 48–51, 65, 71–2, 74–5, 89, 91, 93, 131–2, 143, 144, 162, 179–81, 183, 185, 199, 214, 223, 241, 248, 254, 256–61, 260, 267, 268, 275, 277
health-care industry 134–6
Heilbroner, R. 248
Higgs, R. 25–6, 27, 44, 49, 113, 224–6, 253, 263, 265, 266, 276
High, J. 252
high/low-order goods 261
Hitler, A. 228
Hobbes, T. 250
Hughes, J. 133, 183, 235, 249, 251, 259, 263, 266, 272, 276, 277, 278

ideological change 52–3, 100, 115–18, 125, 146, 159, 160–1, 236; endogenous 35–8; exogenous 24–5; logic of 115–18; in welfare state 176–86
ideology 49, 95, 106, 120–1, 131, 136, 152, 199, 202, 207, 221–2, 236, 276; and directing interventionist process 113–15; role of 112–13
ignorance 97, 108, 120–4, 212; see also radical ignorance
Ikeda, S. 250, 251, 252, 256, 257, 258, 268, 278
immunizing stratagems 223
Impossibility Theorem 70
incentives 5–6, 7, 11, 27, 49, 53, 62, 65, 81, 95–6, 103–4, 105, 106, 155, 173, 177, 261
income, distribution 36, 249, 252; effect of 169; impact of on government growth 18–19;

(in)equality 39, 169; transfer 2–3, 12, 40, 177, 220, 244
India 229–30
indifference curves 273–4
inflation 39
information 90, 128–9, 258, 274; asymmetry of 39; cost of 122, 124; dispersed 3; transmission of 84
instability 265–6
institutions 31, 60–1, 77
intentional redistribution 17
intentions/outcomes 45, 106, 115, 120–1, 263
interest pressure groups 7, 17, 21–2, 147–8
internal contradictions 120–1
internal/external responses 100–2, 103
interventionism 3, 20, 24, 29, 80, 91, 213, 215, 234–5, 254, 257; autistic 245; as begetter of mixed economy 36; binary 245, 246; and calculation debate 92–4; contractionary phase 137–43; cost of 131; crisis and change in 118–19; critique of xi–xii, 1–2, 11–12, 28, 29, 31–2, 41–6, 93, 199–200, 244; defined 31, 35–6, 197; economic case for 38–41; expansionary phase 99–137; general version 112, 119; impact of 52; as intentional transfer 12–13; internal/external responses to 133–6; limitations of critique 46–9; micro aspect of 253; middle way 38; negative consequences of 114; paradox of 46, 53; perverse consequences of 100–7; psychological/moral impact of 26; as self-defeating 45, 48; as self-organizing 143–4; as spontaneous order 143–4, 151; strong version 110–11, 119; total demand for 208–9; triangular 245, 246; typology of 40, 245–6, 245–7, 249; under socialism 34–5; undesirable

consequences of 107–12; weak version 111–12, 119

Johnson, D.B. 118, 251
Johnson, P. 231, 277
judicial system 32, 225, 235–6, 278

Kalt, 253, 272
Kaplan, D.P. 219
Katz, L.F. and Krueger, A.B. 264
Keller, M. 271, 272, 277
Kelman, S. 7, 12; *et al.* 8
Keynes, J.M. 266, 278
Kirzner, I. (Kirznerian) 2, 3, 9, 24, 48, 52, 58, 60, 62–3, 65, 95–8, 100, 107, 158–60, 163, 172, 183, 209, 237, 248, 253, 256–8, 262, 263
Klaus, V. 141
knowledge problem 24, 54, 56, 61, 78, 83–4, 89–90, 93–4, 122, 123, 198, 200, 211, 217, 260; acquisition 22, 32; dispersed xi, 51, 81, 149; division of 93; in government 75–7; lack of 178; manifestation of 51; nature/significance of 50, 94–9; setting of 50–1; solutions to 51–2; use of 188; *see also* perfect knowledge
knowledge-motive matrix 240–1
Kolko, G. 271
Koppl, R. and Yeager, L.B. 195, 271
Kornai, J. 141
Krueger, A.O. 147
Kuhn, T. 275

labor market 169–74
labor/leisure analysis 165, 166–8, 194
laissez-faire 24, 29, 36, 38, 42, 45, 99, 123–4, 130, 148, 217, 224, 225, 238, 267, 278
Landsberg, S.E. 271
Lange, D. 277
Lange, O. and Taylor, F.M. 34
Lavoie, D. 65, 92–3, 199, 214, 228, 243, 246, 248–9, 258, 259, 272
learning 52, 256; class-one/class-

two 120, 130, 201; delays in 106, 120–4; dynamic 97; failure of 52; obstacles to 99; outside of equilibrium 98–9; process of 108; slow 119
Lee, D. 16–17, 253, 274
legitimation crisis 77
Lenin 34
Leys, S. 277
liberalism 237, 278
Lindahl 198
Lindbeck, A. 265, 267, 270, 271
Littlechild, S.C. 248, 263
log-rolling 35, 82, 85, 146
logic of collective action 22

McCormick, R.E. *et al.* 267
Madison, J. 250
Mao Tse Tung 277
market *see* catallaxy
market failure 37–8, 41–2, 255; macroeconomic 39; microeconomic 38–9
market process 57, 96, 157, 165, 238, 251, 257, 268; competition and monopoly in 63–5; differences with government process 73–5; nature of 58–61; normative 61–3; as spontaneous order 61; *see also* Austrian political economy
market socialism 34, 67
Martin, J.J. 254
Marxism 241, 248, 275
maximal state 33
median voters 6, 18–19, 20
Meltzer, A.H. and Richard, S.F. 18, 19
Menem, C. 231
Menger, C. 143, 260
middle way 4, 38, 278
minimal state 30, 36, 90, 92, 215, 225, 253, 256–7; analysis of 199–209; and bureaucracy 210–11; described 197–9; functions of 274; ideology of 221–2; (in)stability of 47, 53, 196–7, 211–12, 213, 214, 221–2;

and monopoly 209–10; and public goods 209, 211–12
minimum wage 157
Mises, L. von (Misesian) 1–3, 9, 11–12, 14, 24, 28, 29, 31–6, 41–50, 52–4, 65, 76, 78, 80, 92–3, 96, 98, 100, 110, 113–14, 124, 126–7, 130–2, 151, 162, 178, 196, 199, 214–15, 219, 227–8, 228, 233, 241–6, 248–9, 251, 252, 254–6, 259, 261, 267
Misesian paradox 215, 233
Mishan, E.J. 255
mixed economy 3, 28, 35–8, 93, 119, 128, 138, 149, 234, 254; as contradictory and illogical 1; crisis of 125–32; crisis in and of 217–18; dynamics of 57, 216–17; prevalence of 215–16, 227; prospects for 236–9
Moe, T. 260, 261
monetary policy 131–2, 161–2, monopoly 63–5, 92, 187–90, 209–10, 257, 260
moral aversion 176–7, 199, 207, 273
Morrison, S. and Winston, C. 123
Mueller, D.C. 5, 87, 250, 251, 252, 253, 259, 272
Munn Doctrine 278
Murphy, K.M. *et al.* 267
Murray, C. 2, 123, 135, 171, 177, 267, 270

narrow (political) self-interest 6, 12–13, 53, 83, 85–6, 131, 145, 146, 148–9, 150, 260, 264; *see also* self-interest
nationalization 47, 53, 92, 105, 133, 152, 174, 186–90, 233, 241–3, 260
Neale, A.D. and Goyder, D.G. 277
Nebbia Doctrine 278
neighbourhood effects 17
neoclassical approach 250, 251; equilibrium in xi, 157–8; limitations of 9–12
Net Harm 171–2
Neumark, D. and Wascher, W. 264
new learning 258

new political economy *see* public choice (choosers)
Nirvana approach 255, 267
Niskanen Jr, W.A. 20, 22, 23, 50, 187, 259
nodal points 115, 117–18, 119, 133, 134, 223
non-equilibrium prices 60, 257
non-price coordination, limitations of 86–9
nonmarket, activity 254–5; failure 251
North, D. 265
Nozick, R. 253, 254, 275

objective facts 268
O'Driscoll, G.P. and Rizzo, M.J. 276
Offe, C. 77, 241, 248, 266, 275
Olson, M. 21–3, 50, 52, 53, 83, 147–8, 151, 229–30, 241, 250, 258, 263, 271
Oppenheimer, F. 253
opportunity costs 166–8
optimization 9
order 74, 259
organization 108, 217
outcomes *see* intentions/outcomes
output restriction 45

Pareto optimality 38, 60, 61, 207
partial reform 267
Pasour, E.C. 253, 274
pattern predictions 3, 103, 222–6, 232, 233, 248, 275–6; examples of 227–32
Peltzman, S. 18–19, 21, 154, 250; and Becker, G. 252
perfect competition 23
perfect knowledge 9, 10, 42; absence of 46–9; *see also* knowledge problem
Peron, J. 231
Persson, G. 277
Peukert, D.J.K. 277
piecemeal intervention 44–5, 130, 139–41, 148
plan (dis)coordination 74, 76, 85, 88, 118, 128, 149, 261

Polanyi, M. 34, 256, 259
political, capitalism 36; market 86
Popper, K. 223
Posner, R.A. 40, 153, 250, 277
pressure groups 17
price 67–8, 74, 78, 81, 84, 88, 92, 98–9, 122, 125, 182–5, 189–90, 216, 278; ceiling 42–3, 113–14, 255; control 43–5, 220; distortion 122, 123, 154–9, 166–8; dynamics of 3; impact of income transfer on 174–5; and non-price regulation 157–9; (non)equilibrium 62; regulation 152; subsidies 47–8, 243–5; *see also* relative price
prisoners' dilemma 116, 253, 278
production 179–81; and distribution 179–81; organizations 210; restriction 163
productivity 19
profit and loss 52, 59–60, 88, 97, 262
profit-seekers 44, 49, 60, 79
Progressive Era 271–2
property rights 63, 125, 165; absence of 66–7; impact of income transfers on 174–5; private 261; role of 66; under collectivism 68–72
Prychitko, D.L. 124, 248, 250, 254, 266
public authorities 5
public choice (choosers) 4, 12, 29, 31, 36, 49–50, 76, 120–1, 145, 149–50, 173, 212, 216, 217, 219, 229, 230, 233, 235, 238–9, 249–52; Chicago variant 252; defined 5–6, 11; general approach to 4–15; limitations of 132; models of 14–28; normative 7–9, 11; positive 8; as rascals 7; reform of 7; and rejection of interventionism 134, 138; suitability of 9–14; and systemic breakdown 123–4, 125, 126
public goods 197, 201–4, 209, 211–12, 254, 272, 278

public interest 42, 91; benevolent 145–51, 150
public-spiritedness 37, 82, 83–5, 88, 104, 114, 260
public/private sectors 94–5, 116

quality control 164

radical ignorance 3, 12, 59, 60, 81, 100, 122, 124, 126, 149, 219, 221, 255, 258, 263; see also ignorance
RAND Graduate School of Policy Studies 248–249
Rawls, J. 39
Reagan, R. 118
recidivism 141–2
redistribution 11, 16–17, 18, 27, 42, 170–1, 195, 268, 269, 270; effects of 126; (un)intentional 128
regulatory dynamics 4–5, 13, 14, 40, 48; comparison with transfer dynamics 182–5
regulatory state 29, 34, 36–7, 39–40, 45, 47, 53, 148, 152, 153–4, 182, 233, 244, 250; categories of 161; and ideological change 160–1; and insecurity 160–1; and monetary manipulation 161–2; outline of 159–60; and price control 162; and price/non-price distortions 154–9; and production restriction 163; and quality control 164
relative price, change in 265; distortion 173, 236, 242–3, 244, 258; see also price
rent-seeking 17, 22, 147, 149, 251, 260, 261, 263, 267
reserve fund 100, 123, 124, 215, 216, 217; depletion of 125–7, 129, 130, 134; and measurement/measurment problem 129–30; replenishment of 127–8
rising expectations 177, 182–3
Rizzo, M.J. 99, 129, 260, 262, 275
Rosenberg, N. and Birdzell, L.E. Jr 182
Rothbard, M. 35, 40, 153, 203, 241, 243–9, 253, 257, 268, 277

Rowley, C.K. 250
rules 55, 157, 256
Russia 228

safety-rule 157
Scherer, F.M. 250
Schmidtz, D. 253, 278
Schultze, C. 22, 101
Schumpeter, J. 182, 237–8
security 27, 160–1, 182, 183–4, 185, 264
self-fulfillment thesis 27, 49, 179–81, 184
self-interest 6, 8, 9, 10, 42, 53, 147–8; simple 146; see also narrow (political) self-interest
Sharp, A.M. et al. 136
Simon, H.A. (Simoneon) 20–1, 100, 160, 255, 266
Skidelsky, R. 266, 278
Smith, H. 70
social, justice 27, 180, 184; policy 26
socialism 33, 250, 254
socialist-calculation debate 58, 64, 65–72, 92–4, 271
Sowell, T. 174, 251
spill-over effects 17, 94)5
Spinoza, B. 250
spontaneous order 15, 55, 143–4, 151, 217, 256
stability 272
state see government
Steele, C.N. 265
Stigler, G. 10, 250
subjective facts 268
subsidies 43, 104, 106, 114, 130, 170, 173, 190, 243–5, 270
substitution effect 169
suffrage 18, 19
supply and demand 19, 204–5
Sweden 230–1, 277
system-wide process 11, 218, 233, 234
systemic breakdown 123–4, 125, 126; and radical reform 128–9

Tanzi, V. 16–17
tax 18, 43, 96, 101, 104, 105, 178,

190, 201–8, 255, 270, 273; and
government expenditure 169–74
Taylor, F.M. 258
Thatcher, M. 231
Thomsen, E.F. 257
Thornton, M. 120, 263
Tocqueville, A. de 250
totalitarianism 234, 238, 277
transaction costs 7
transfer dynamics 3, 12–13, 14, 40,
153, 159, 164–5, 244; budget
deficit 192; comparison with
regulatory dynamics 182–5; and
degradation of price signals 165;
direct income 191; (in)direct 40;
new social regulation 192; and
price distortions 166–8; and
property rights/prices 174–5;
and unintended consequences of
tax/subsidies 169–74;
(un)intentional 41
Tucker, W. 111, 264, 267
Tullock, G. 7, 147, 241, 250, 257,
268
turning points 218–20, 224–5

unemployment 39, 101, 109–10
unintended consequences 11, 13,
20–2, 49, 100, 101–2, 156, 158,
159, 173, 190, 208, 217–18, 236,
252; as negative 100, 104–6, 109,
110–12, 136–7; of tax/subsidies
169–74; as undesirable 107–10;
weak version 184, 217, 271
Unintended Rewards 171

United States 229–30, 276
University of Chicago 5
University of Virginia 5
utility maximization 6, 8, 20, 253

voting mechanisms 82, 84, 85, 86–8,
146, 149

wage/price control 39, 162
Wagman, R. 76, 259
Wagner, R. 10–11, 14, 151, 154, 169,
241, 249, 252, 253, 254, 269, 270
war/domestic conflict 226–9
Wasley, T.P. 135
Weber, M. 259
Weiss, L.W. and Klass, M.W.
139–140
welfare state 2, 7, 12–13, 29, 37,
39–40, 46, 47, 53, 92, 148, 152–3,
194, 225, 233, 244, 250, 252, 265;
and degradation of price signals
in 165–75; and ideological
change in 176–86; relative
stability of 220–1
Williams, W.E. 264
Wilson, J.Q. 2, 8, 79–80, 84, 110,
178, 210, 236, 264, 267, 278
winners and losers 104, 108, 155
Wolf, C. 52, 109, 122, 248–9, 251,
254, 255, 256, 259, 262, 264, 271

Zwangswirtschaft (German/
Hindenburg pattern) 33–4, 92,
175, 227
Zycher, B. 264

AAO- 4081